The 6Ps of the BIG 3™

The **6Ps**
of
the **BIG 3**™

for Job-Seeking JDs

60+ Ways to Get Hired Using Social Networking

Amanda C. Ellis, Esq.

Published by Something Different Publishing, Inc.

P. O. Box 25211
Dallas, TX 75225

www.6psbig3.com

ISBN: 978-0-5780530-3-9

Printed in the United States of America

Contents

Acknowledgments 1
Disclaimer 3
Premise of the 6Ps of the BIG 3 5
   What is a Job Search Campaign? 5
   What Role Does Social Networking Play in a Campaign? 7
   What is Social Networking? 7
   What are the Big 3? 8
      Facebook 8
      LinkedIn 9
      Twitter 9
   What are the 6Ps? 10
      Professionalism 11
      Profile 11
      Privacy 11
      Performance 11
      Practice 11
      Protocol 11
   Why is Social Networking an Essential Component
   to Your Job Search Campaign? 12
      Search 12
      Social Recruiting 13
      Warm Calls 13
      Seven Touches 13
      Client Development 14
      The In-house Social Media Attorney 14
      Perpetual Network 15
      Passive Candidate 15
   How to Use this Book 15

PART 1: PREPARE TO USE THE BIG 3 SITES IN YOUR JOB SEARCH.................................... 18

CHAPTER 1. PROFESSIONALISM........................... 19

Facebook is Partly Professional.............................. 20
    Majority View: 5-40% Professional Content.............. 21
    Minority View: Up to 80% Professional Content 21
LinkedIn is Primarily Professional 22
    100% Professional Content 22
Twitter is Primarily Professional............................. 23
    80% Professional Content 24
Points: Professionalism 24

CHAPTER 2. PROFILE..................................... 25

PROFILE PICTURE... 25
Why Does a Profile Picture Improve Your Profile? 26
What Type of Picture Should You Include? 27
    Recent 27
    Quality... 27
    Headshot 27
    Partly Professional v. Primarily Professional............... 28

BIOGRAPHICAL INFORMATION 34
Facebook 34
Current City and Hometown 36
    Helpful... 36
    Harmful... 36
Birthday 36
    Harmful... 36
Political Views and Religious Views......................... 36
    Harmful... 36
Relationships.. 37
    Helpful... 37
    Harmful... 37
Likes and Interests....................................... 38
    Helpful... 38
    Harmful... 38
Education and Work...................................... 38
    Helpful... 38

Contact Information 40
    Helpful 40

LinkedIn 40
  Snapshot 42
    Name 42
    Professional Headline 43
    Location 45
    Industry 45
    Status Update 45
    Public Profile 46
  Summary 48
    Professional Experience & Goals 48
    Specialties 48
  Applications 48
    Blog 48
    Slide Presentations 49
    Articles 50
    Travel 51
    Books 52
    Events 52
    Legal Updates by JD Supra 54
  Education 54
  Experience 54
    Past Professional Positions 54
    Numbers & Amounts 54
    Concise 55
    Details 55
  Recommendations 57
    Receiving Recommendations – Attorney Advertising? 57
    Giving Positive Recommendations –
    Evidence in Discrimination Lawsuits? 57
  Additional Information 58
    Websites 58
    Twitter 60
    Interests 60
    Groups 60
    Honors and Awards 60
  Personal Information 60
    Phone 60
    Address 60

Birthday 60
Contact Settings 60
Career Opportunities 60
Consulting Offers. 60
New Ventures. 60
Job Inquiries. 60
Reference Requests 60

Twitter 61
Name 61
Twitter Username 61
Location 62
Web 62
Bio 63
Optional Backgrounds. 64

POINTS: PROFILE 67

CHAPTER 3. PRIVACY 69

SECTION 1: FACEBOOK 70
Privacy Tools 70
Privacy Levels 70
Lists 72
Profile Preview 73
Privacy Recommendations for Job Seekers. 76
Pictures. 79
Status Update 81
Work and Education. 83
Contact Information. 84
Searches 84

SECTION 2: LINKEDIN 88
Personal Information. 89
Recommendation for Job Seekers 89
Opportunity Preferences 90
Recommendation for Job Seekers 92
Connections Browse 92
Recommendation for Job Seekers 94
Profile Views 97
Recommendation for Job Seekers 99

Status Visibility 101
    Recommendation for Job Seekers 102
Profile and Status Updates 102
    Recommendation for Job Seekers 102

SECTION 3: TWITTER 103
  Privacy Options 103
    Tweets - Recommendation for Job Seekers 104
    Lists - Recommendation for Job Seekers 105
  Always Public 106
    Twitter Profile 106
    Twitter Favorites 107

POINTS: PRIVACY 109

PART 2: PERFORM YOUR JOB SEARCH
ON THE BIG 3 SITES III

CHAPTER 4. PERFORMANCE 113

SECTION 1: FACEBOOK 115
  Step 1: Connect with Friends, Family, Select Professional Contacts 115
  Profile Page 116
    Who: Level of Scrutiny to Connect with Friends 116
    How: Connection Methods 117
  Fan Pages & Groups 122
    Who: Level of Scrutiny to Connect with Pages/Groups 122
    How: Connection Methods 122
  Step 2: Assimilate Information to Use in Your Job Search 125
    1. Review Friends' Status Updates 125
    2. Review Friends' Wall Posts & Notes 126
    3. Review Events in News Feed 127
    4. Search BranchOut 128
    5. Search Marketplace 129
    6. Review Firm Pages for Practice Area Insight 130
    7. Review Job Postings on Firm Pages 131
    8. Review Career-Related Articles on
       Law Schools' Career Pages 131
    9. Search Community Pages to Learn about Firms 132
  Step 3: Participate to Remain on Your Network's Radar Screen 134

1. Update your Status with Personal Updates 134
2. Post Status Updates about Your Job Search 135
3. Market Your Expertise in Your Status Updates 136
4. Tag Friends in Status Updates. 137
5. Share Articles Reflective of Your Practice Area. 138
6. Share Legal News 139
7. Share Posts & Tag Friends. 140
8. Leave Note after Networking 141
9. Wish Friends 'Good Luck' on Professional Endeavors. . . . 141
10. Congratulate Friends on Personal Achievements. 141
11. Wish Friends 'Happy Birthday'. 141
12. Like (Thumbs Up) Your Friends' Content 142
13. Comment on Target Firms' Pages 143
14. Like (Thumbs Up) Firms' Content. 143

SECTION 2: LINKEDIN 145
Step 1: Connect with Classmates, Colleagues, Legal Professionals. . 145
Who: Level of Scrutiny to Connect with Contacts. 145
How: Grow Your 1st Degree Connections 147
Write Introduction to 1st Degree Connections 152
Ask for Introductions to 2nd & 3rd Degree Contacts 155
Step 2: Assimilate Information to Use in Your Job Search. 159
1. Search Companies (Firms) 159
2. Search People (Attorneys, Recruiters) 166
3. Search Job Board 169
4. Identify Lost Contacts through Group Search. 170
5. Identify Firms/Attorneys in Target Practice Area
through Group Search 171
6. Search Group Job Openings 171
7. Discover Interview Talking Points through Group Search. 172
8. Review Status Updates for Job Leads 174
9. Review Profile Updates for Job Leads 175
10. Find Networking Events to Attend. 175
11. Monitor Application Updates. 175
12. Learn about Practice Areas through
Legal Updates by JD Supra. 176
Step 3: Participate to Remain on Your Network's Radar Screen. . . . 178
1. Update Your Status. 178
2. Comment on Your Contacts' Status Updates 179
3. Like (Thumbs Up) Your Contacts' Updates 180
4. Share Your Contacts' Links to Articles/Posts 180

    5. Share Articles with Group(s). 180
    6. Initiate or Participate in Group Discussion. 181
    7. Market Yourself to a Group 183
    8. Update Your Profile Information 184
    9. Send a LinkedIn Message 184

SECTION 3: TWITTER. 186
  Step 1: Connect with Anyone—Focus on Legal Professionals. 186
    Who: Level of Scrutiny to connect with Followers. 186
    How: Connection Process 187
    How: Find Legal Professionals. 187
  Step 2: Assimilate Information to Use in Your Job Search. 201
    1. Monitor Your Contacts' Tweets for Job Openings. 201
    2. Discover Job Opportunities through Twitter Search 204
    3. Search for Job Opportunities on TwitJobSearch.com 206
    4. Monitor Your Contacts' Tweets
       for Potential Job Openings 207
    5. Prepare for Interview by Searching Firms 207
    6. Prepare for Interviews by Searching Attorneys 208
    7. Research Practice Areas. 209
    8. Identify Media Opportunities. 211
    9. Identify Writing/Speaking Opportunities 213
    10. Identify Conference Opportunities. 214
    11. Obtain Legal News & Developments 215
  Step 3: Participate to Remain on Your Network's Radar Screen. . . . 216
    1. Tweet about Your Job Search. 216
    2. Tweet about Your Practice. 219
    3. Share Links to Articles/Blog Posts. 220
    4. Retweet. 223
    5. Respond to @replies/Mentions, Retweets 227
    6. Comment on Other Users' Links 228
    7. Ask Job Search Questions 229
    8. Participate in #LawJobChat 231
    9. Participate in Conference Tweets 232
    10. Socialize 233
    11. Connect Offline 233

POINTS: PERFORMANCE 236

PART 3: POLISH YOUR PERFORMANCE 241

CHAPTER 5. PRACTICE 243

Block Your Time 243
  Time Blocking in Recruiting 243
  Time Blocking in Job Search. 244
Block Certain Information you Assimilate. 245
  Mobile Applications for Status Updates 245
  Facebook Lists 247
  Facebook Hidden Activities 247
  LinkedIn Category View. 249
  Twitter Lists 252
  Twitter Favorites. 252
Measure Activity Responses. 255
  Track Clicks on Short URLs. 256
  Comments 257
  Likes. 259
  Share 259
  Retweets. 260
Measure Activity Goals 262
  CAP Goals 262
  Target Goals 264
  First-Year Plan 265
Practice with Six-Week Schedule 267
  Practice Improves Performance. 267
  Six-Week Schedule 267
Points: Practice. 269

CHAPTER 6. PROTOCOL 271

PINSTRIPES. 271
  Desired Behavior on the Big 3 Sites. 272
    Fresh Status Updates on the Big 3. 272
    Don't Sync Status Updates on the Big 3 272
    Don't Sound Desperate. 273
    Read Links before Sharing or Retweeting 274
    Avoid Negative Comments about Job Interviews 274
  Desired Behavior on Facebook. 274
    Edit Your Facebook Wall. 274
    Exercise Caution with Certain Facebook Activities 275

Desired Behavior on LinkedIn. 276
    Fresh LinkedIn Profile 276
    Exercise Caution with LinkedIn Introductions 277
    Don't Spam LinkedIn Groups. 279
Desired Behavior on Twitter 279
    Avoid Twitter Annoyances 279
    Exercise Caution with Certain Twitter Activities. 281
PEARLS 282
Create Your Brand with Strategic Content. 282
Editorialize Shared Links. 285
Promote Your Brand when Growing Your Network. 287
Listen, Learn, Publish 288
Lead on Twitter 289
Follow Different Users, Share Different Content. 289

POINTS: PROTOCOL 290

PART 4: PROOF LAWYERS GET HIRED USING THE 6Ps SYSTEM

PART 4: PROOF LAWYERS GET HIRED
USING THE 6Ps SYSTEM. 291

CHAPTER 7. PARAGONS. 293

Meet the Paragons. 294
    The Snarky Waitress – Bobbi-Sue Doyle-Hazard 294
    The Social Media Maven – Laura Bergus 297
Spot the 6Ps. 301
    Professionalism. 301
    Profile. 302
    Privacy 302
    Performance 302
    Practice. 302
    Protocol 302
See the Significance 303
    Search. 303
    Warm Calls. 303
    Seven Touches. 303
    In-house Social Media Attorney 303
    Perpetual Network 303
    Passive Candidate 303
Points: Paragons 304

Parting Words 305

Primer   307

Appendix A – Law School Career Offices' Facebook & Twitter Pages. . . . 317

Appendix B – Law Firms' Facebook Career Pages. 323

Appendix C – Twitter Legal Job Boards 325

Appendix D – Sample Law Student First-Year Plan 327

Appendix E – Sample Social Networking Schedule 335

Appendix F – Chapter Notes 337

ACKNOWLEDGMENTS

I gratefully acknowledge:

Ann Levine, one of my first contacts on Twitter who published her own book in 2009. I've never met Ann in person but consider her my virtual mentor.

Karen Sargent, for discovering the blog post I wrote on Ann Levine's blog and asking me to speak to her students. I never imagined that presentation would lead to future speaking engagements and a book. I was a legal recruiter, not an author.

Chali Linke and Heather Harrigan, for inquiring about a presentation regarding Facebook, LinkedIn, and Twitter. The "6Ps of the Big 3" were born when I created the presentation for their program in July 2009.

Pia Thompson, for reading my LinkedIn status updates, noting my first presentation of the "6Ps," and inviting me to share the program with her firm.

Jeanne Arden, Jennifer Wallace, and Kathryn Moran, for reading this book in its early stage and providing feedback. And, Kathryn Moran, for traveling with me to the NALP Conference to promote the book.

Greta Tackebury and Ginna Galbraith, for providing input on any issue when I asked.

Melissa Sachs, for her patience in working with me on a never-ending project, and her continuing encouragement.

Evan Fogelman, for his wisdom and guidance on trademark and media law issues, not to mention his continuing encouragement

Laura Bergus and Bobbi-Sue Doyle Hazard, the paragons of social networking—I was fortunate to discover you through Twitter. You are an inspiration for all job-seeking JDs! Chapter 7 was my favorite chapter to write because of your stories.

For my cast of characters, thank you for allowing me to use your pictures, names, and content. Your examples bring the 6Ps to life!

Regina Adams   Jennifer Ingram

Yana Knutson   Neda Mirafzali

Steve Silton

Amy Hein

Amy Pfeiffer

Jennifer Taddeo

James Wingfield

Evan Fogelman

Kathryn Moran

Philip Guzman

Melissa Sachs

Jerry Levine

Todd Smith

Ashley Clark

Jason Tenenbaum

Marina Feehan

Van Pham

Pia Thompson

Chad Ruback

Ashley Hunter

Etan Tepperman

Erin Johnston

Kathleen Pearson

Ellen Faba

Drew Carls

Michael Maslanka

Rachel London

Luke Gilman

Sohana Barot

Laura McWilliams

Kelly Hoey

And, my dear family (especially my mother), Brian, and Brian's family—for their love and support and for listening to me during this roller coaster experience.

Disclaimer

THIS book is designed to help you use Facebook, LinkedIn, and Twitter in your search for attorney jobs. Every required effort has been made to comply with each site's terms of service and permissions. Facebook, LinkedIn, and Twitter do not necessarily endorse this book.

There is no guarantee that anything in this book will get you a job. Moreover, because of the rapid pace of technologies and marketing, some information might become outdated.

Everything the book suggests or explains must be taken with State and Federal Professional Responsibility Compliance and all laws concerning communications, media and the workplace. No attorney-client relationship is created by this book, and all legal issue questions should be directed to your own attorney. Similarly, site use questions should be directed to Facebook, LinkedIn, and Twitter.

No express or implied representations or warranties, including warranties of performance, merchantability and fitness for a particular purpose, is given or created by any information in the book, the book itself and/or your purchase of the book.

Facebook, LinkedIn and Twitter own their Trademarks, copyrights and other intellectual property interests. Individuals own their own posted content and related rights unless site terms of service indicate otherwise.

Any and all requests for permissions to utilize the book's content must be made in writing. Use the book at your own risk, but with our wishes for your own success!

PREMISE OF THE 6Ps OF THE BIG 3

WHAT can you learn from President Barack Obama and U.S. Senator Scott Brown about getting hired? Obama and Brown obtained their current jobs through successful campaigns focused on social networking. How many law students and lawyers incorporate social networking in their job search campaigns? Very few. Should you? Absolutely! You should craft a job search campaign that capitalizes on social networking.

WHAT IS A JOB SEARCH CAMPAIGN?

I receive calls from lawyers daily, and most are looking to leave their current jobs immediately. Some have been told by firm management to start looking for new opportunities. Others have grown tired of their current firms or law practice in general. And, some have already been laid-off and need to find a new position immediately.

I remind all of the lawyers that a job search is a marathon, not a sprint—a campaign, not an application. And, I share the story of a young attorney, Amy, who landed her dream job after months of planning, networking, and leading various legal organizations in her community. Amy began her legal career working for a federal judge. She knew the position would end at a certain time; it was only a one-year term. She formulated a plan which she began implementing on her first day of the clerkship:

- get involved with a young lawyer organization by assuming a leadership role on a committee
- polish her profiles on LinkedIn and Facebook
- schedule one information interview a month with attorneys in her city
- update and share information on LinkedIn and Facebook weekly
- blog about life as a new lawyer

- attend two networking events each week

After adhering to this plan for eight months, one of Amy's contacts on LinkedIn, Jane, read Amy's status update about a mentoring event Amy was organizing for the young lawyer organization. Jane, the contact from LinkedIn, attended the networking event and introduced Amy to Tom, a law firm partner who spoke at the event. Jane and Tom previously practiced together.

After the event, Amy followed up with Tom and connected with him on LinkedIn. Amy frequently shared links to her blog posts on LinkedIn and Tom noticed. Amy wanted to learn more about Tom's practice, so Amy invited Tom for coffee one month following the young lawyer mentoring event. Tom's firm wasn't hiring, but he was impressed with Amy's leadership and writing. One month after their meeting, Tom's section grew busier and Tom lobbied for the firm to hire another associate. Tom invited Amy to interview for the position and Tom's firm ultimately hired Amy; Amy secured a job one month prior to the end of her clerkship.

You can learn the following lessons in marketing, networking, and planning from Amy's successful job search:

- **Marketing Lesson:**
  Tell potential employers why they should hire you by sharing your work. Amy wrote a blog which she frequently shared on her social networking profiles. Tom read her work and saw value in her work. Moreover, he remembered Amy's work when an opening arose in his firm and called Amy to interview.
- **Networking Lesson:**
  Network in a variety of forums, including online. Amy networked in a variety of forums—online, offline, one-on-one, group events—and, *all* contributed to her job search success. Moreover, Amy's online activities on LinkedIn led to offline activities (*i.e.,* introduction to Tom and a subsequent interview with Tom for a position in his firm).
- **Planning Lesson:**
  Campaign before you need a job. Amy didn't start looking for a new position one month before her clerkship ended. Rather, she commenced her campaign on the first day of her clerkship, and it took eleven months to secure a position.

What Role Does Social Networking Play in a Campaign?

Amy's social networking contributed to her getting hired just as social networking contributed to Obama's and Brown's victories.[1,2] Through social networking, Obama and Brown engaged supporters and motivated them to turn their online enthusiasm into on-the-ground, grassroots activities.[3] It was Obama's and Brown's *performance*—their engagement—on social networking sites, not their mere *presence*, that contributed significantly to their victories.

Amy's *performance* on social networking sites—LinkedIn specifically—was a contributing factor to her job search success. Her LinkedIn profile alone did not land the job; rather, it was her performance on the LinkedIn site. Jane learned of the mentoring event by reading Amy's comment on LinkedIn and then attended the event. At the event, Jane introduced Amy to Tom who ultimately hired Amy. While it's possible that Amy and Tom would have met without Jane's introduction, the introduction made Amy's follow-up with Tom warmer. Moreover, Amy followed up with Tom via LinkedIn which allowed Tom to view Amy's writing or product. It was Tom's impression of Amy's writing that led him to call her when an opening arose in his firm.

A job search campaign, like a political campaign, is comprised of various pieces. One piece that can no longer be ignored in either campaign is social networking. Social networking alone can't win elections or jobs, but it can contribute significantly when performed correctly.

Chapter 4 outlines over 60 ways you can perform your job search with social networking.

What is Social Networking?

Definition

A social network is any website designed to allow multiple users to publish content themselves.[4] The subject matter of the information shared by users varies, depending on the audience which can range from family and friends to professional contacts and strangers. Thus, social networking is simply one tool, like a telephone or e-mail, used to communicate and share information with your networks.

Varieties

If you maintain a profile on a site like MySpace, Facebook, Twitter, Flickr, YouTube, Digg, StumbleUpon, Del.icio.us, or LinkedIn, you already have a presence on a social networking site. You might even have a profile on one of the social networking sites designed specifically for lawyer-to-lawyer networking: Martindale Hubbell Connected, Legal OnRamp, Legally Minded, Avvo, or a state bar association's social networking site.

Obama and Brown used a variety of social networking sites to reach their potential employers, the voters. Obama used, among others, Facebook, Eons, MiGente.com to reach young voters, baby boomers, and Latinos, respectively.[5] Brown used, among others, Ning to organize campaign volunteers, an iPhone application to assist canvassers with their scripts, and YouTube to reach young voters.[6]

You need a variety of social networking sites to reach potential employers and referral sources, and I recommend the Big 3 social networking sites.

WHAT ARE THE BIG 3?

The Big 3 social networking sites—Facebook, LinkedIn, and Twitter (collectively, the "Big 3")—are the three most popular social networking sites in terms of registered users.[1] For best results, you should use all three sites because each site attracts a different audience that can contribute to your job search success.

Facebook

With over 500 million users (as of July 2010), Facebook is the largest of the Big 3.[7]

- *Audience*: Most people use the site to connect with friends, family, former or current classmates, and even some professional colleagues. Facebook originated as a social networking site for college students but

---

[1] Please review the Big 3 sites' terms of service and agreements for guidance on appropriate use:
Facebook: http://www.facebook.com/terms.php.
LinkedIn: http://www.linkedin.com/static?key=user_agreement&trk=hb_ft_userag.
Twitter: http://twitter.com/tos.
Additionally, many states' rules governing attorney professional conduct and advertising address attorneys' use of social networking sites such as the Big 3, and you should review the rules for the state(s) in which you are licensed.

attracted older members in droves in 2009; the majority of Facebook users fall in the 35-54 age range.[8]

- *Features*: Facebook allows users to share information by writing status updates, sharing websites, videos and pictures, writing on other users' walls (or pages), and sending private e-mail messages. The people you are connected to are known as your friends, and Facebook reminds you of your friends' birthdays. There are a host of applications, games, and quizzes available on Facebook as well.

- *Role in Job Search*: You need a presence on Facebook because your best referral network is on Facebook—family and friends who know, like, and trust you and are likely to refer you for jobs. You need to continually nurture this already strong network.

LinkedIn

LinkedIn is a professional social networking site with over 70 million users (as of June 2010).[9]

- *Audience*: Most people use LinkedIn to connect with other professionals, including former colleagues and classmates, current colleagues, clients, and even strangers who happen to work in the same industry.

- *Features*: Many attorneys create LinkedIn accounts, accept invitations when people invite them to connect, but then never use the site. You can, however, share information like a status update, events you are attending, your travel schedule, blog, articles, and book reviews. The information you share on LinkedIn is more professional in nature; you wouldn't post family vacation pictures on LinkedIn.

- *Role in Job Search*: LinkedIn is an excellent research tool and one that journalists, recruiters, and hiring managers often use to find lawyers. You will miss opportunities if you do not participate on LinkedIn.

Twitter

Twitter, the newest of the Big 3, is still a mystery to many. Twitter had over 75 million visitors in January 2010[10]; yet, its active user base is much smaller—about 15 million active users.[11] Many people create Twitter accounts and then abandon them, possibly because they don't spend enough time learning how Twitter works.

- *Audience*: Twitter is literally everywhere—every major news outlet tweets as well as your favorite TV, movie, music, and sports personalities. More people learned of Michael Jackson's death on Twitter than from major news outlets. But, professionals tweet as well, including many in the legal profession. And, many legal media outlets tweet. Thus, Twitter is a great source for legal news and connections.
- *Features*: Twitter asks users to answer, "What's happening?" in no more than 140 characters. In effect, Twitter is just the exchange of short status updates. People post thoughts, ask for feedback, share links to articles or blogs, review a movie or restaurant they recently tried, and discuss current events.
- *Role in Job Search*: Of the Big 3 sites, Twitter is the best platform for forging new relationships. You can meet new contacts on Twitter because the Twitter platform is conducive to conversation that leads to offline relationships.

WHAT ARE THE 6PS?

As in political campaigns, your *presence* on the Big 3 social networking sites is not enough to get hired. It's your strategic *performance* on the Big 3 social networking sites that makes social networking a winning piece of a job search or political campaign. The purpose of this book is to outline a system to help you incorporate the Big 3 social networking sites in your job search campaign.

The system consists of six components, hence the 6Ps, required to get you hired using social networking. Chapters 1-6 focus on one component or "P."

Part 1: Prepare to Use the Big 3 Sites in your Job Search

Chapters 1-3 are the preparation phase. The chapters in this section discuss actions you must take *before* using the Big 3 in your job search—steps you must perform initially but not daily. The chapters in this section include:

1. *Professionalism (Chapter 1):* All online social networking sites serve a professional purpose to some degree. You must understand the varying degrees of professionalism required on the Big 3 sites so you can perform your job search accordingly.

2. *Profile (Chapter 2):* What information should you share on your profiles on the Big 3? Is there information you should omit? You must complete a profile on each site, but how much information you share varies according to the professionalism of the site and your use of the site.

3. *Privacy (Chapter 3):* What information should you protect? After you complete your profile, you'll want to protect certain information.

Part 2: Perform your Job Search on the Big 3 Sites

After understanding the degrees of professionalism, completing your profiles, and setting your privacy controls, you are ready to use the Big 3 sites to perform your job search campaign. It is your performance, not your mere presence, on social networking sites that will get you hired.

4. *Performance (Chapter 4):* There are three levels of performance, and you must complete all three levels on all three sites in order to CAP or maximize your job search success: (1) Connect; (2) Assimilate; and (3) Participate. Chapter 4 outlines over 60 ways to use the Big 3 sites in your job search.

Part 3: Polish your Performance

The final part of the 6Ps system consists of steps to help you polish your performance and increase your chances of getting hired using the Big 3 social networking sites.

5. *Practice (Chapter 5):* Chapter 5 covers how to use the Big 3 sites efficiently, and there are three required steps: (1) block (time and activities); (2) measure (activity responses and activity goals); and (3) practice (includes sample schedule).

6. *Protocol (Chapter 6):* Chapter 6 contains pinstripes (desired behaviors) and pearls (distinguishing activities).

Part 4: Proof Lawyers Get Hired Using the 6Ps System

The last chapter, **Chapter 7 - Paragons**, is not part of the 6Ps system; rather, it profiles two paragons of social networking—one law student and one practicing lawyer who successfully used social networking to get hired. Chapter 7 outlines the paragons' stories, analyzes the presence of the 6Ps in the paragons' job searches, and draws on examples from the paragons' searches to illustrate the importance of incorporating social networking in your job search.

WHY IS SOCIAL NETWORKING IMPORTANT?

As you read this book, you'll see why social networking is an important tool and why face-to-face meetings, phone calls, and e-mails, alone, are not always sufficient for getting hired. Consider the following eight reasons why you should understand the Big 3 social networking sites, and look for discussions and illustrations in the noted chapters.

1. *Search*. Studies show that potential employers search and review candidates' profiles on social networking sites.

   - *79% search online.* Research commissioned by Microsoft in December 2009 found that 79 percent of United States hiring managers and job recruiters surveyed reviewed online information, including social networking sites, about job applicants.[12]
   - *70% reject based on negative information.* In the Microsoft study, 70 percent of the hiring managers admitted to rejecting candidates based on negative information on the candidates' online profiles.[13]
   - *85% influenced by positive profiles.* Sharing positive information on your social networking profiles might help your chances of obtaining a job. In the same Microsoft study, 85% of the recruiters and hiring managers said a candidate's positive online reputation influences his or her hiring decisions to some extent.[14]

     Bottom line: Employers search candidates' online profiles. Be sure the online profiles you craft give employers a reason to hire you rather than to reject you. Chapter 2 discusses how to craft positive profiles on the Big 3.

2. *Social Recruiting*. As you'll see in Chapter 4, numerous methods exist for employers to post or announce job openings on the Big 3 sites; therefore, you should know how to navigate the sites to find the openings.

3. *Warm Calls*. Online social networking and traditional offline networking are not mutually exclusive. Chapters 4 and 7 are filled with examples that illustrate how your conversations with strangers on Twitter fuel offline communications. The online conversations "warm" the offline cold introductions when you meet potential employers for coffee, an information interview, or even a job interview. For example, you may already know the person's favorite kind of coffee or taste in movies. Introverts, especially, can appreciate knowing something about the other person and using that information as a conversation starter.

Marketing Principle: Cold Call v. Warm Call

A cold call is a sales term referring to a call or visit made to a stranger, often in order to sell something. A cold call, however, may also apply to job seekers who must contact potential employers they don't know to inquire about jobs or referrals. Salespeople prefer warm calls, contacting a prospect with whom you've had some form of prior communication, to cold calls. Warm calls are still made to people you don't know well; however, they differ from cold calls because they involve some prior communication or contact.

4. *Seven Touches*. Networking, whether online or offline, is a high touch business. It takes at least seven touches or interactions with someone before they are likely to hire you.[15] In other words, you must remain on your network's radar screen in order for them to refer you or hire you. The Big 3 allow job seekers to share information with their networks on a regular basis and remain on their radar screens.

Chapter 4 outlines how you can use the Big 3 sites to remain on your networks' radar screens.

Marketing Principle: Seven Touches

Another marketing principle applicable to job seekers and empowered by online social networking is the rule of seven touches. It takes, on average, seven "touches" to convert a cold customer to a sale. The same seven touches theory applies when developing new contacts in your job search. It takes at least seven touches or interactions with someone before you develop a relationship that will generate a referral or job lead.

5. ***Client Development***. Knowing how to navigate the Big 3 social networking sites may get you hired by clients. For example, an energy company based in Houston, Texas, recently required law firms to state in a tweet on Twitter why the Houston company should hire the law firm.[16] Of the 50 law firms that downloaded the company's Request for Proposal (RFP), only eight firms complied with the instructions to tweet and made the final cut. Thus, knowing how the social networking sites work and how to use them might give you a competitive advantage when seeking new work.

   At a minimum, the skills you learn in Chapter 4 transfer to your business development activities. Your performance on the Big 3 social networking sites can help you to get hired by employers or clients.

6. ***The In-house Social Media Attorney***. As more companies embrace social networking in their marketing practices, more legal issues about social networking will arise. For example, Clorox Corporation recently advertised for a Corporate Counsel – Social Media/Talent Rights position.[17] Perhaps more companies will need attorneys with this specialization as corporations continue to lead the push in social media.

Chapter 7 also illustrates how law firms may use social media attorneys in the future.

7. ***Perpetual Network.*** The contacts you build on the Big 3 social networking sites now are an investment; these contacts, if nurtured, can serve as resources in future job searches or client development. The need to network does not die when your job search ends. You will need a strong network at other points in the future; thus, your work to build your network is actually an investment.

Chapter 7 illustrates the benefit of a perpetual network.

8. ***Passive Candidate.*** In the world of legal hiring, there are two types of candidates: (1) active; and (2) passive. An active candidate is one who is actively looking for a job, screening job boards, and submitting resumes. A passive candidate is one who is happy with his or her current job and not actively looking; he or she might, however, listen to potential employers or recruiters if they should contact him or her about a better opportunity.

Your performance on the Big 3 social networking sites can lead potential employers and recruiters to find you even when you aren't actively seeking a new job. For example, your postings and conversations on Twitter, over time, might reveal that you are an expert in retail bankruptcy proceedings. A potential employer or recruiter may have a need for someone with that expertise.

Chapter 7 illustrates how one passive candidate obtained a job through her use of social networking.

HOW TO USE THIS BOOK

I wrote this book to help job-seeking lawyers and law students at *all* levels. You should note some features of the book and how they apply to your specific level.

1. *Primer.* There is a Primer at the end of the book to help beginners understand the basics of Facebook, LinkedIn, and Twitter. I encourage beginners to start with the Primer before diving into the chapters. Everyone else may want to refer to the Primer as needed.

2. *Points.* There is a checklist called Points at the end of each chapter. Each Points Page serves as a bullet point summary with points you should have learned in the previous chapter.

3. *Practice.* After completing all seven chapters of the book, go back to the Practice section and follow the suggested schedules or create your own. I recommend following a schedule for at least six weeks.

4. *Protocol.* Advanced users may want to re-read the Protocol chapter and outline their strategy for using the Big 3 sites in branding and differentiation.

5. *Reference.* Refer back to particular sections of the book as often as needed during your regular use of the Big 3 sites. The detailed Table of Contents can help you navigate to the appropriate section to address your questions.

NETWORKING NECESSARY, TECHNOLOGY BACKGROUND OPTIONAL

This is a book about networking—specifically, networking to advance your legal career. While the networking tools discussed in this book involve technology (using online social networking sites), you don't need a technology background to understand this book or succeed at social networking. The social networking sites are simply additional tools resulting from technological advancements to aid with your job search, similar to the fax machine, e-mail, and online job boards of the 1980s, 1990s, and 2000s, respectively.

FINAL CAVEAT

The Big 3 sites continue to evolve. During the time I worked on this book, controls on all three sites changed at least twice. I encourage you to read for substance and strategy. I will, however, write about any changes and their impact on the legal job search on my blog: www.6psbig3.com.

PART 1

PREPARE TO USE THE BIG 3 SITES IN YOUR JOB SEARCH

You must prepare *before* you actually use the Big 3 social networking sites in your job search. The steps outlined in the following three chapters are steps you must perform initially but not daily.

The chapters in this section examine the degree of professionalism for each of the Big 3 sites (Chapter 1), the information to include and omit from your profiles on the Big 3 sites (Chapter 2), and the information you may want protect before rushing to use the Big 3 sites in your job search (Chapter 3).

CHAPTER 1

Professionalism

All online social networking sites serve a professional purpose to some extent.

YOU have read or will read many blogs and articles suggesting that job seekers must determine whether they are using a social networking site for a personal or professional purpose. Erase this advice. There is no such clear distinction for attorneys because certain friends are both professional colleagues and friends (*i.e.,* law school classmates). As you will learn throughout this book, *all* social networking sites serve a professional purpose to some degree for attorneys.

The degree of professionalism you exhibit on social networking sites is directly related to the audience composition of each social networking site. This chapter examines the audience composition of the Big 3 social networking sites and recommends how much professional content you should share on the sites. Each of the Big 3 sites can be classified as either:

1. ***Partly Professional:*** less than 50% of your time and content will be devoted to professional content, and
2. ***Primarily Professional:*** more than 50% of your time and content will be devoted to professional content

FACEBOOK

Platform:	Personal
Audience:	
Majority View	People you know/have known plus *select* professional colleagues
Minority View	People you know/have known plus *any* professional colleague, client
Purpose:	Communicating with people you know and have known, your best referral network
Degree of Professionalism:	
Majority View	*Partly Professional* (5-40% professional content)
Minority View	*Primarily Professional* (up to 80% professional content)

Facebook provides a platform for users to share *personal* information such as birthdays, anniversaries, interests, religious and political views, and pictures— family pictures, old pictures, vacation pictures, and pictures celebrating milestones of life such as births and weddings.

Purpose

Because of the volume of personal information shared on Facebook, most lawyers use Facebook to connect and communicate *only* with people they know well such as childhood friends, college friends, law school friends, family and select professional colleagues.

Although secondary, Facebook may also be an opportunity for professional networking. Many employers hire job seekers they know, like, and trust—your family and friends on your Facebook page probably know, like, and trust you or they wouldn't be connected to you. Thus, your Facebook contacts, while probably not all professional contacts, just might be your strongest professional network. Your Facebook friends are likely to refer you to their contacts because they know, like, and trust you. Information in Chapter 4 will explain how your performance on Facebook can help your job search as you interact with friends and family, sharing information with them regarding your job search.

Audience

Lawyers adopt one of two views when selecting their Facebook friends.

Majority View

Most lawyers use Facebook to connect and communicate only with people they know well, such as childhood friends, college friends, law school friends, family, and *select* professional colleagues.

Minority View

Some lawyers use Facebook to connect with people they know well *plus any* professional colleague, including clients. Under this minority view, lawyers may accept a friend request from just about anyone on Facebook if they think that contact will lead to business or a career opportunity. Or, some lawyers following the minority view accept friend requests from people they've never met in person.

Chapter 4 explains two rules for connecting with people on Facebook in detail. It's worth introducing the two differing views now so you can see how each view affects other decisions you'll make when using the Big 3 sites, such as choosing a profile picture (Chapter 2 Profile) or controlling your privacy settings (Chapter 3 Privacy).

Degree of Professionalism

Your degree of professionalism on Facebook will vary depending on whether you follow the Majority View or the Minority View of defining your audience. Attorneys following the Majority View could share between 5-40% professional content, whereas attorneys following the Minority View might share up to 80% professional content.

I adopt the Majority View, and, thus, the views in this book reflect the Majority View unless specifically noted. It's also important to note that your view might change during your career. Think about which view is best for you as you continue to read through the book.

LinkedIn

Platform:	**Professional**
Audience:	**Past/present colleagues and classmates, others in your industry**
Primary Purpose:	**Connecting and communicating with colleagues, classmates, industry professionals**
Degree of Professionalism:	**Primarily Professional (100% professional content)**

LinkedIn is a professional networking site that reached over 70 million users in June 2010. The number of legal professionals using LinkedIn nearly quadrupled between June 2008 (216,000) to June 2009 (840,000),[18] and the number of lawyers with LinkedIn profiles crossed over the 1 million mark at some point in fall 2009 (1,359,590).[19]

Purpose

Most lawyers view LinkedIn as a static site where they can list their education and experience and connect with other professional contacts. Thus, LinkedIn functions as your online resume and rolodex.

Although LinkedIn is not as social as Facebook or Twitter, it, too, allows you to communicate with your LinkedIn contacts via applications to your profile, updates to your profile, and group discussions. All of these uses are explained further in Chapter 4.

Audience

Your LinkedIn audience is professional and may include past/present colleagues and classmates, including professionals in your industry even if you don't know them.

Degree of Professionalism

Because LinkedIn has a professional platform, it falls into the Primarily Professional category, and 100% of the content you share should be professional in nature.

TWITTER

Platform:	**Hybrid – Professional and Personal**
Audience:	**Anyone (Target = 80% Professional)**
Purpose:	**Communicate with people you don't know but want to get to know and forge new relationships**
Degree of Professionalism:	**Primarily Professional (80% professional content)**

One feature unique to Twitter is the ability to connect with other users without obtaining their approval. With Facebook and LinkedIn, you must request to connect with other users and the users must approve your request. On Twitter, however, you can connect with and "follow" anyone; there's no approval process unless a person's account is protected (discussed in Chapter 3).

Purpose

The combination professional-personal nature of Twitter makes it an effective site for communicating with people you don't know but want to get to know—from celebrities and professional athletes to people who are more likely to be a resource in your job search, like law school career counselors, law firm recruiters and hiring personnel, third party legal recruiters or headhunters, lawyers, law students, legal marketing professionals, legal technology professionals, and law firm consultants.

And, Twitter is so much more than small talk about what you had for lunch. The amount of information you can gain from people on Twitter is infinite and invaluable—from job leads, to new contacts, to tips about hot practice areas or professions. The best part about Twitter is that only a few attorneys are using it in their job search (or even know how to use it), so those who do use it instantly have access to untapped resources.

Audience

Remember, you can connect to just about anyone. I recommend that job seekers follow 80% professional contacts and about 20% other contacts.

Degree of Professionalism

Accordingly, Twitter falls into the Primarily Professional category, and 80% of your content on Twitter should be professional in nature.

POINTS – PROFESSIONALISM

	Platform	Audience	Purpose	Professionalism
Facebook	Personal	**Majority View** - People you know/ have known plus *select* professional colleagues	Communicating with people you know and have known, your best referral network	**Majority View** – *Partly Professional* (5-40% professional content)
		Minority View - People you know/ have known plus *any* professional colleague, client		**Minority View** – *Primarily Professional* (up to 80% professional content)
LinkedIn	Professional	Past/present colleagues and classmates, others in your industry	Connecting and communicating with colleagues, classmates, industry professionals	*Primarily Professional* (100% professional content)
Twitter	Hybrid	Anyone (Target = 80% Professional)	Communicating with people you don't know but want to get to know and forging new relationships	Primarily Professional (80% professional content)

CHAPTER 2

Profile

THE first rule of marketing is to put yourself and/or your product out there.[20] Today, that means having some online presence. Politicians create an online presence immediately upon announcing their candidacy for the jobs they seek, and some even create unofficial sites prior to their official announcement.[21] They create websites, blogs, and social networking profiles. You must do the same in your job search.

As noted in the Premise, 79% of hiring managers and recruiters search candidates' online social networking profiles, and 85% have found a candidate's positive online profile to influence their hiring decision to some extent.[22]

This chapter examines how to craft a positive profile that will get you hired. The first part of the chapter focuses on your profile picture on the Big 3 social networking sites, and the second part of the chapter focuses on the biographical information you share.

PROFILE PICTURE

When I speak about the Big 3 sites, someone always asks if he or she must include a picture on his or her social networking profile. Have you ever seen a politician who is campaigning for his job omit his picture from his social networking profile? Probably not—your profile picture is the product image that potential employers (or voters) will identify with and remember. You should include a profile picture on the Big 3 sites as well. Your profile picture improves your social networking profile in at least three ways.

Why does a profile picture improve your profile?

1. *It humanizes you.* Employers want to hire humans. A profile picture shows your human side. A picture also confirms that you are not a spammer. To avoid spammers, many people will not reciprocate friend requests from people without profile pictures.

2. *People remember you!* Consider the following scenario:

   • Natalie and Ashley are both real estate lawyers but practice in different geographical areas; they have never met or exchanged any type of communication. Natalie read an article Ashley authored for a real estate law publication; Natalie was impressed with the article and went to LinkedIn to learn more about Ashley. After reading Ashley's LinkedIn profile, Natalie concluded that they might be able to collaborate and refer matters to each other in the future. Natalie sent Ashley a request to connect.

   Ashley reviewed Natalie's profile, including the picture, and accepted Natalie's LinkedIn request. A few days later, Natalie found Ashley on Twitter and started following her. Natalie's Twitter profile didn't contain a picture, but Ashley associated Natalie's name with the picture on her LinkedIn profile.

   Studies suggest that we remember information, such as someone's name or profile information on a social networking site, if a picture is associated with it. The above scenario illustrates the point.

   Thus, if you want potential employers, recruiters, and hiring personnel to remember you and your social networking profiles, include a profile picture.

3. **People recognize you.** I attended a networking event last year where a man approached me and thought he knew me from somewhere. At first, I couldn't figure out how I knew him. As we continued to talk, we realized that we followed each other on Twitter. But, I would not

have recognized him from across the room because his Twitter profile picture is his company logo. He recognized me, however, because of my Twitter profile picture.

The opposite is also true. As recommended in Chapter 4, you should connect online with contacts you make offline at conferences and networking events. It's helpful for you to identify contacts if their profiles contain a picture. For example, I made over 30 new professional contacts at the last conference I attended. Two days following the conference, I sat down to connect with these people on LinkedIn. The profiles with pictures were so much better; I remembered our conversations, and I knew I had the right person (especially if the person had a common name and there were over 300 Amy Smiths in the LinkedIn database).

What type of picture should you include?

Your profile picture on all of the Big 3 sites should meet the following requirements:

1. ***Recent.*** Your profile picture on all of the Big 3 sites should be a recent picture—one taken in the past five years. This is especially important on LinkedIn and Twitter where you often connect with people you've never met or haven't seen for some time. If you meet in person, you want to be recognizable.
2. ***Quality.*** Avoid blurry pictures—especially on LinkedIn and Twitter where the pictures are so small; the small size makes the poor quality even worse.
3. ***Headshot.*** Use a headshot where the picture is of your shoulders up and focuses on your face (Image 2.1) rather than a full length picture (Image 2.2) where your face isn't clear.

Image 2.1
Headshot – YES

Image 2.2
Full Length – NO

v.

4. ***Partly Professional v. Primarily Professional:*** You learned in
    Chapter 1 that all of the Big 3 social networking sites serve a profes-
    sional purpose to some degree. Your profile picture on each site should
    correspond to the degree of professionalism of the site—either Partly
    Professional or Primarily Professional.

    Partly Professional: Facebook – Majority View

    If you follow the Majority View, you use Facebook primarily to
    connect with family, friends, and select colleagues—people who know
    you well. As a result, you can enjoy greater flexibility with the type of
    profile picture you choose, as follows:

    1. <u>Casual</u> – A casual profile picture is acceptable on Facebook if
        you adhere to the Majority View. You don't have to use a profes-
        sional, formal headshot. In fact, you probably should include a
        casual picture to show your personality.

        Compare the following pictures of Regina Adams, an attorney
        in Houston, Texas. Regina uses the casual picture shown in
        Image 2.3 as her Facebook profile picture instead of her profes-
        sional headshot in Image 2.4 which she uses on LinkedIn.

Image 2.3
Casual– YES

Image 2.4
Professional – Not Preferred

v.

2. **Rotate pictures** – Under the Majority View, your Facebook friends include people who know you well and know what you look like; thus, it's okay to change your profile picture. You don't need to maintain one picture so your audience will identify with it; they already know what you look like.

For example, Regina, the attorney profiled above, frequently changes her profile picture to reflect a season or holiday, as illustrated by the Halloween picture in Image 2.5 and vacation picture in Image 2.6. Note that the pictures are still headshots, recent, and of good quality.

Image 2.5
Holiday Pictures
(Halloween) –YES

Image 2.6
Vacation Pictures - YES

v.

Or, you may participate in the Facebook theme weeks, a format through which Facebook designates the type of profile picture to include for a certain time period. For example, Facebook has in the past designated Retro Week for posting a childhood picture and Doppleganger Week for posting a picture of a celebrity you resemble. The variety and change is what makes Facebook fun and interactive.

3. **Non-human picture** – A picture of you is preferred, but, occasionally, you may want to use a picture of an animal, object, or cartoon character. You may also want to join or support a cause or campaign by using the cause's logo as your profile picture.

    One caveat to note, when using non-human pictures: use them for a *limited period of time.*

4. **Others in your picture** – You will find that lawyers following the Majority View will sometimes post pictures of their children or friends as their profile picture. Including pictures of others is acceptable on Facebook under the Majority View. Chapter 3 (page 79) addresses potential privacy concerns some people have with using pictures that include others.

5. **Office Desk Photo Rule** – And, finally, your Facebook profile picture should pass the Office Desk Photo Rule for the following reasons:

    Google Effect: As you will learn in Chapter 3, your profile picture is one piece of information that Facebook makes available to the entire public, including people not on Facebook. If someone searches for your name on a search engine like Google, a thumbnail picture of your profile picture will appear—even if your privacy settings are set so that only your friends can view your pictures.[2]

---

[2] It is possible to remove your profile from Internet search results—see Chapter 3, page 86.

As you learned in the Premise, 79% of human resource managers search candidates' names on the internet; thus, it is likely a potential employer will search your name and see your Facebook profile picture, even if your profile is protected.

Pages & Groups: Also, if you are a member of a professional group (or "like" a business page) on Facebook (discussed in Chapter 4), other members of that group (or page) can see your profile picture even if all of your other information is set to private and even if you removed yourself from search engine indexing.

Your profile picture is visible when you comment on friends' pages or you RSVP to events (discussed in Chapter 4). As more bar associations, law school alumni groups, and professional organizations create groups and pages on Facebook, it's highly likely that you are connected to one of these pages. Therefore, your profile picture is widely visible, and you should choose your profile picture accordingly.

My recommendation is the **Office Desk Photo Rule**: choose a profile picture that you would display on your office desk. Thus, the picture can be casual—just not too casual.

At a minimum, avoid using a profile picture if it's one of you taking shots or passed out at a party. You probably wouldn't display such picture on your office desk, so why include it on Facebook where your colleagues and clients/potential clients can see it? Avoid any type of nude picture even if it's a picture of your nude back. I realize this might seem obvious, but I have seen lawyers use such pictures as their profile pictures.

Remember, it doesn't matter how tight your privacy settings are, your profile pictures are still visible; that's why it's better to stick with only casual pictures you would display on your office desk.

Primarily Professional: Facebook – Minority View, LinkedIn, Twitter

If you follow the Minority View on Facebook, you use Facebook to connect with anyone—family, friends, and all colleagues, clients, and people you've never met; you are not as selective with your friend selections as those who follow the Majority View. As a result, you cannot enjoy the same flexibility afforded to users following the Majority View. Because you are connecting with people you have not met or people who know you only from a professional context, you'll want to use a professional profile picture like you do on LinkedIn and Twitter, the other Big 3 sites that are primarily for professional networking.

The professional picture does not need to be a picture taken by a professional photographer (Image 2.7), but it should represent the "professional" image you want to project to employers or clients (Image 2.8).

**Image 2.7
Professional
Photograph – YES**

**Jennifer Ingram
Attorney, Dallas, TX**

**Image 2.8
Professional
Image – YES**

**Yana Knutson
Law Student,
St. John's Law School**

Also, keep in mind that your LinkedIn and Twitter pictures are tiny—80 x 80 pixels—and LinkedIn and Twitter will crop the picture you upload for your profile picture. Keep this in mind when selecting a picture.

Image 2.9
Picture Uploaded

Image 2.10
Picture Cropped
by LinkedIn

I recommend that job seekers consider using the same professional picture on both Twitter and LinkedIn. If you are using the sites in your job search, you might encounter the same people on both sites—people you have not met in person but with whom you've developed a relationship online. Using the same picture helps brand you and others will quickly identify you on the other site.

BIOGRAPHICAL INFORMATION

The second component of a politician's or job seeker's profile is the biographical information—the description of the product you are marketing—YOU!

FACEBOOK

Your Facebook profile is comprised of the following categories shown in Image 2.11:

Image 2.11

The profile picture was discussed above so this section focuses on the biographical information contained in the other profile categories: basic information, relationships, likes and interests, education and work, and contact information.

You should note a few general points about the biographical information requested:

1. *Optional.* Most of the biographical information requested for your Facebook profile is optional. Share only information you feel comfortable sharing.
2. *Privacy.* You can, however, protect most of the information you share. Refer to the privacy controls discussed in Chapter 3.
3. *Helpful v. Harmful.* I recommend that job seekers analyze whether the

information requested could help or harm their chances of obtaining a job. If it could help, include it and make sure the information is visible to potential employers (discussed in Chapter 3). If the information could harm your chances, you may want to exclude it or you may want to use a privacy setting (in Chapter 3) to protect the information.

This section focuses on how certain biographical information could either help or harm your job chances.

Category: Basic Information

Basic Information is comprised of the categories of information in Image 2.12. Certain categories—current city, hometown, birthday, political views, and religious views—are discussed below Image 2.12.

Image 2.12

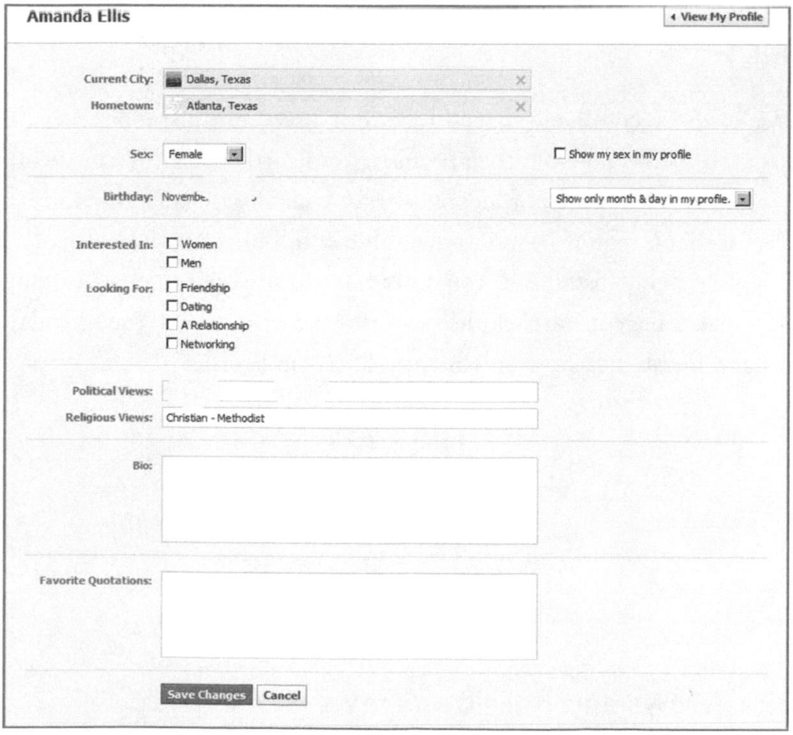

Current City and Hometown

Helpful: A potential employer from your hometown might find your profile and contact you to see if you are interested in returning to your hometown to practice. Or, if you are applying for jobs in your hometown, potential employers might search for you on Facebook or Google. Employers like to see ties or connections to the markets in which candidates are applying, so including this information could help your job search.

Harmful: In rare cases, job seekers sometimes tell potential employers that they "recently relocated to X city" when actually they are just testing the waters and will only move to X city if there are employment opportunities. Again, this doesn't happen often, but be careful if you try this approach. The potential employer might search your Facebook profile or Google you as part of his or her due diligence. Seeing another city listed as the current city on your profile might raise a red flag.

Birthday

Harmful: I recommend that all Facebook users, not just job seekers, omit their birth year from their profiles. Your birth year is one piece of information that can assist identity thieves, so why make it available? Facebook requires you to provide your full birthday, including the year, when you register. But, you don't have to display the year. As you can see in Image 2.13, click the drop down menu next to the birthday box and highlight "show only month & day in profile."

Image 2.13

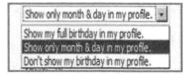

Political Views and Religious Views

Harmful: Some job seekers question whether their religious and political views will harm their chances at certain jobs. While employers shouldn't discriminate based on this information, the possibility exists. If you are concerned, omit the information or protect it through a privacy setting discussed in Chapter 3. Chapter 6 also addresses political views from an etiquette standpoint.

Category: Relationships

Image 2.14

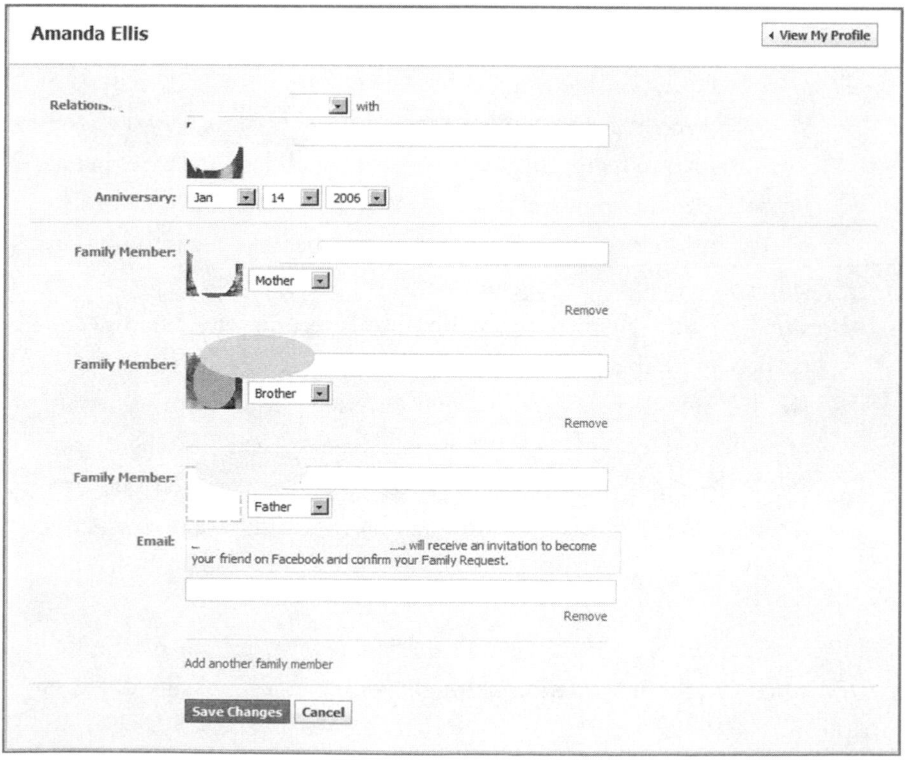

Under the Relationships category, Facebook allows you to identify and link to family members and significant others who also have Facebook accounts.

Helpful. A potential employer who finds your profile through a due diligence search might not recognize your name but might recognize your sibling or someone else with whom you have a relationship. Such information could influence the employer's decision to interview you.

Harmful. On the other hand, if the employer has a negative relationship with or impression of one of your related Facebook members, it might harm you.

Use your discretion. Omit or protect the information through privacy settings if your related Facebook users are contentious people.

Category: Likes and Interests

The Likes and Interests section on Facebook is similar to the Activities/ Interests section on your resume.

Helpful. It is questionable whether listing your activities and interests on your resume will help you land a job. When I became a legal recruiter, I was trained to remove this section from candidates' resumes because it was irrelevant. However, I know many law school career counselors who advise students to include this section because the information can aid in conversation during an interview.

Harmful. It's unlikely the information in this section would harm your chances of getting a job unless you list questionable activities. I've had law firm recruiters tell me that they have rejected candidates because of questionable activities, such as pole dancing, listed on their resume. While the candidate was probably referring to the popular pole dancing aerobics class, perhaps the word "aerobics" would have been a better word choice.

Exercise discretion. Omit the information if you feel uncomfortable, or control who sees the information through your privacy settings discussed in Chapter 3.

Category: Education and Work

The Education and Work section is perhaps the most helpful section for job seekers, yet many job seekers omit this information from their profiles.

Helpful. Education and Work is the most important category of information because it can help your job search in several ways.

1. ***Personal Referrals.*** If you are using Facebook to communicate primarily with friends and family, you may think your friends and family don't care about your professional life, such as the education and work section. As you will see in Chapter 4, this idea is a bit misguided since that group—your friends and family—can be one of your best referral sources. Your referral sources need information about your professional life in order to know what you do and how, when, or if you may be a candidate referral.

2. ***Professional Referrals.*** As discussed earlier regarding your profile picture, your profile picture and name are visible on the Facebook groups you join or the fan pages that you like. More bar associations, law school alumni groups and professional organizations now have group or fan pages that you will likely join or like. Other Facebook users who are members of the groups or like the page will probably see your name and picture—especially if you engage by commenting or responding to an event. If the person doesn't know you, he or she might click on your name to view your Facebook profile. Since these users are possibly professional colleagues, it would help if they could see some professional information about you such as your work and education. Perhaps they even know of a job opportunity and can let you know if they have information about your background.

3. ***BranchOut.*** BranchOut launched in July 2010, and the Facebook application allows you to see where your Facebook friends (and, your friends' friends) work or previously worked. BranchOut only identifies you if you include your work information. You may miss opportunities if you don't provide your work information. For example, if a potential employer performed a search to identify his or her friends (and, friends' friends) who previously worked at a certain firm, you would only appear in the search results if you listed the firm on your Facebook profile. Chapter 4 addresses how to use BranchOut.

If you simply don't want to take the time to complete your professional information, at least include a link to your LinkedIn profile where your friends and family can go to find these details, as shown in Images 2.15 and 2.16.

Image 2.15

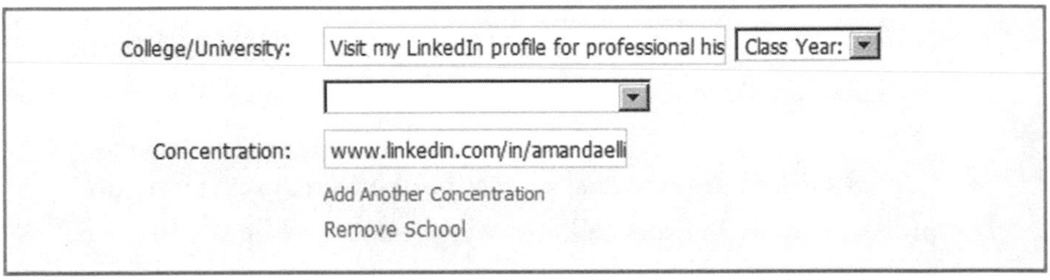

College/University:	Visit my LinkedIn profile for professional his	Class Year: ▼
		▼
Concentration:	www.linkedin.com/in/amandaelli	
	Add Another Concentration	
	Remove School	

Image 2.16

Education and Work

College: www.linkedin.com/in/amandaellis

Category: Contact Information

Another overlooked category of helpful information is the Contact Information section.

> *Helpful.* You want your Facebook friends to contact you if they hear of career opportunities. You need at least one contact number or e-mail in case your Facebook friends want to contact you about a career opportunity.

I realize some people cringe at the thought of listing contact information online. You can control who sees the information through the privacy settings discussed in Chapter 3.

LINKEDIN

Like your Facebook profile, your LinkedIn profile also allows you to share information in multiple categories. A few things to note before looking at the various categories:

LinkedIn v. Facebook Distinction

The primary distinction between your Facebook and LinkedIn profiles is that most of the information sought is professional in nature. It's to your advantage to complete your LinkedIn profile in detail, whereas it was okay to omit information from your Facebook profile.

A Law Student's Bio

If you are a law student, it's even more important for you to create a detailed profile because your LinkedIn profile serves as your online professional bio. Employers can view a practicing attorney's firm bio or profile before deciding whether to interview or hire. Law students, however, have no such listing. Therefore, a law student who creates a detailed profile on LinkedIn may be providing valuable information for a discerning employer.

Re-arranging Sections

Your LinkedIn profile is comprised of nine categories of information that can be re-arranged. For example, if you are a student, you may want your education to appear before your experience, while a practicing attorney might want his experience to appear before his education.

To move a section, look for the four arrow symbol to the left of the section heading (as shown in Image 2.17) and drag it to the area of your profile where you want it to appear.

Image 2.17

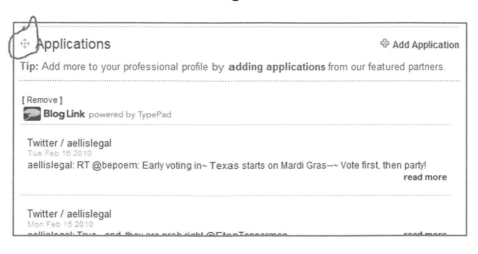

The nine categories of information you can share on LinkedIn include:

1.   Snapshot
2.   Summary
3.   Applications
4.   Education
5.   Experience
6.   Recommendations
7.   Additional Information
8.   Personal Information
9.   Contact Settings

(1) Snapshot

The Snapshot section is the overview of your LinkedIn profile that people read first. Some of the information displayed in your snapshot is pulled from other sections of your profile, while other information is unique to the Snapshot section, including:

- Name
- Professional headline
- Location
- Industry
- Status Update
- Public Profile

It is worth noting some features of the categories unique to the Snapshot section.

Name

Use the same name that appears on your resume so recruiters or hiring authorities find your profile if they look on LinkedIn.

Professional headline (Title)

You can use your professional headline to differentiate yourself and stand out from other law students or practicing attorneys. Like your profile picture, your headline is something employers are likely to remember, so create a unique headline.

Law Students:

Most law students use their headline to list their law student status. For example,

- Law Student at Vermont Law School, or
- 3L at Vermont Law School

Consider distinguishing yourself by providing a specific title or leadership position you hold. This practice makes potential employers more likely to remember your distinct title. For example, there is probably only one Associate Editor of a law school's Air Law Symposium, so the student in Image 2.18 is more memorable to employers than the hundreds of students who use "law student" as their title.

Image 2.18

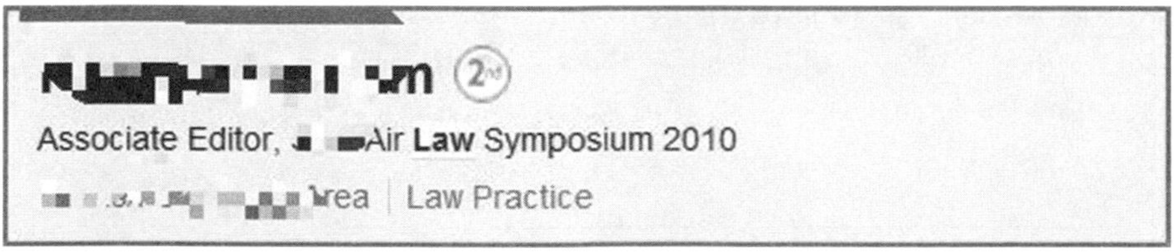

Another idea for law students is to include the title for your clerkship, internship, or clinic position. You can even combine a leadership or clinic title with your law student title. In Image 2.19, Neda Mirafzali, a May 2010 graduate of Michigan State University College of Law, indicated that she was a law student and a law clerk at The Health Law Partners, P.C.

Image 2.19

Neda Mirafzali ①ˢᵗ
Law Clerk at The Health Law Partners P.C., 3L at Michigan State
University College of Law
Greater Detroit Area | Law Practice

In Image 2.20, Yana Knutson, a law student at St. John's University School of Law, also combined her law school role and her internship title.

Image 2.20

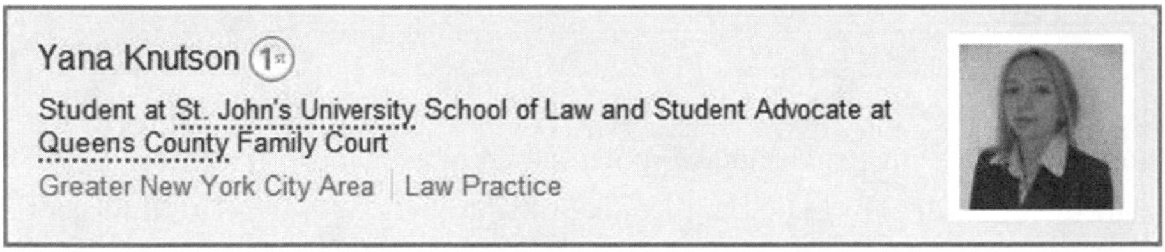

Yana Knutson ①ˢᵗ
Student at St. John's University School of Law and Student Advocate at
Queens County Family Court
Greater New York City Area | Law Practice

Practicing Lawyers:

Attorneys who are practicing in firms may want to state their practice area expertise (Image 2.21) and the name of the firm because many reporters/journalists search LinkedIn headlines when they need an expert in a particular area of the law.

Image 2.21

Jennifer Ingram ①ˢᵗ
Attorney - Commercial/Intellectual Property Litigation at Munck Carter,
P.C.
Dallas/Fort Worth Area | Law Practice

A growing trend is for attorneys to freelance or take on projects on an independent contract basis. Law firms seeking to hire a freelance or independent contract attorney may search LinkedIn for qualified candidates, so it is important to share your freelance or independent contractor status in your LinkedIn title, as shown in Image 2.22.

Image 2.22

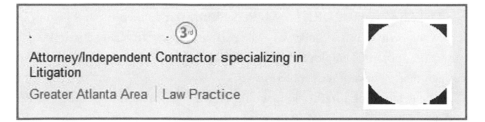

Location

LinkedIn requires you to enter your zip code and then it generates your location—such as Dallas/Fort Worth or the Greater Atlanta Area.

Industry

LinkedIn provides a list of industries from which you must select one. Most attorneys and law students choose "Law Practice" or "Legal Services."

Status Update

LinkedIn allows you to include a status update similar to the Facebook status update feature. If you include a status update, it appears below your name, title, location, industry, and picture, as shown in Image 2.23.

Image 2.23

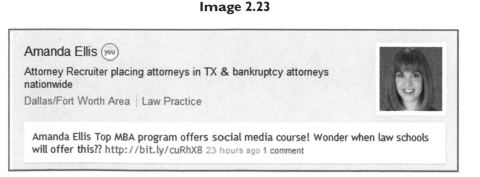

Chapter 4 discusses how to use the status update feature, including how to use the status update to market yourself and remain on the radar screen of your network.

Public Profile

LinkedIn assigns a URL or website link to your LinkedIn page—think of it as your own website. Since you will probably want to share this link with others (*i.e.,* potential employers or referral sources), you want the link to be short enough that it's easy to remember or share.

The default link is rather long with a weird combination of numbers at the end, as shown in Image 2.24. It's not one that is easy to remember or share.

Image 2.24
Default Public Profile:

Public Profile	http://www.linkedin.com/pub/evan-fogelman/1/897/211

You can, however, customize the link so that it's easier to remember and share, as shown in Image 2.25.

Image 2.25
Custom Public Profile:

Public Profile	http://www.linkedin.com/in/amandaellis

To customize your LinkedIn URL, click on Edit My Profile in the Profile section of your main menu. Then, click on Edit next to your current Public Profile, as shown in Image 2.26.

Image 2.26

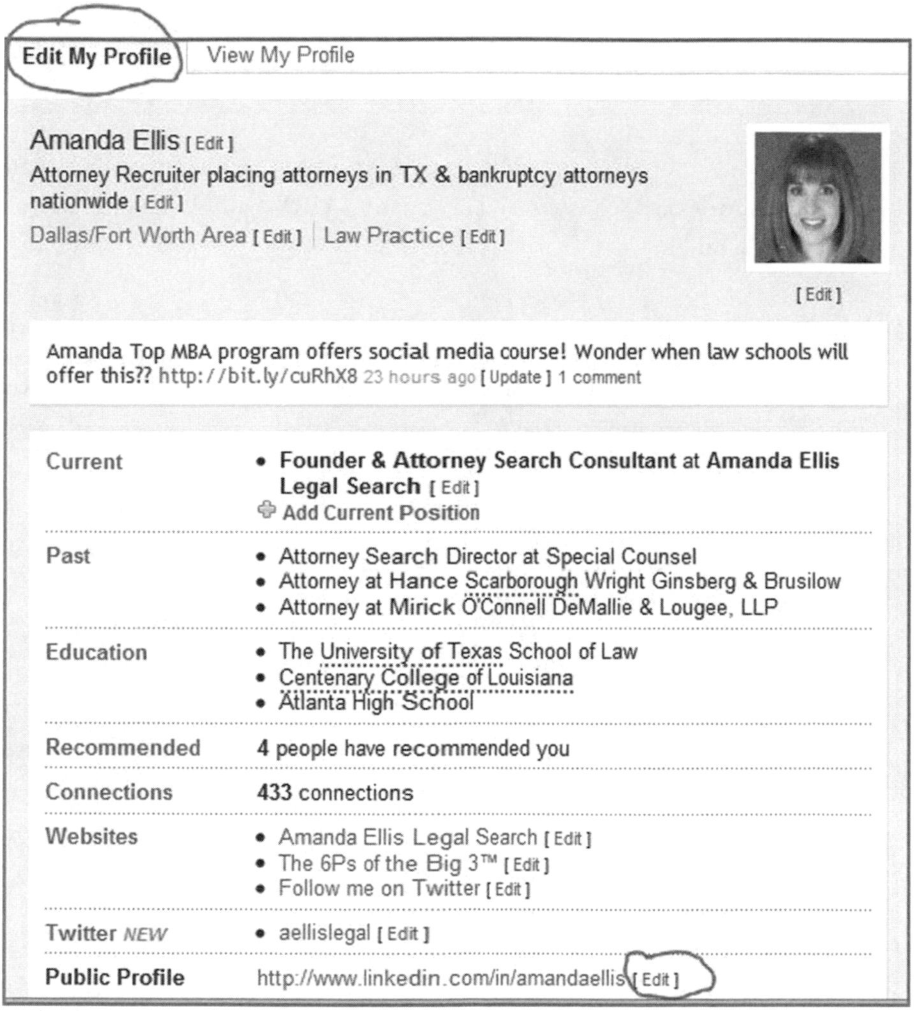

A new window opens and shows you your current public profile. Click Edit to create your own.

Image 2.27

Your Public Profile URL http://www.linkedin.com/in/amandaellis   [Edit]

Once you customize your public profile, include the link in your e-mail signature, business card, or resume. The custom URL will also increase your profile's Google ranking.

(2) Summary

The second section of your LinkedIn profile is the Summary. There are two sections of your Summary:

- Professional Experience & Goals. In this sub-section, you can provide an overview of your experience or share information that is not on your resume.
- Specialties. In this sub-section, you can use key words or short phrases to describe your particular expertise.

Take advantage of completing both parts of the Summary section because this section is important in indexing key words for Google searches. When potential employers, recruiters, or journalists perform a search, the words in the Summary section are searched first.

(3) Applications

LinkedIn offers a variety of free applications that allow you to market yourself and your talents to employers. All job seekers should take advantage of at least one application, if not more. Several popular applications include:

Blog

While you can include the link to your blog(s) under website, you can link directly to your blog feed through one of the blog applications; the most recent blog entries will display on your LinkedIn profile, as shown in Image 2.28.

Image 2.28

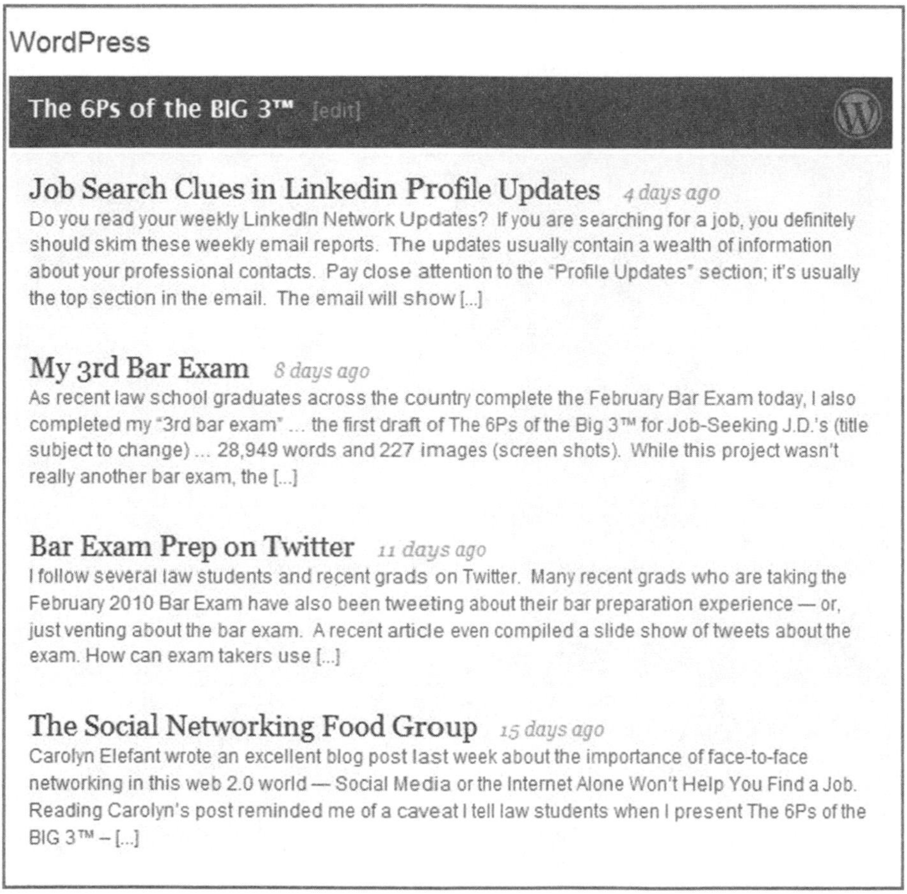

WordPress

The 6Ps of the BIG 3™ [edit]   (W)

Job Search Clues in Linkedin Profile Updates   *4 days ago*

Do you read your weekly LinkedIn Network Updates? If you are searching for a job, you definitely should skim these weekly email reports. The updates usually contain a wealth of information about your professional contacts. Pay close attention to the "Profile Updates" section; it's usually the top section in the email. The email will show [...]

My 3rd Bar Exam   *8 days ago*

As recent law school graduates across the country complete the February Bar Exam today, I also completed my "3rd bar exam" ... the first draft of The 6Ps of the Big 3™ for Job-Seeking J.D.'s (title subject to change) ... 28,949 words and 227 images (screen shots). While this project wasn't really another bar exam, the [...]

Bar Exam Prep on Twitter   *11 days ago*

I follow several law students and recent grads on Twitter. Many recent grads who are taking the February 2010 Bar Exam have also been tweeting about their bar preparation experience — or, just venting about the bar exam. A recent article even compiled a slide show of tweets about the exam. How can exam takers use [...]

The Social Networking Food Group   *15 days ago*

Carolyn Elefant wrote an excellent blog post last week about the importance of face-to-face networking in this web 2.0 world — Social Media or the Internet Alone Won't Help You Find a Job. Reading Carolyn's post reminded me of a caveat I tell law students when I present The 6Ps of the BIG 3™ – [...]

Slide Presentations

Think of presentations you've given at some point in your career or education—for example, a presentation at a conference, a seminar, or a class. You can upload the presentation slides directly to your LinkedIn Profile and potential employers or hiring personnel can view the presentations from your profile. For example, Image 2.29 contains a presentation by Steve Silton, a commercial bankruptcy lawyer.

Image 2.29

Articles

Most lawyers and law students have written at least one article. You can also upload articles to your LinkedIn profile. For example, Image 2.30 is from the LinkedIn profile of Neda Mirafzali, the recent law school graduate pictured on page 44 who clerked at a health law firm. She uploaded an article she wrote about identity theft programs for anesthesia centers.

Image 2.30

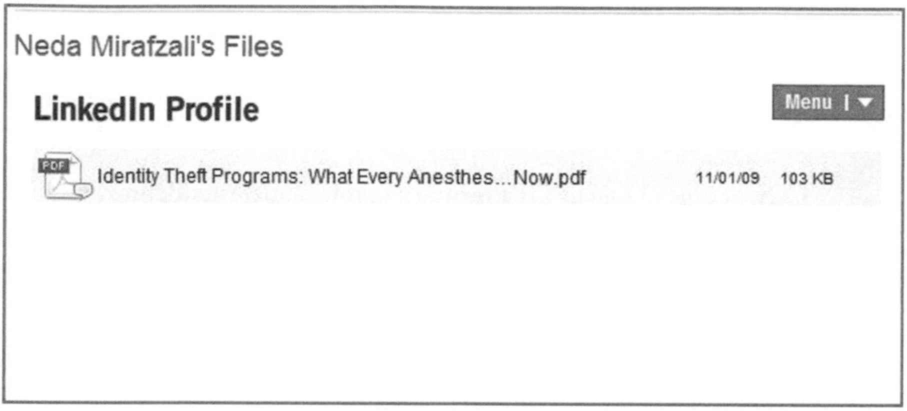

Neda Mirafzali's Files

LinkedIn Profile   Menu | ▼

📄 Identity Theft Programs: What Every Anesthes…Now.pdf   11/01/09   103 KB

Travel

One application allows you to share your travel schedule. This application allows you to arrange to meet people in your network who live in the city(ies) you are visiting. If you are searching for a job in another market, using this application is a great way to let firm recruiters or your network contacts in that market know when you'll be in town and available for interviews or informational interviews. You can even share details about the purpose of your trip, as shown in Image 2.31.

Image 2.31

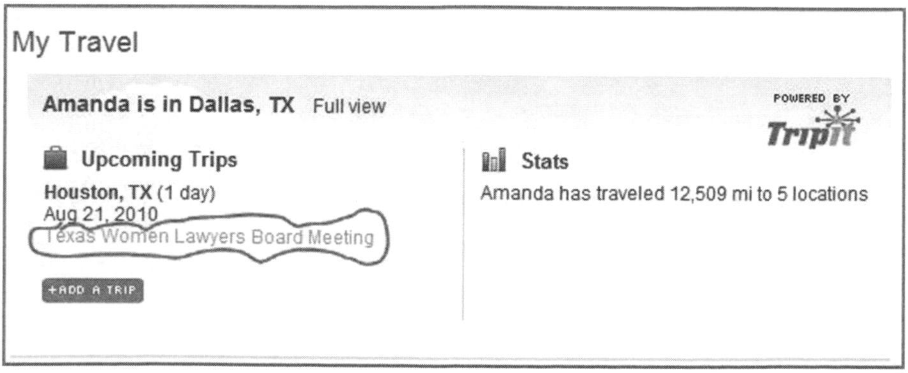

My Travel

Amanda is in Dallas, TX Full view   POWERED BY
                                                                 TripIt

🧳 **Upcoming Trips**   📊 **Stats**
Houston, TX (1 day)   Amanda has traveled 12,509 mi to 5 locations
Aug 21, 2010
Texas Women Lawyers Board Meeting

+ADD A TRIP

Books

The Reading List by Amazon allows you to share books you are reading and write reviews of books you've read. This tool may be used as a conversation starter if an employer or interviewer sees this information on your profile.

> *Caveat:* Since LinkedIn is a primarily professional site (defined in Chapter 1), I recommend sharing professional books in your Amazon reading list, as shown in Image 2.32.

Image 2.32

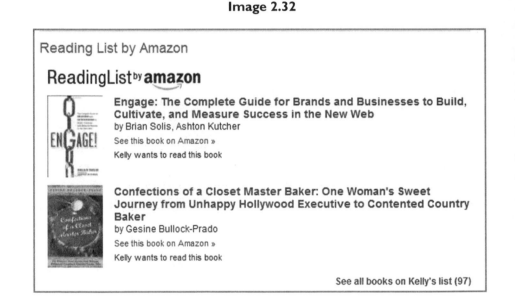

Events

The events application allows you to find various networking events in your area or anywhere in the country. You can search by event type—conferences, tradeshows, networking meetups, fundraisers, training and seminars, and other—as shown in Image 2.33.

Image 2.33

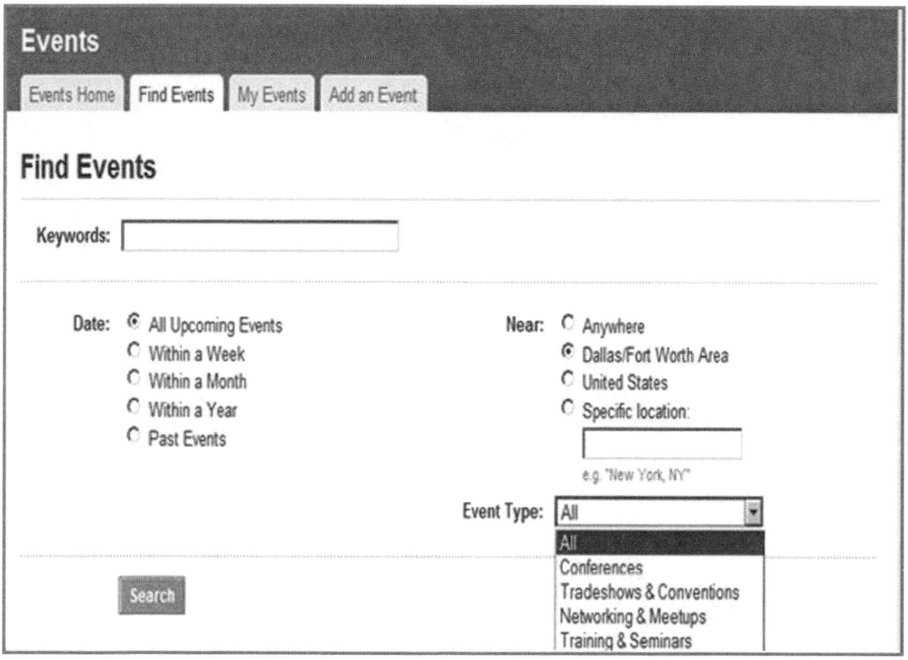

Once you find and RSVP for events, your events appear on your LinkedIn profile, as shown in Image 2.34.

Image 2.34

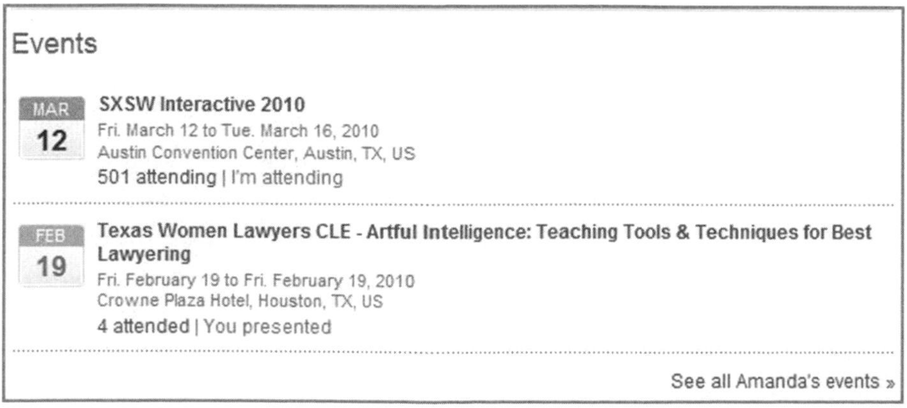

If an event you are organizing or attending is not listed on LinkedIn Events, create an event profile. People who access your profile will view you as a leader, and you will be able to publicize your event to others on LinkedIn.

Legal Updates by JD Supra

If you have a JD Supra account, you can disseminate your articles and content to your LinkedIn network with the Legal Updates LinkedIn application. Legal Updates is another way to share your portfolio directly on your LinkedIn profile, making your portfolio visible to recruiters and potential employers.

(4) Education

You want to complete your education information in detail, including the years you attended each school. You will see in Chapter 4 that one way to get started connecting with people on LinkedIn is through LinkedIn's suggestions of your former classmates. LinkedIn recommends former classmates you may know, based on the years you attended each institution. Include the information for your law school, college, high school, and any other graduate school you attended.

(5) Experience

To make your Experience section stand out, consider the following:

Past Professional Positions: You want to err on the side of including too many past positions, even if they were not in the legal field. For example, if you worked as an engineer prior to attending law school, include your engineering experience as well. You will see in Chapter 4 that LinkedIn also recommends former colleagues you may know. The recommendations are based on where you worked in the past and during what time period you worked at each place. Thus, the more positions you list, the more potential contacts LinkedIn will identify for you.

Numbers & Amounts: You must quantify your experience to set yourself apart. You need numbers, percentages, and dollar amounts. For example, notice how the descriptions in Column B sound more interesting than the descriptions in Column A in Table 2.1:

Table 2.1 - Quantify Experience

Without Numbers (A)	With Numbers (B)
Litigated and settled numerous preference and fraudulent transfer actions	Litigated and settled 300+ preference and fraudulent transfer actions, yielding $45 million for the debtor's estate
Reviewed and objected to proofs of claim filed against debtor's estate	Reviewed over 21,000 proofs of claim (totaling over $42 billion) filed against the debtor's estate; objected to inappropriate claims, reducing claims by 60%
Served on membership committee for Chicago Women's Bar Association	Chaired the 2007 membership drive for the Chicago Women's Bar Association, resulting in a 60% increase in new members
Implemented blog for firm's practice group	Launched *Toxic*, a legal blog for the firm's Products Liability Section with over 125,000 readers
Chaired 2009 Seattle Make-A-Wish Ball	Chaired 2009 Seattle Make-A-Wish Ball which raised nearly $40 million for cancer research

Concise: Your audience doesn't comprehend long phrases or sentences. Studies show that sentences between one and eight words yield 100% comprehension, yet comprehension plunges to 8% in sentences with 44 or more words. Comprehension ranks at 75% for sentences with 20-22 words. Aim for short phrases in your profile—think 25 or fewer words per sentence or phrase.[23]

Details: You can share information on your LinkedIn profile that you wouldn't include on your resume. For example, you might want to explain why you left one position for another. In Image 2.35, the attorney recruiter left her position as a third-party recruiter at Robert Half to work directly for one of her law firm clients. The notation on the recruiter's LinkedIn profile not only tells why the recruiter left her position at Robert Half, but it also illustrates that this particular client liked her work so much that the client decided to hire her.

Note: Elaborate does not mean that you must use long phrases or hundreds of words in your description. Remember, brevity is bliss. You can elaborate succinctly, and the description in Image 2.35 is an example. The attorney used short phrases to explain her departure from a previous position.

Image 2.35

Recruiting Manager
Robert Half International ⌕
Public Company; 10,001 or more employees; RHI; Staffing and Recruiting industry
August 2005 – January 2007 (1 year 6 months)
Legal recruiter placing attorneys and key staff in Dallas, Texas. Recruited to go in-house to client Locke, Liddell.

You can also elaborate by describing a firm where you worked. This might be helpful if you worked at a small firm in one region of the country and are seeking a job in a different legal market where the small firm might not be particularly well-known. In Image 2.36, the attorney describes her small Philadelphia firm by noting it was founded by Duane Morris alumni. This attorney relocated to Texas. Texas firms might not recognize the name of the small Philadelphia firm, but they would likely recognize Duane Morris, an AmLaw firm.

Image 2.36

Attorney
Smith Giacometti
Partnership; 1-10 employees; Law Practice industry
October 2002 – November 2004 (2 years 2 months)
Commercial litigation and bankruptcy practice in AV rated boutique law firm in Philadelphia. Smith Giacommetti was founded by Duane Morris alumni.

(6) Recommendations

Most job search articles regarding LinkedIn advise job seekers to obtain LinkedIn recommendations—endorsements from your LinkedIn contacts. However, this matter is one unsettled area for attorneys, so I wouldn't stress about obtaining a LinkedIn recommendation just to complete your profile. As you'll read in the following section, it's unclear whether such recommendations violate attorney ethics rules regarding advertisements, and, therefore, questionable whether you should receive recommendations. It is also questionable whether you should give recommendations.

Receiving Recommendations - Attorney Advertising?

The recommendations section is potentially troubling because it is unclear whether a recommendation on LinkedIn constitutes a testimonial. Certain states' ethics rules prohibit testimonials, while other states have limitations on what can be said in a testimonial and may even require a disclaimer.

One of the best writings I've seen addressing this issue was on Doug Cornelius's *Compliance Building* blog on March 24, 2009, "Compliance and Recommendations on Social Networking Sites."[24] Cornelius advises attorneys to keep recommendations off their LinkedIn profiles, and I agree.

Perhaps your state bar will address this issue in the future and you may choose to embrace recommendations. To my knowledge, Florida, a state that prohibits testimonials in attorney advertising, is the only state at this time to exempt recommendations on social networking sites like LinkedIn from this regulation prohibiting testimonials.[25]

Giving Positive Recommendations – Evidence in Discrimination Lawsuits?

The other issue surrounding LinkedIn recommendations affects employers: can an employer's positive recommendation of an employee be used against the employer in a future discrimination or harassment suit? An article advising against giving positive recommendations to employees appeared in *The National Law Journal* on July 6, 2009—"Lawyers Warn Employers Against Giving Glowing Reviews on LinkedIn."[26] Thus, many people may have their own policies against giving recommendations.

(7) Additional Information

The seventh profile section, Additional Information, allows you to share a myriad of information on your LinkedIn profile, including:

- Websites
- Twitter account
- Interests
- Groups
- Honors and awards

While this information seems self-explanatory, it's worth noting a few practice pointers.

Websites

You may add up to three websites.

Include at least one website: If you have a blog, you could include it. Or, if you are currently employed, you could link to your bio on your firm's website. Or, perhaps you hold a leadership role in a professional organization. You could include a link to the organization's website.

Caveat: Don't list your Facebook or MySpace profile as your website. Remember, LinkedIn is a primarily professional site (defined in Chapter 1), and the content you share, including links to websites, should be primarily professional. As discussed in Chapter 1, Facebook is a partly professional site.

Customize the link to your website: LinkedIn provides you with various options to use as a title for your website link, including My Company, My Blog, My Website, My RSS Feed, or My Portfolio. The title you choose appears in your LinkedIn Snapshot, as shown in Image 2.37.

Image 2.37

Websites	• My Website

Consider customizing your website title by choosing "other," then provide a title such as the name of your firm or organization or the name of your blog. For example, in Image 2.38, I chose "other" and then listed Amanda Ellis Legal Search.

Image 2.38

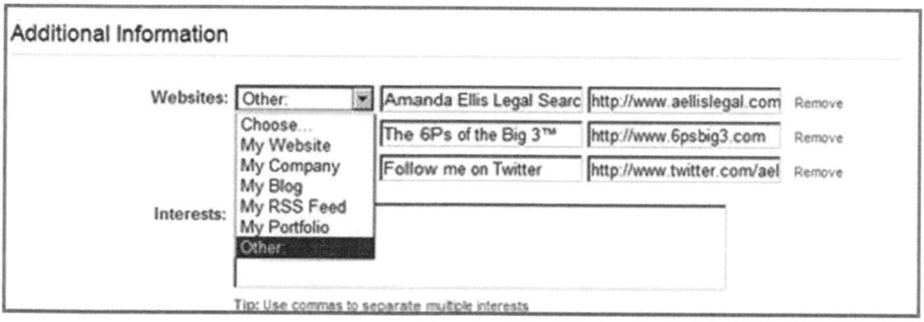

Additional Information

Websites: [Other ▼] [Amanda Ellis Legal Searc] [http://www.aellislegal.com] Remove
          Choose...
          My Website   [The 6Ps of the Big 3™] [http://www.6psbig3.com] Remove
          My Company
          My Blog   [Follow me on Twitter] [http://www.twitter.com/ael] Remove
Interests: My RSS Feed
          My Portfolio
          Other

Tip: Use commas to separate multiple interests

As you can see in Image 2.39, the result is a more descriptive link in your Snapshot—just another way to differentiate yourself and your profile.

Image 2.39

Websites	• Amanda Ellis Legal Search
	• The 6Ps of the Big 3™
	• Follow me on Twitter

Another idea for blog links is to use a title that describes the blog—not just the title of the blog. Think of terms that would lead your viewers to click on the link. For example, I list the title of my blog, *The 6Ps of the Big 3*™. Perhaps something like, "Social Networking Job Search Tips for Lawyers," would be more descriptive. Or, if you are a law student blogging about life in law school, perhaps something like, "My life as a 1L."

Twitter

If you have a Twitter account, you can list your Twitter username which will link directly to your Twitter page.

Interests

If you wish to list personal interests you can do so here, although it's not required. As discussed in the section about Facebook on page 38, interests can be conversation starters as long as you don't list questionable activities or interests.

Groups

As you join Groups on LinkedIn, the group name and logo appear in this section.

Honors & Awards

Include professional honors and awards that are unique in this section.

(8) Personal Information

You can share information such as phone number, IM, address, birthday, and marital status. Many people leave this information blank. You may want to include business phone and address. Or, as explained in Chapter 4 – page 89, you may want to create a secondary personal e-mail account and include the address in case an employer or recruiter is interested in your profile

(9) Contact Settings

Your contact settings let your connections (and hiring managers and recruiters) know *why* you want to be contacted. Options include: career opportunities, consulting offers, new ventures, job inquiries, and reference requests. As explained in Chapter 4 – page 90, if you are employed and don't want your current employer to know you are job searching, you may want to omit certain options, like career opportunities, new ventures, consulting offers, and job opportunities.

TWITTER

A Twitter profile contains significantly less biographical information than a Facebook or LinkedIn profile. However, because the purpose of Twitter is to communicate with people you don't know and to meet new contacts in your industry, you want your profile to be as descriptive as possible in the short space provided.

The box in the upper right side of a Twitter user's profile page contains the user's bio consisting of the following information: name, location, web, and bio.

Image 2.40

Name Amanda Ellis
Location Dallas, TX
Web http://www.aellis...
Bio Attorney Recruiter,
Speaker/Author of 2 books for
law students, attorney job
seekers, law firm recruiters
about social networking + job
search www.6psbig3.com

Job seekers should note a few things about the information provided in the bio:

Name

List your real name, not your Twitter username. As you will see in Chapter 4, listing your full name is valuable when using the "Find People" search feature. If you don't list your full name, you won't be found in searches for your name.

Twitter Username

Your Twitter username appears to the left of your Twitter bio, next to your profile picture, as shown in Image 2.41.

Image 2.41

aellislegal

That's you!   Lists ▾

Name Amanda Ellis
Location Dallas, TX
Web http://www.aellis...
Bio Attorney. Recruiter.
Speaker/Author of 2 books for
law students, attorney job
seekers, law firm recruiters
about social networking + job
search www.6psbig3.com

Practice Pointer

Choose your Twitter username wisely.

1. *Short.* Your tweets, including your username, are limited to 140 characters so a short username is preferred.
2. *Memorable.* Avoid numbers and symbols; choose a name that's easy to remember and spell. You want a username that people will remember if they try to find you or want to direct a tweet to you.
3. *Brand.* You may incorporate your brand into your username. For example, you may use your firm's domain name if you are a solo attorney. Or, you may use some combination of your firm name and your practice area.

Location

List the city and state in which you live. If you live in the suburbs of a major city, you may want to provide the name of the metropolitan area—for example, Dallas/Fort Worth Area instead of Frisco, TX, a suburb of Dallas.

You might see users list their locations with the letters "UT" and then a string of numbers, like 92.343451,-41.012372. The "UT" stands for Uber Twitter, a twitter application that pinpoints your location at any given moment. Listing your geographical market rather than your Uber Twitter map coordinates is preferred.

Web

If you are a practicing attorney with a firm website profile, you should link to that bio in the website section. Or, if you write a blog, you might want to link to your blog. You can even link to your LinkedIn profile, especially if it is more detailed than your firm bio or profile.

Law students should link to their LinkedIn profile or blog since they don't have a firm bio or profile.

> ***Caveat:*** Don't list your Facebook or MySpace profile as your website. Remember, Twitter is a primarily professional site (defined in Chapter 1), and the content you share, including links to websites, should be primarily professional. As discussed in Chapter 1, Facebook is a partly professional site.

Bio

You have 160 characters to use to write your Twitter bio. Think concise—this is your elevator speech. You can mix in personal points. Remember that Twitter is about 80% professional and 20% personal. Your bio can reflect this equation, as illustrated in the example in Image 2.42.

Image 2.42

Name Pia Norman Thompson
Location Chicago, IL
Web http://www.linked...
Bio experienced bkrtcy, creditor's rights and workout atty, Wellesley grad, economist, college football & movie fan & a mom

480	269	10
following	followers	listed

Omitting any of the above information—name, location, web, bio—will make you less credible. Many spammers create Twitter accounts but don't list their full names or list just a first name or an initial. Thus, if you skimp on providing the information, you may be viewed as a spammer.

Optional Backgrounds

You have several options with the background of your Twitter page. If you go into your settings tab and click on design, you'll see that you have about 20 different backgrounds from which to choose, as shown in Image 2.43. All of the backgrounds in Image 2.43 are acceptable.

Image 2.43

You may, however, prefer to customize your background, and there are several free sites that help you do this. As you can see in Image 2.44, Amy Hein, a second-year law student at the University of Iowa College of Law, customized her Twitter background to reflect her professional background, degrees, and interests—information valuable to recruiters and potential employers.

Image 2.44

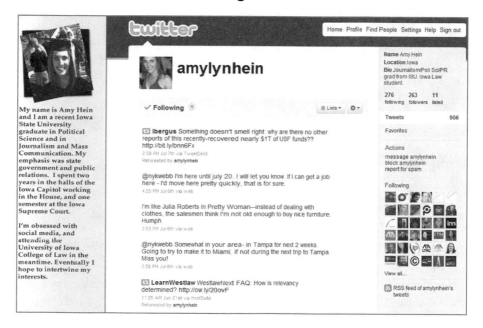

As you can see in Image 2.44, the custom background allows this law student to share information that normally wouldn't appear in her Twitter bio, such as her undergraduate studies, work experience, and interests.

And, Image 2.45 contains the custom background of Dallas appellate attorney Chad Ruback. Ruback customized his Twitter background to make his contact information stand out.

Image 2.45

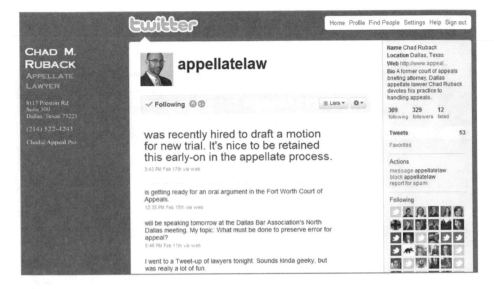

To craft a positive profile on the Big 3 social networking sites, keep each site's and each audience member's degree of professionalism in mind. You may freely share as much detail in the space provided on primarily professional sites like LinkedIn and Twitter. You may give more thought, however, about the information you share on a partly professional site like Facebook where much of the information requested is personal in nature. Analyze how the information may help or harm your goals, and remember that you may want to omit information or protect information with the privacy controls discussed in the next chapter.

Points – Profile

	Picture	Bio		
Facebook • Optional • Privacy • Helpful v. Harmful	Majority View – Partly Professional • Recent, Quality, Headshot • Acceptable: Casual, Rotate, Non-human • Office Desk Rule Minority View – Primarily Professional • Recent, Quality, Headshot • NOT Acceptable: Casual, Rotate, Non-human • Professional Image • Match LinkedIn & Twitter		Helpful	Harmful – omit or protect with privacy controls
		Current City & Hometown	Returning to hometown	"Recently relocated to X city"
		Birthday		Omit birth year
		Political & Religious Views		Protect with privacy setting if concerned
		Relationships	Employer recognizes relative	Employer's negative relationship or impression of relative
		Likes & Interests	Conversation ice-breaker	Omit questionable activities
		Education & Work	Referral sources, fan pages, BranchOut	
		Contact Information	Phone or e-mail	

	Picture	**Bio**
LinkedIn • More details than FB • Law student's bio • Re-arrange sections	Primarily Professional • Recent, Quality, Headshot • Professional Image	**Snapshot** (name, headline, location, industry, status, public profile) • Unique headline, custom public profile
		Summary (SEO)
		Applications (blogs, slide presentations, articles, travel, books, events)
		Education (detail)
		Experience (past positions, numbers/amounts, concise, details)
		Recommendations (unsettled)
		Additional Information (websites, Twitter, interests, groups, honors/awards) • 1 website minimum, customize
		Personal Information (phone or e-mail)
		Contact Settings (why you want to be contacted)
Twitter • Detailed elevator speech	Primarily Professional • Recent, Quality, Headshot • Professional Image	Name • First and last name
		Username • Short, logical, brand
		Location • Metro area
		Web • Firm bio, LinkedIn profile, blog
		Bio • 160 characters, brand
		Optional background

CHAPTER 3

Privacy

POLITICIANS' employers, the voters, frequently search the internet during political campaigns to learn more about the candidates. You should be prepared for such scrutiny from potential employers when planning your job search campaign. Employers such as law firms also search online to learn more about candidates. As noted in the Premise, 79% of hiring managers and recruiters search candidates' online profiles, and 70% admit to rejecting candidates because of negative information on the candidate's social networking profiles.[27]

The tweet in Image 3.1 by a law school career services professional illustrates that employers sometimes reject candidates based on information they find on social networking sites, such as pictures of candidates drinking and partying.

Image 3.1

> Met alum who interviewed job candidate then checked Facebook. Found many party/drinking pics. No job offer. Lesson: Privacy settings!
>
> about 13 hours ago from

Chapter 2 examined how to craft a positive profile to impress employers. This chapter examines how to protect information that may disappoint employers. The best way to prevent unwanted information from reaching potential employers or clients is to omit such information from your social networking profile. At a minimum, you should adjust your privacy settings.

This chapter outlines privacy settings applicable to job seekers, including how to protect information that might harm your job search. But, privacy extends beyond protecting potential harmful information and includes protecting *any* kind of information. And, in certain situations, you may want to relax privacy settings to make information available for potential employers to find.

FACEBOOK

Of the Big 3 sites, there are more opportunities for privacy blunders on Facebook than on LinkedIn or Twitter because of the volume of personal information that is shared on Facebook. However, lawyers and law students can use the privacy settings to prevent the blunders.

This section examines:

1. *Privacy Tools* - three Facebook tools that protect the information you share on Facebook.
2. *Privacy Recommendations* – instruction on how to use the tools to protect information you share that can influence your job search—either negatively or positively.

Privacy Tools

The three Facebook Privacy Tools you may want to use include:

1. Privacy Levels
2. Lists
3. Profile Preview

(1) Privacy Levels

The information you share on Facebook is visible to others based on the privacy level assigned to the information. There are four privacy levels:

1. *Everyone.* Everyone on the internet can see the information.
2. *Friends of Friends.* Your Facebook friends and their friends can see the information, even if you aren't friends with your friends' friends.
3. *Friends Only.* Only your Facebook friends can see the information.
4. *Customize.* You can name specific friends or groups of friends who can or can't have access to the information.

Facebook assigns a default privacy level to each piece of information you share on Facebook. Table 3.1 lists the default privacy level for each piece of information.

Table 3.1 – Facebook Default Privacy Levels

Information	Default Privacy Level
BASIC DIRECTORY INFORMATION	
Search for me on Facebook	Everyone
Send me friend requests	Everyone
Send me messages	Everyone
See my friend list	Everyone
See my education and work	Everyone
See my current city and hometown	Everyone
See my interest and other pages	Everyone
THINGS I SHARE	
Posts by me (status updates)	Everyone
Family	Everyone
Relationships	Everyone
Interested in and Looking for	Everyone
Bio and favorite quotations	Everyone
Website	Everyone
Religious and political views	Friends of Friends
Birthday	Friends of Friends
Edit Album privacy (Photos)	Everyone

THINGS OTHERS SHARE	
Tagged photos/videos	Friends of Friends
Comment on posts	Friends Only
Friends can post on my wall	Friends can post on Wall Enabled
Can see Wall posts by friends	Friends of Friends
CONTACT INFORMATION	
Mobile phone	Friends Only
Other phone	Friends Only
Address	Friends Only
IM Screen name	Friends Only
E-mail	Friends Only

You can change the default settings. The **Friends Only** setting generally offers the most protection to job seekers *if* you are careful about who you allow to be your Facebook friend (see Strict Scrutiny Test discussion on page 116 in Chapter 4).

However, the **Customize** setting may offer more protection if you want to share information with only certain (but, not all) of your Facebook friends. For example, you may share a photo album with certain Facebook friends but not all of your Facebook friends.

The Privacy Recommendations part of this chapter (beginning on page 76) recommends privacy levels for certain categories of information in Table 3.1 that can influence your job search.

(2) Lists

One other tool available with the **Customize** privacy setting is the lists feature. You can arrange some or all of your Facebook friends into lists and share information with certain lists but not all of your Facebook friends.

The lists feature allows you to assign your friends to a list and then share information, including permission to see your photos, to certain lists. For example, an attorney job seeker might divide his Facebook friends into the following lists:

1. Family
2. Childhood friends
3. College friends
4. Law school friends
5. Lawyer friends
6. Book club friends
7. Former law firm colleagues
8. Current law firm colleagues
9. Law firm hiring contacts
10. Referral sources
11. Clients

To create a friends list:

- Select **Friends** from the menu down the left side of your Facebook home page
- Then, click **Create a List**
- A box will appear and you will be asked to **Enter Name** of your list (*i.e.*, family)
- Then, select the friends you wish to place in this category. You can click on their picture or begin typing their name in the box that says **Start Typing Name.**

The Lists tool is discussed further in the section on protecting photo albums on page 80.

(3) Profile Preview

Before adjusting your privacy levels, check to see what information is currently visible to others. The Profile Preview tool allows you to test your privacy levels and see how other Facebook users, including non-friends such as potential employers, recruiters, or hiring managers, view your profile. Once you know what is visible to others, you'll know what, if anything, you need to hide.

1. Place your cursor on the **Account** tab in the menu bar across the top of your page and click on **Privacy Settings**.

Image 3.2

2. The **Choose Your Privacy Settings** box will appear. Click on **View Settings** next to **Basic Directory Information.**

Image 3.3

Choose Your Privacy Settings

Basic Directory Information
To help real world friends find you, some basic information is open to everyone. We also suggest setting basics like hometown and interests to everyone so friends can use those to connect with you. View settings

Sharing on Facebook

		Everyone	Friends of Friends	Friends Only	Other
Everyone	My status, photos, and posts			•	
Friends of Friends	Bio and favorite quotations			•	
Friends Only	Family and relationships			•	
	Photos and videos I'm tagged in				•
Recommended	Religious and political views			•	
	Birthday			•	
Custom ✓	Can comment on posts			•	
	Email addresses and IM				•
	Phone numbers and address				•

✎ Customize settings   ✅ This is your current setting.

3. From the **Basic Directory Information Menu**, click on **Preview My Profile**.

Image 3.4

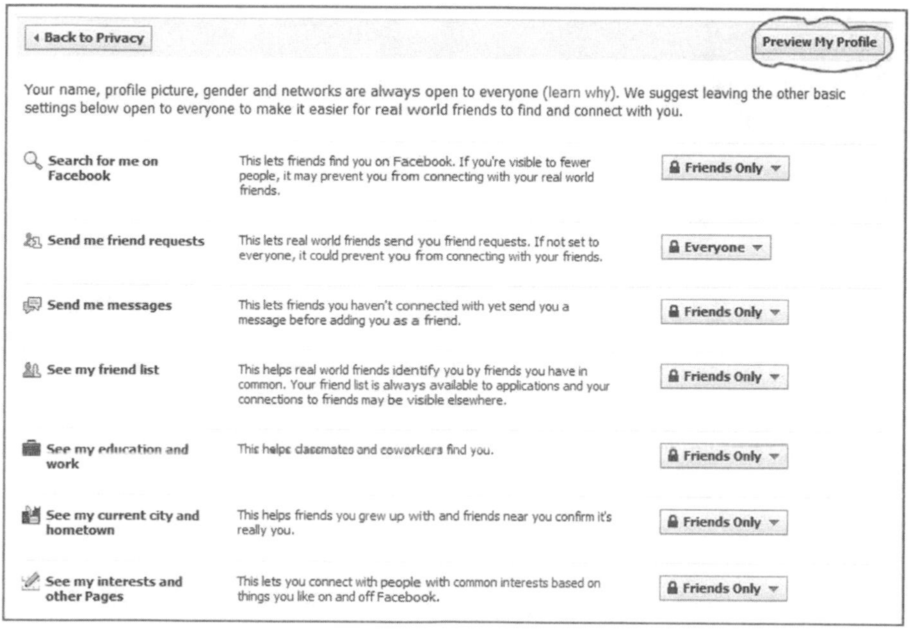

4. Image 3.5 shows the information visible to Facebook users who are not my Facebook friends when each category (except "Send me friend requests") is set to **Friends Only**, the most restrictive setting.

Image 3.5

A potential employer will see my profile picture and name in the **Only Friends** setting.

In the Privacy Recommendations section, you'll see which categories of information you might want to share with **Everyone,** and which information to keep private and share with **Friends Only.**

Privacy Recommendations

The three Privacy Tools—Privacy Levels, Lists, and Profile Preview—help you control the information you share on Facebook. Table 3.2 outlines the information you share on Facebook, the default privacy level, and the recommended level for job seekers. Certain categories of information warrant more discussion and are discussed in Sections 1-5 following Table 3.2.

Table 3.2 – Recommended Facebook Privacy Levels for Job-Seekers

Information	Default Privacy Level	Recommended Privacy Level for Job Seekers	Notes
BASIC DIRECTORY INFORMATION			
Search for me on Facebook	Everyone	Everyone	Discussed in Section (5)
Send me friend requests	Everyone	Everyone	
Send me messages	Everyone	Everyone	Discussed in Section (4)
See my friend list	Everyone	Friends Only	
See my education and work	Everyone	Everyone	Discussed in Section (3)
See my current city and hometown	Everyone	Everyone	Refer to Hurt v. Harm analysis in Chapter 2
See my interests and other pages	Everyone	Friends Only	Refer to Hurt v. Harm analysis in Chapter 2
THINGS I SHARE			
Posts by me (status updates)	Everyone	Friends Only	Discussed in Section (2)
Family	Everyone	Friends Only	Refer to Hurt v. Harm analysis in Chapter 2

Relationships	Everyone	Friends Only	Refer to Hurt v. Harm analysis in Chapter 2
Interested in and Looking for	Everyone	Friends Only	
Bio and favorite quotations	Everyone	Everyone	Refer to Hurt v. Harm analysis in Chapter 2
Website	Everyone	Everyone	Refer to Hurt v. Harm analysis in Chapter 2
Religious and political views	Friends of Friends	Friends Only	Refer to Hurt v. Harm analysis in Chapter 2
Birthday	Friends of Friends	Friends Only	
Edit Album privacy (Photos)	Everyone	Friends Only	Discussed in Section (1)
THINGS OTHERS SHARE			
Tagged photos/videos	Friends of Friends	Customize – Only Me	Discussed in Section (1)
Comment on posts	Friends Only	Friends Only	
Friends can post on my wall	Friends can post on Wall Enabled	Friends can post on Wall Enabled	
Can see Wall posts by friends	Friends of Friends	Friends Only	

CONTACT INFORMATION			
Mobile phone	Friends Only	Friends Only	Discussed in Section (4)
Other phone	Friends Only	Friends Only	Discussed in Section (4)
Address	Friends Only	Friends Only	Discussed in Section (4)
IM Screen name	Friends Only	Friends Only	
E-mail	Friends Only	Everyone	Discussed in Section (4)

(1) Pictures

There are three different types of pictures on Facebook—Profile Picture, Photo Albums, and Tagged Photos—and you control the privacy settings for each separately.

Profile Picture

As discussed in Chapter 2, your profile picture is one piece of information that you can't restrict, and potential employers will see your profile picture if they Google your name or review a Facebook fan page or group with which you are affiliated—even if other information in your Facebook profile is restricted.

Recommendation for Job Seekers

I recommended that you follow the **Office Desk Photo Rule** described in Chapter 2. This rule states that you should choose a profile picture that you would display on your office desk.

The picture you choose will vary depending on your personal preferences. For example, a female attorney job seeker who may not want potential employers to think her family responsibilities might interfere with her ability to perform the job, may choose a picture that doesn't include her children. Another female job seeker might choose to be depicted as a family person and display a photo with her children. After all, would a male job seeker be as concerned about displaying family pictures?

A more serious consideration is the avoidance of using a profile picture showing you taking shots or passed out at a party. A male or female risks becoming another statistic of not being hired because of his or her Facebook picture being an inappropriate professional image.

Photo Albums

Most Facebook blunders occur because Facebook users don't protect their photo albums. As a result, their photo albums can be viewed by Facebook users who aren't their friends.

You can, however, select one of the four privacy levels to protect your photo albums. The **Friends Only** level offers maximum protection for most users *if* they are careful about their friend selections and follow the Strict Scrutiny Test outlined in Chapter 4.

If you choose to use the list feature described on page 72, you may want to choose the **Customize** privacy level and give permission to only a certain list to view a photo album. For example, your Facebook friends might consist of some professional colleagues you know well, plus old college friends and high school friends. If you do not want your professional colleagues to see your college photo album, you can create a list for college friends and share your college album only with your college friends list.

Recommendation for Job Seekers

I recommend the **Friends Only** setting for most job seekers. If you are Facebook savvy, the **Customize** level with the list feature might be attractive, yet too labor intensive for the average Facebook user.

You must select privacy settings for *each* photo album you upload to Facebook because no global setting exists. If you have five photo albums on Facebook, select a privacy level for each album. Check your existing Facebook photo albums and change the privacy level accordingly. Going forward, select the privacy level when you create a photo album on Facebook and upload pictures.

Tagged Photos

When another user posts a picture of you and tags you, the picture appears on your profile page. The default privacy level for tagged photos is **Friends of Friends**. Thus, if your college friend Frank tags you in a picture where you are passed out at a party, that picture will appear on your profile page and be visible to all of your Facebook friends, plus all of Frank's Facebook friends.

You can't prevent other users from posting pictures and tagging you, but you can prevent the tagged pictures from appearing on your profile. If you choose the **Custom** privacy level, select the **Only Me** setting. This level offers the most protection. At this level, your tagged photos will never be visible to friends on your profile page.

Some may find this setting too restrictive. If so, you may control the setting on a more limited basis. Your tagged photo setting applies to all tagged pictures in which you appear, whereas the settings for pictures you post are determined on an album-by-album basis—some can be more restrictive than others. Some users want their friends to see the tagged pictures—they just don't want the entire world or Facebook world to see them. For a less restrictive privacy level, choose **Specific People** from the **Custom** menu. You can enter specific friends or lists that you would like to see your tagged pictures.

Recommendation for Job Seekers

I recommend the **Only Me** privacy level. If you are tagged in photos which you want to share with friends, save the photos and post them to one of your Facebook albums where you can control who sees each picture.

(2) Status Update

The default privacy level for status updates is **Everyone**, which includes everyone on the internet.

Recommendation for Job Seekers

I recommend the **Friends Only** privacy level for status updates. You can change the level as you update your status if you wish to share the update with more people or restrict certain friends from reading your status update. There is a drop down menu in the status update box that is marked with a lock symbol (Image 3.6).

Image 3.6

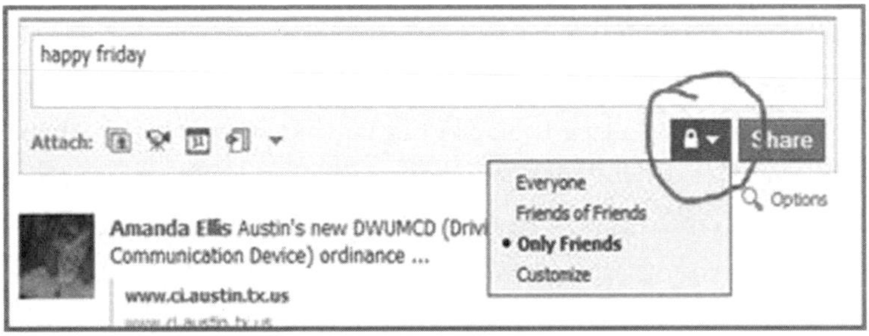

As you can see in Image 3.7, my default status update setting is **Friends Only**. However, if I want to post an update that I don't want certain friends to see I can choose **Customize** and list the names of the friends I do not want to see the update.

Image 3.7

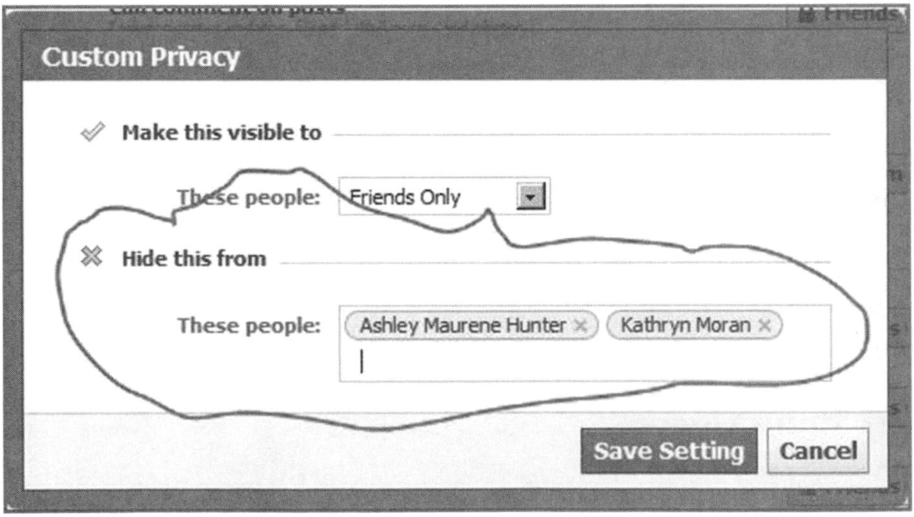

If you are a practicing attorney searching for a job, you may not want your current colleagues to know about your job search. Yet, you may want to use the status update feature to share information with your friends and family about your job search, as discussed in Chapter 4. You can exclude your current colleagues from viewing your job search related status updates by customizing the privacy settings on those particular updates and hiding the update from certain friends, as shown in Image 3.7.

Or, if you are Facebook friends with multiple work contacts, you may want to create a List of work contacts and hide the status update from the entire list.

Image 3.8

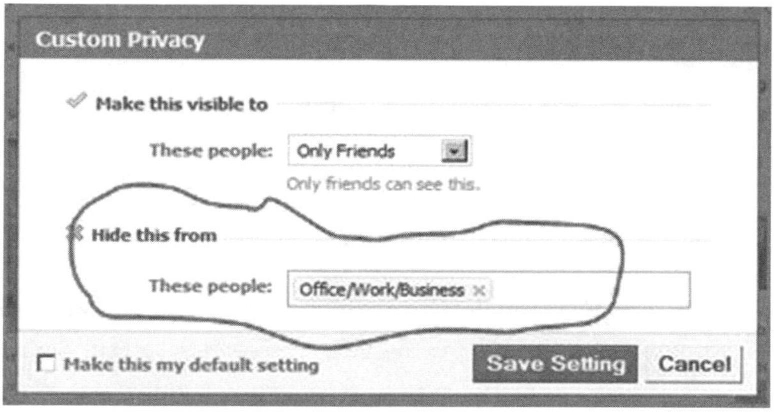

(3) Work and Education

The default privacy setting for status updates is **Everyone**, which includes everyone on the internet.

Recommendation for Job Seekers

I recommend that you keep the **Everyone** privacy level. As discussed in Chapter 2, your work and education information may influence your job search in a positive manner, so you may want everyone to see this information.

For example, if you are a member of a bar association group page on Facebook and comment (or RSVP) on the group's Facebook page about an event the group is hosting, all other group members can see your comment. Another member who doesn't know you might click on your profile. Even if your profile is restricted, the person can still see your work and education information if you keep the default setting. Perhaps that person's firm is hiring and he is impressed with the work information listed on your Facebook page. Even if you aren't actively searching for a new job, the person who found your page may be a useful contact for future referrals.

(4) Contact Information

You need to list some method by which potential employers or referral sources can contact you if they come across your profile and sense an interest in you.

Recommendation for Job Seekers

I recommend listing at least one communication option. In Table 3.2, I kept the **Everyone** default setting for "Send me messages," and I changed the default setting for "E-mail" from **Friends Only** to **Everyone**. Potential employers can contact me by sending a Facebook message or sending an e-mail to the e-mail address I listed.

You might choose to provide a telephone number instead of an e-mail address. My personal preference is to create a secondary e-mail address and provide it instead of my primary e-mail address. It's easier (and cheaper) to create a secondary e-mail address rather than a phone number.

(5) Searches

There are two types of searches potential employers might conduct to find your Facebook profile: (a) Facebook search; and (b) Internet search.

Facebook Search

Employers can search your name on the Facebook site. The default privacy level for a Facebook search is **Everyone** so a potential employer can find your profile. However, potential employers can only see the information you give "everyone" permission to view. To see what "everyone" can view, check your Profile Preview discussed on page 73, and you will see the information available to employers if they searched your name on the Facebook site.

If you don't want employers or recruiters to find your Facebook profile through a Facebook search, select the **Friends Only** privacy level. However, people you know won't be able to find you through a Facebook search if you use the **Friends Only** setting.

To change your privacy level for Facebook search, click on **Privacy Settings** from the Account tab in the main menu bar. Click on **View Settings** under **Basic Directory Information**. Choose the privacy level from the drop down menu shown in Image 3.9.

Image 3.9

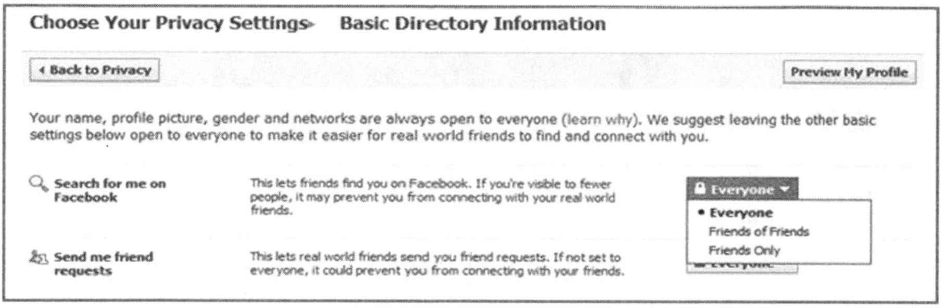

Recommendation for Job Seekers

I recommend keeping the default Facebook search level of **Everyone** so people you know can find you. Then, adjust the privacy levels on other information such as photos and contact settings so that such information is available to only friends. People will be able to find your profile through a Facebook search, but they won't be able to view all of your information.

Internet Search

In addition to searching for your name on the Facebook site, employers may also search the Internet through Google or another search engine. They are likely to find your Facebook profile listed among the top search results for your name because of Facebook's search engine optimization.

If you allow Facebook to index your profile, certain (limited) information from your Facebook profile will appear if employers search your name on the search engines. If you remove your profile from the search engine index, nothing will appear in a Google search.

If your profile is indexed on the search engines, the following information will appear:

1. Profile picture
2. Name
3. Gender
4. Networks

Image 3.10 is an example of how the information appears.

Image 3.10

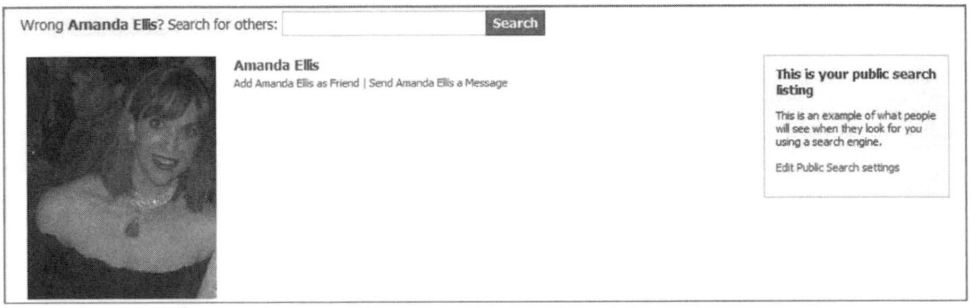

Wrong Amanda Ellis? Search for others:
Search
Amanda Ellis
Add Amanda Ellis as Friend | Send Amanda Ellis a Message
This is your public search listing
This is an example of what people will see when they look for you using a search engine.
Edit Public Search settings

If you are concerned about employers seeing any of the above information, you should remove your profile from the search engine index so that nothing appears in a Google or similar search. To do so:

1. Place your cursor on the **Account** tab in the menu bar across the top of your page
2. Click on **Privacy Settings**

Image 3.11

Home
Profile
Account
Amanda Ellis
Edit Friends
Account Settings
Privacy Settings
Application Settings
Credits Balance
Help Center
Logout

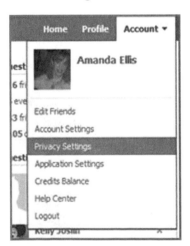

3. Then, click **Applications and Websites.**

Image 3.12

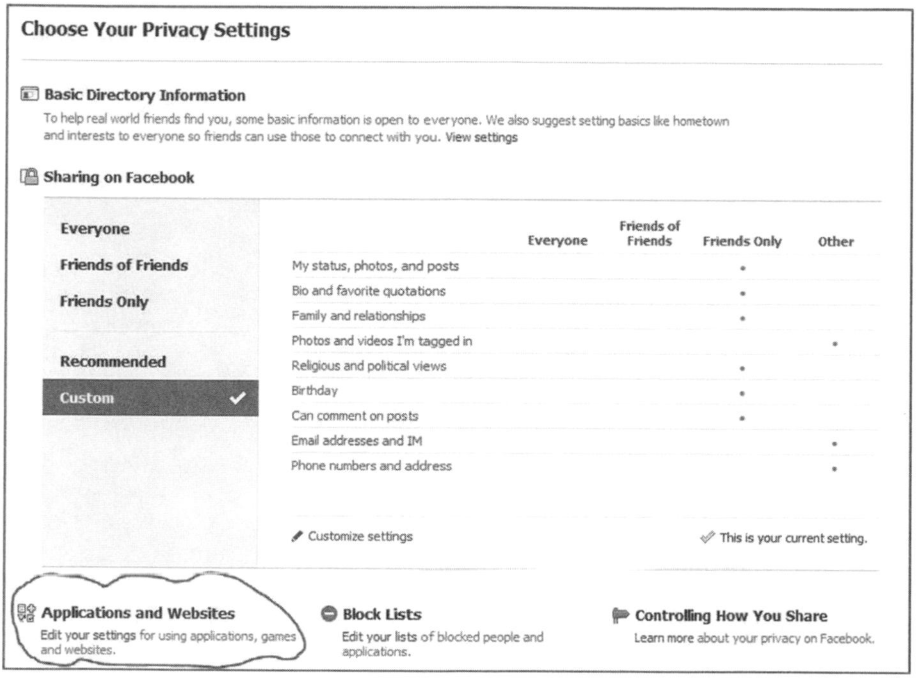

Choose Your Privacy Settings

▭ **Basic Directory Information**
To help real world friends find you, some basic information is open to everyone. We also suggest setting basics like hometown and interests to everyone so friends can use those to connect with you. View settings

▣ **Sharing on Facebook**

		Everyone	Friends of Friends	Friends Only	Other
Everyone					
Friends of Friends	My status, photos, and posts			•	
Friends Only	Bio and favorite quotations			•	
	Family and relationships			•	
	Photos and videos I'm tagged in				•
Recommended	Religious and political views			•	
Custom ✔	Birthday			•	
	Can comment on posts			•	
	Email addresses and IM				•
	Phone numbers and address				•

✎ Customize settings   ✅ This is your current setting.

🖳 **Applications and Websites**   ⊖ **Block Lists**   ⚑ **Controlling How You Share**
Edit your settings for using applications, games   Edit your lists of blocked people and   Learn more about your privacy on Facebook.
and websites.   applications.

4. The last category is Public Search. Click **Edit Settings**.

Image 3.13

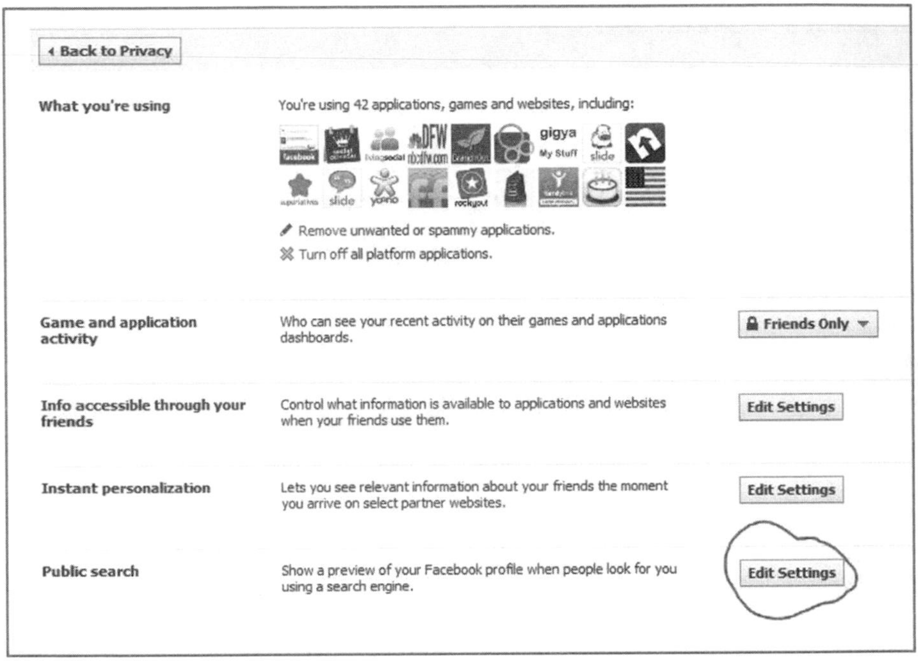

And, then make sure the **Enable Public Search** box does not contain a check mark.

Image 3.14

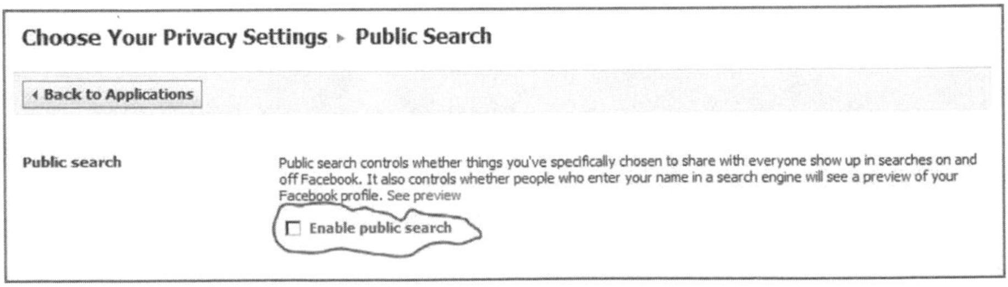

LinkedIn

There are fewer privacy settings on LinkedIn, primarily because it is purely a professional network. You don't share as much personal information like you do on Facebook. In fact, you don't have to share any personal information.

However, there are still a few settings you may wish to change, especially if you are currently employed and searching for a new job and don't want your current firm to know you are looking:

- Personal Information
- Opportunity Preferences
- Connections Browse
- Profile Views
- Status Visibility
- Profile and Status Updates

(1) Personal Information

As you learned in Chapter 2, there is a section where you can share personal information on your LinkedIn profile. Image 3.15 shows the information you can provide if you wish. If you omit this information, this section doesn't appear on your public profile.

Image 3.15

⊕ **Personal Information** [Edit]

Phone:	Add a phone number to your profile.
Address:	Add your address to your profile.
IM:	Add an IM to your profile.
Birthday:	Add your birthday to your profile.
Marital status:	Add your marital status to your profile.

Recommendations for Job Seekers

You may want to provide some form of contact information—either an e-mail address or a phone number—in case an employer or recruiter is interested in your profile. As I suggested with Facebook, my personal preference is to create a secondary e-mail address and provide it instead of my primary e-mail address.

If you provide your birthday, omit the year to prevent identity theft. And, never provide your home address.

(2) Opportunity Preferences

Your Opportunity Preferences tell other users *why* you'd like to be contacted, including if you'd like to hear about job opportunities. Your Opportunity Preferences appear in the Contact Settings section of your profile, as shown in Image 3.16.

Image 3.16

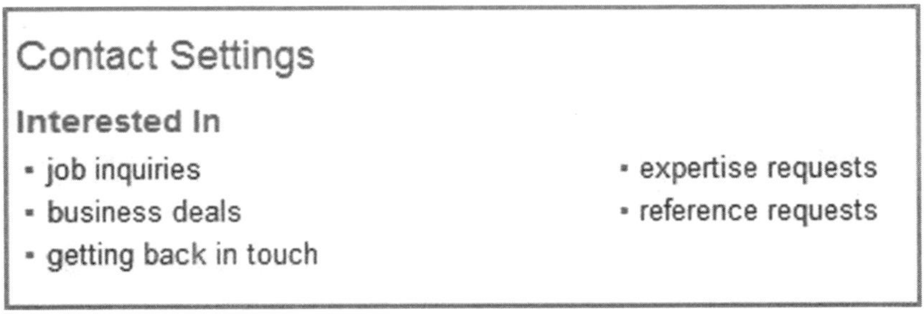

Contact Settings

Interested In

- job inquiries
- business deals
- getting back in touch
- expertise requests
- reference requests

According to the information listed in Image 3.16, this person is interested in hearing about job opportunities.

If you are currently employed and searching for a new opportunity but don't want your current employer to find out, you may not want "job inquiries" listed. Follow these steps to change your Opportunity Preferences:

1.   Select **Profile** from the top menu bar.

Image 3.17

Linked **in** ®   Home   Profile   Contacts   Groups   Jobs   Inbox (94)   More...

2.   Scroll down to the **Contact Settings** at the bottom of your profile page. Click **Edit** next to **Contact Settings**

Image 3.18

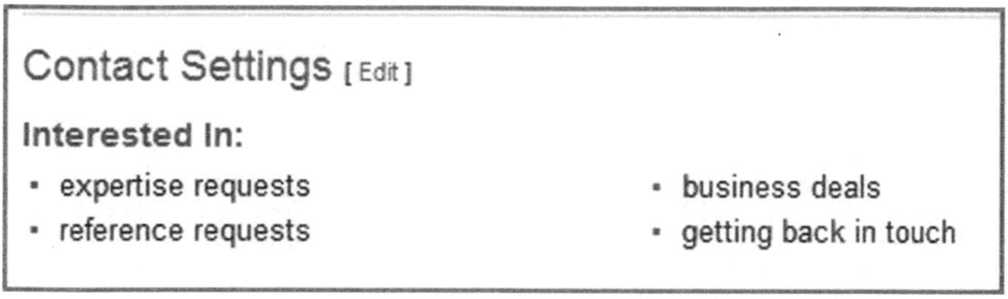

Contact Settings [Edit]

Interested In:

- expertise requests
- reference requests

- business deals
- getting back in touch

Look at the second section of the new page – **Opportunity Preferences**. You will see that you can select up to eight reasons why you would like people to contact you on LinkedIn.

Image 3.19

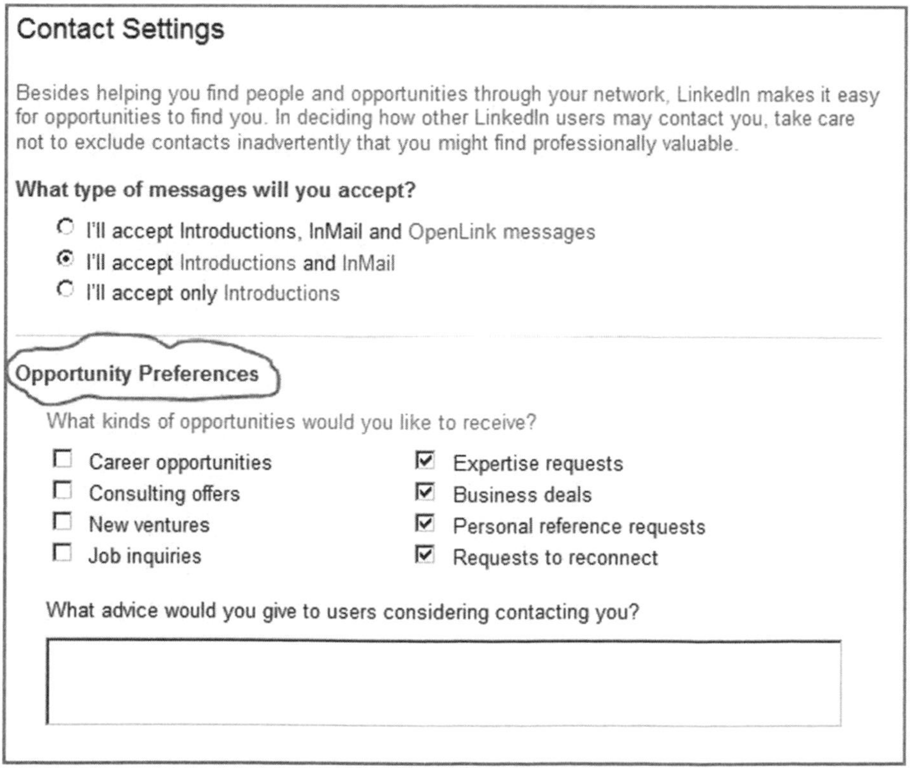

Contact Settings

Besides helping you find people and opportunities through your network, LinkedIn makes it easy for opportunities to find you. In deciding how other LinkedIn users may contact you, take care not to exclude contacts inadvertently that you might find professionally valuable.

What type of messages will you accept?

- ○ I'll accept Introductions, InMail and OpenLink messages
- ◉ I'll accept Introductions and InMail
- ○ I'll accept only Introductions

Opportunity Preferences

What kinds of opportunities would you like to receive?

- ☐ Career opportunities
- ☐ Consulting offers
- ☐ New ventures
- ☐ Job inquiries

- ☑ Expertise requests
- ☑ Business deals
- ☑ Personal reference requests
- ☑ Requests to reconnect

What advice would you give to users considering contacting you?

If you check one of the eight options listed under Opportunity Preferences, that option(s) will appear on your LinkedIn profile page.

Recommendation for Job Seekers

If you are currently employed and don't want your employer to find out that you are looking for new opportunities, you may want to leave the following categories unchecked: **Career opportunities, New ventures, Consulting offers, and Job inquiries**. Recruiters and employers who are interested in your profile will likely contact you anyway, without paying attention to your opportunity preferences.

In order to receive messages from recruiters and employers, you must choose to accept InMail messages, as shown in Image 3.19 above Opportunity Preferences.

(3) Connections Browse

By default, your connections on LinkedIn can view a list of all of your other connections. Select one of your connections and go to his or her profile page. Look down the right side of the page and you will see a box with his or her connections. Here's the box from one of my contacts.

Image 3.20

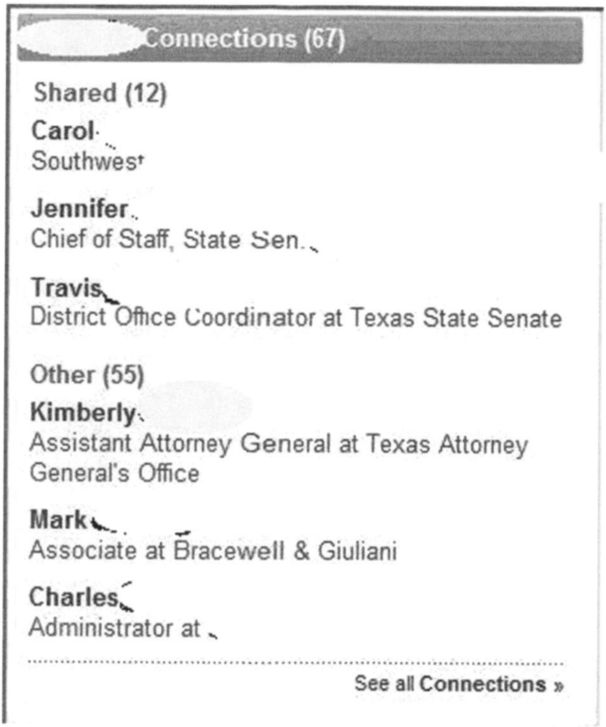

> **Connections (67)**
>
> Shared (12)
> **Carol**
> Southwest
>
> **Jennifer**
> Chief of Staff, State Sen.
>
> **Travis**
> District Office Coordinator at Texas State Senate
>
> Other (55)
> **Kimberly**
> Assistant Attorney General at Texas Attorney General's Office
>
> **Mark**
> Associate at Bracewell & Giuliani
>
> **Charles**
> Administrator at
>
> See all **Connections** »

Look below the sample names in Image 3.20, and you'll see a hyperlink called "see all connections." Clicking on that link will show you *all* of your contact's connections, as in Image 3.21.

Image 3.21

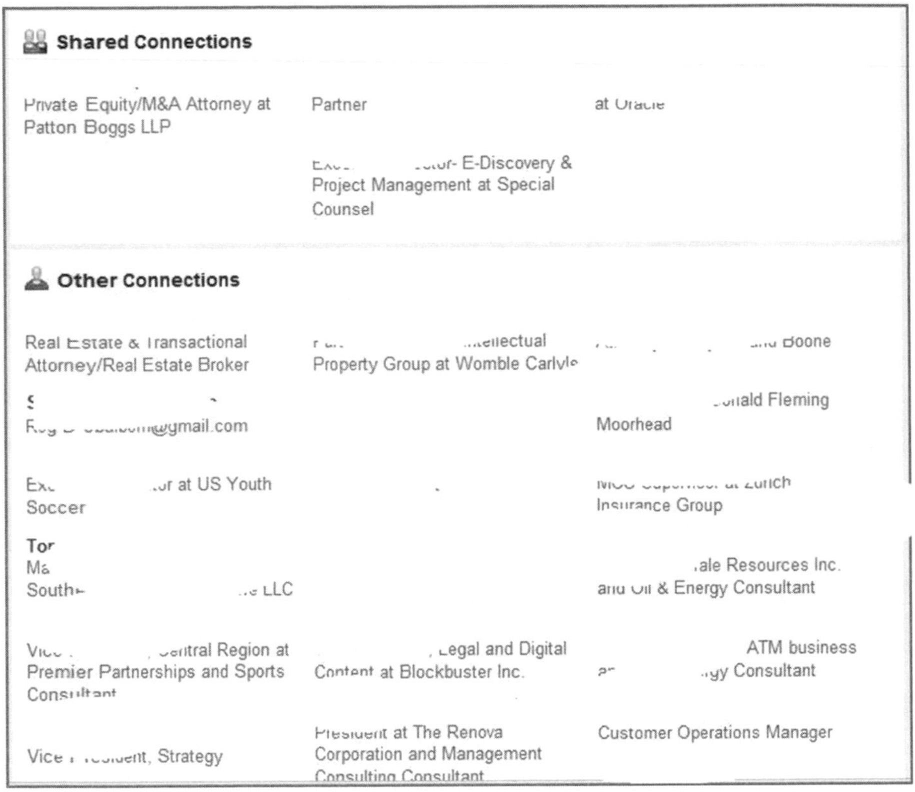

👥 **Shared Connections**

Private Equity/M&A Attorney at Patton Boggs LLP	Partner	at Oracle
	Exec ___ ctor- E-Discovery & Project Management at Special Counsel	

👤 **Other Connections**

Real Estate & Transactional Attorney/Real Estate Broker	...ellectual Property Group at Womble Carlyle	...u Boone
S F.~g ~ ~~~~~~@gmail.com		...nald Fleming Moorhead
Exc ...or at US Youth Soccer		MCC Supervisor at Zurich Insurance Group
Tor Ma South~ ...s LLC		...ale Resources Inc. and Oil & Energy Consultant
Vice ...entral Region at Premier Partnerships and Sports Consultant	Legal and Digital Content at Blockbuster Inc.	ATM business ...gy Consultant
Vice President, Strategy	President at The Renova Corporation and Management Consulting Consultant	Customer Operations Manager

---

Recommendation for Job Seekers

I recommend hiding your connections for the following reasons:

1. Just because you are connected to someone on LinkedIn doesn't mean you like them, endorse them, or would recommend them for a job. Some of your contacts might approach your other contacts directly and use you as the introduction even if it's someone you normally wouldn't recommend or introduce.

2. Some of your connections are competitors in your industry. You may not want them to have access to all of your contacts and connections.

To change the default setting and hide your connections, follow these steps:

1. Click on **Settings** across the menu bar in the upper right side of the page.

Image 3.22

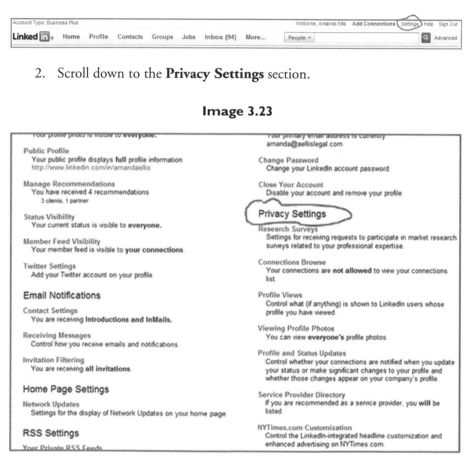

2. Scroll down to the **Privacy Settings** section.

Image 3.23

3. Then, click **Connections Browse**.

Image 3.24

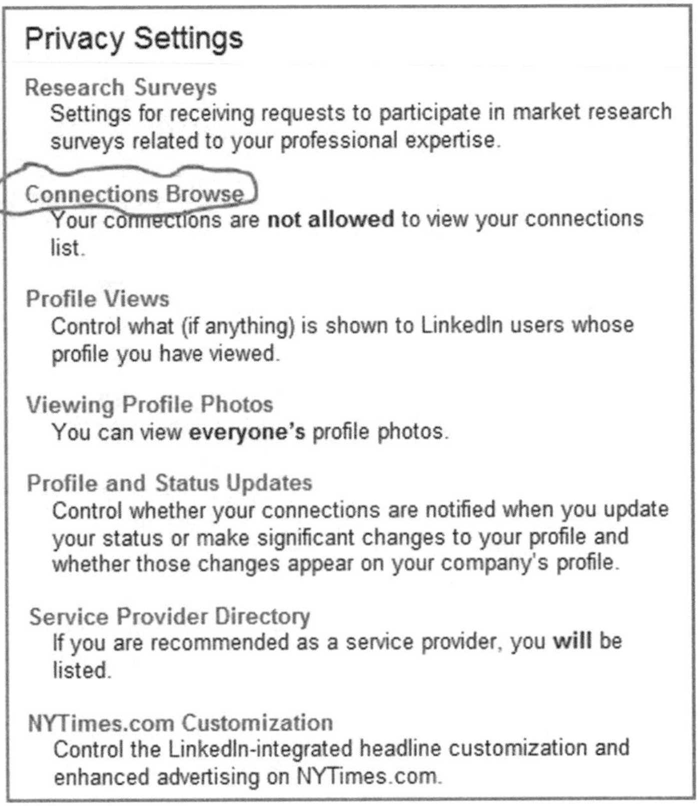

Privacy Settings

Research Surveys
   Settings for receiving requests to participate in market research
   surveys related to your professional expertise.

Connections Browse
   Your connections are **not allowed** to view your connections
   list.

Profile Views
   Control what (if anything) is shown to LinkedIn users whose
   profile you have viewed.

Viewing Profile Photos
   You can view **everyone's** profile photos.

Profile and Status Updates
   Control whether your connections are notified when you update
   your status or make significant changes to your profile and
   whether those changes appear on your company's profile.

Service Provider Directory
   If you are recommended as a service provider, you **will** be
   listed.

NYTimes.com Customization
   Control the LinkedIn-integrated headline customization and
   enhanced advertising on NYTimes.com.

---

4.   You can then select to hide your list of connections.

Image 3.25

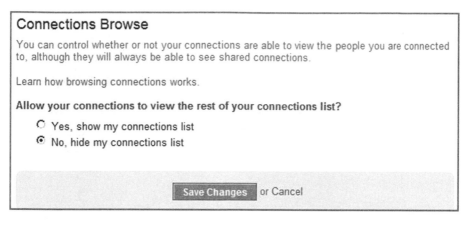

Caveat: You can only control whether or not your connections are able to view the people you are connected to, but your connections will always be able to see shared connections.

(4) Profile Views

About mid-way down your LinkedIn homepage, you'll see a box on the right side labeled, "Who's viewed my profile?" There are two reasons why you should pay attention to this box: (1) you want to see who is viewing your profile; and (2) you want to see how LinkedIn describes you when you view someone else's profile.

1. Find the **"Who's viewed my profile?"** box on your homepage.

Image 3.26

You'll note that it shows you how many people have viewed your profile in a certain number of days as well as how many times your name has appeared in search results.

2. Click on the text in this section and a new box will appear which displays who viewed your page.

Image 3.27

Your profile has been viewed by 11 people in the last day, including:

Someone in the Business Administration function in the Luxury Goods & Jewelry industry from Greater New York City Area

Someone in the Legal function in the Law Practice industry from Greater Philadelphia Area

Director at Calfee, Halter & Griswold LLP

Someone in the Leadership function in the Law Practice industry from Houston, Texas Area

Someone in the Leadership function in the Law Practice industry from Greater New York City Area

Someone in the Clerical function in the Staffing and Recruiting industry from Dallas/Fort Worth Area

Attorney at Bowman and Brooke LLP

Someone in the Legal Services industry from Greater Chicago Area

Someone in the Leadership function at UnitedLex Corporation

Assistant Attorney General at New Jersey Department of Law & Public Safety, Division of Law

Examiner at National Labor Relations Board

You'll note that the descriptions range from generic descriptions about a person's industry and location to more specific descriptions such as a person's title and firm or company.

You should check this listing routinely. Perhaps you applied for a job and your resume contains the link or address to your LinkedIn profile. Check this listing to see if the person you sent your resume to has viewed your profile. If he or she hasn't, and, if sufficient time has passed since you initially submitted your resume, perhaps you should follow up to make sure he or she received the resume.

Also, think about how you wish to be described when you view other LinkedIn users' profiles. You have three options:

1. Your name and headline can be shown.
2. Only anonymous profile characteristics such as industry and title can be shown.
3. You can select that nothing be shown—LinkedIn won't show other users that you viewed the profile.

Recommendation for Job Seekers

Choose the option to include your name and headline when you view another user's profile. A potential employer might feel flattered to see that you've reviewed his or her profile and, in turn, he or she might be led to view your profile.

At some point in your legal career, you may wish to change this setting. For example, if you begin to use LinkedIn to gain a competitive advantage and look at your competitors' profiles or opposing counsel's profile, you may want very little or no information about you to appear.

To control how your title is displayed, follow these steps:

1. Start at the **Settings** tab in the upper right menu

Image 3.28

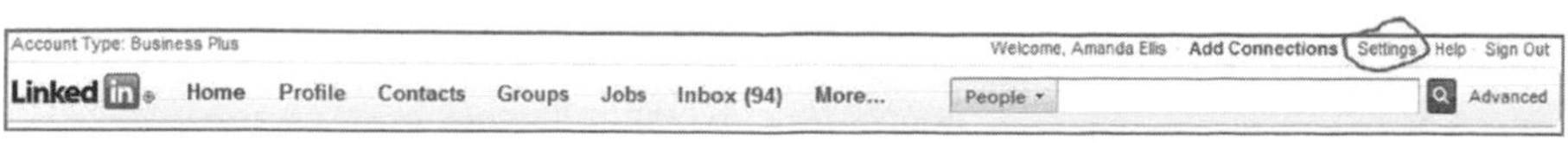

Account Type: Business Plus

Linked in®   Home   Profile   Contacts   Groups   Jobs   Inbox (94)   More...   People ▾   Q Advanced

Welcome, Amanda Ellis   Add Connections   Settings   Help   Sign Out

2. Scroll down to the **Privacy Settings** and select **Profile Views**.

Image 3.29

Privacy Settings

Research Surveys
Settings for receiving requests to participate in market research surveys related to your professional expertise.

Connections Browse
Your connections are **not allowed** to view your connections list.

Profile Views
Control what (if anything) is shown to LinkedIn users whose profile you have viewed.

Viewing Profile Photos
You can view **everyone's** profile photos.

Profile and Status Updates
Control whether your connections are notified when you update your status or make significant changes to your profile and whether those changes appear on your company's profile.

Service Provider Directory
If you are recommended as a service provider, you **will** be listed.

NYTimes.com Customization
Control the LinkedIn-integrated headline customization and enhanced advertising on NYTimes.com.

3. You will then see your three options. Select the one that fits your need.

Image 3.30

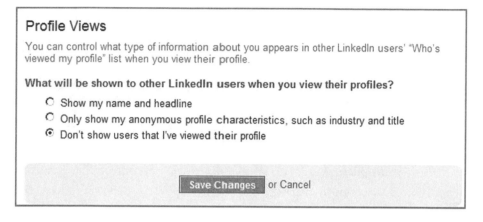

(5) Status Visibility

One LinkedIn profile feature mentioned in Chapter 2 was the status update, an update that points to what you are working on in your professional life or to a link to an article you wish to share. As you'll learn in Chapter 4, you can use your status to update your contacts about your job search, practice, and law school activities.

Your status update is visible to anyone by default, including people you are not connected to on LinkedIn but who happen to find your profile, unless you restrict the visibility to your connections only. When you post your update, you can change the visibility by clicking on the drop down menu next to "visible to" and selecting "connections only," as shown below in Image 3.31.

Image 3.31

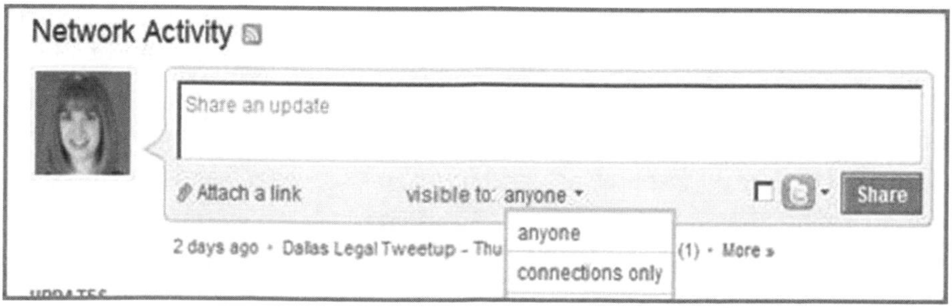

Recommendation for Job Seekers

You'll want to choose "anyone" for your visibility level for most status updates because you want potential employers who are not your connections to hear about your search.

If, however, you share particular firm names in a status update, consider sharing that update with connections only.

(6) Profile and Status Updates

When you update your status or make changes to your profile, LinkedIn alerts your connections by sharing notice of the update in their news feed. For example, the following notice in my news feed tells me that my contact recently updated the Education portion of her profile.

Image 3.32

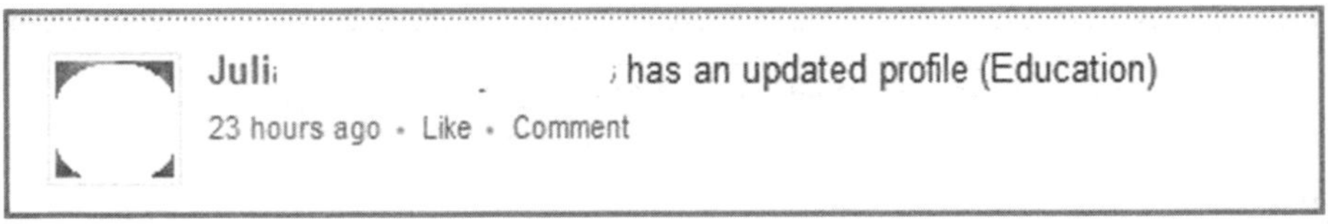

> Juli: , has an updated profile (Education)
> 23 hours ago · Like · Comment

Recommendation for Job Seekers

I recommend that you allow LinkedIn to share notices to your connections when you update your status or change your profile information because these notices often drive your connections to your profile.

However, I would disable this notification when you make substantive revisions to your profile. For example, I recommend in Chapter 6 that you update your LinkedIn profile on a quarterly basis. You don't want to clog your connections' news feed with multiple notices that you've updated multiple parts of your profile. I would disable the notification feature and then turn it back on when I get ready to make the last update.

To disable the notification, go to your **Privacy Settings** from the **Settings** menu and click on **Profile** and **Status Updates**. Then, click on "No" under both questions.

Image 3.33

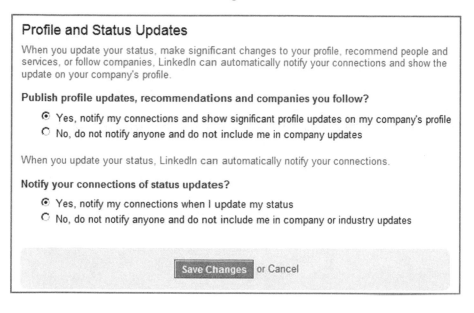

Profile and Status Updates

When you update your status, make significant changes to your profile, recommend people and services, or follow companies, LinkedIn can automatically notify your connections and show the update on your company's profile.

Publish profile updates, recommendations and companies you follow?

⦿ Yes, notify my connections and show significant profile updates on my company's profile
○ No, do not notify anyone and do not include me in company updates

When you update your status, LinkedIn can automatically notify your connections.

Notify your connections of status updates?

⦿ Yes, notify my connections when I update my status
○ No, do not notify anyone and do not include me in company or industry updates

[Save Changes] or Cancel

TWITTER

Twitter is the simplest of all three sites in terms of privacy settings and options. You should note the information that is always public and the information you can make private.

(1) Privacy Options

You can protect your tweets and Twitter lists.

Tweets

By default, everything you tweet is public. To change this status, though, click on **Settings** from the top menu bar.

Image 3.34

Home Profile Find People Settings Help Sign out

Scroll down and you'll see a box labeled **Protect my tweets**. If you check this box, only people you approve will be allowed to see your tweets.

Image 3.35

☐ Protect my tweets
Only let people whom I approve follow my tweets. If this is checked, you
WILL NOT be on the public timeline. Tweets posted previously may still be
publicly visible in some places.

If you choose to protect your tweets, other users will see the following message if they go to your page. They will need to send you a request which you will then approve or deny. Only after your approval of a request will they be able to view your tweets.

Image 3.36

This person has protected their tweets.

You need to send a request before you can start following this person.

Send request

Recommendation for Job Seekers

If you follow my advice in Chapter 1 and treat Twitter as a primarily professional site, do not protect your tweets. Most people in the legal profession don't protect their tweets because they want people to connect with them. People may not connect with you if they can't see how often you tweet, the subject matter of your tweets, and whether you engage in conversation versus just promote your own material.

Lists

As you'll learn in Chapter 4, you can group the people you follow into lists. For example, you may have different lists for favorite people, litigation attorneys, corporate attorneys, legal journalists, and legal careers.

The lists you create are public by default, but you can make some or all of your lists private.

Image 3.37

Recommendation for Job Seekers

Most of your lists should be public. As you advance through your career, you may want to make certain lists private. For example, if you are a real estate attorney and create a list of real estate developers on Twitter, you may wish to keep that list private so other real estate attorneys can't see the list of potential clients you have created.

(2) Always Public

Your Twitter profile and Twitter Favorites are public.

Twitter Profile

Your Twitter Profile is public, even if you protect your tweets as described in the previous section. For example, Amy Pfeiffer, a May 2010 graduate of Barry University School of Law, protects her tweets, but I can still see her profile information in Image 3.38. Note that Amy's profile and Twitter background are still professional and appropriate for Twitter. If a recruiter or potential employer finds Amy's profile, they will learn that she's a recent law school graduate. They can send her a follow request if they are interested in connecting with Amy.

Image 3.38

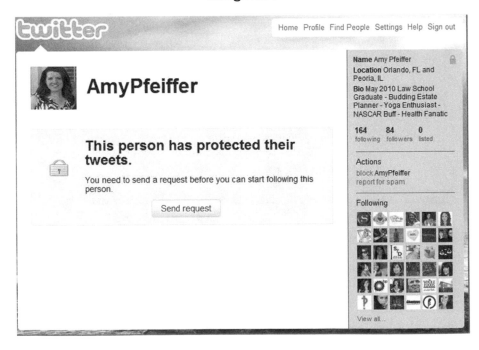

Twitter Favorites

You may choose to mark certain tweets as your favorites. I frequently do this when tweets contain a hyperlink and sound interesting. Then, when I have more time, I click on the Favorites link from my Twitter profile, as shown in Image 3.39.

Image 3.39

Note that anyone can click on your Favorites link because the tweets you add to your Favorites are public. Image 3.40 shows how Twitter displays the tweets marked as "favorite," and Chapter 5 discusses how to use your Favorites and other users' Favorites.

Image 3.40

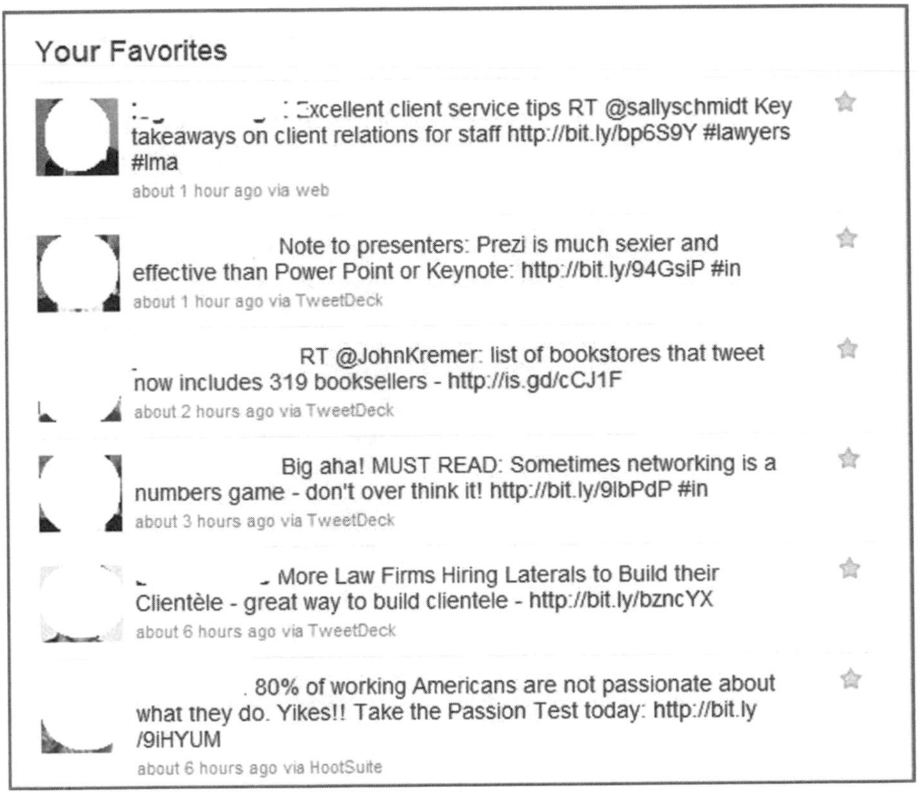

Your Favorites

: Excellent client service tips RT @sallyschmidt Key
takeaways on client relations for staff http://bit.ly/bp6S9Y #lawyers
#lma
about 1 hour ago via web

Note to presenters: Prezi is much sexier and
effective than Power Point or Keynote: http://bit.ly/94GsiP #in
about 1 hour ago via TweetDeck

RT @JohnKremer: list of bookstores that tweet
now includes 319 booksellers - http://is.gd/cCJ1F
about 2 hours ago via TweetDeck

Big aha! MUST READ: Sometimes networking is a
numbers game - don't over think it! http://bit.ly/9lbPdP #in
about 3 hours ago via TweetDeck

More Law Firms Hiring Laterals to Build their
Clientèle - great way to build clientele - http://bit.ly/bzncYX
about 6 hours ago via TweetDeck

. 80% of working Americans are not passionate about
what they do. Yikes!! Take the Passion Test today: http://bit.ly
/9iHYUM
about 6 hours ago via HootSuite

POINTS – PRIVACY

Facebook Privacy Recommendations

Information	Default Privacy Level	Recommended Privacy Level for Job Seekers
BASIC DIRECTORY INFORMATION		
Search for me on Facebook	Everyone	Everyone
Send me friend requests	Everyone	Everyone
Send me messages	Everyone	Everyone
See my friend list	Everyone	Friends Only
See my education and work	Everyone	Everyone
See my current city and hometown	Everyone	Everyone
See my interests and other pages	Everyone	Friends Only
THINGS I SHARE		
Posts by me (status updates)	Everyone	Friends Only
Family	Everyone	Friends Only
Relationships	Everyone	Friends Only
Interested in and Looking for	Everyone	Friends Only
Bio and favorite quotations	Everyone	Everyone
Website	Everyone	Everyone
Religious and political views	Friends of Friends	Friends Only
Birthday	Friends of Friends	Friends Only
Edit Album privacy (Photos)	Everyone	Friends Only
THINGS OTHERS SHARE		
Tagged photos/videos	Friends of Friends	Customize – Only Me
Comment on posts	Friends Only	Friends Only

Information	Default Privacy Level	Recommended Privacy Level for Job Seekers
Friends can post on my wall	Friends can post on Wall Enabled	Friends can post on Wall Enabled
Can see Wall posts by friends	Friends of Friends	Friends Only
CONTACT INFORMATION		
Mobile phone	Friends Only	Friends Only
Other phone	Friends Only	Friends Only
Address	Friends Only	Friends Only
IM Screen name	Friends Only	Friends Only
E-mail	Friends Only	Everyone

LinkedIn Privacy Recommendations

Information	Recommended Privacy Level for Job Seekers
Personal Information	Provide one method of contact
Opportunity Preferences	Employed job seekers should omit Career Opportunities, New ventures, Consulting offers and Job inquiries
Connections Browse	Hide Connections
Profile Views	List name and title
Status Visibility	Anyone unless mentioning specific firm
Profile and Status Updates	Allow to share on news feed unless you are performing multiple updates

Twitter Privacy Recommendations

Information	Recommended Privacy Level for Job Seekers
Tweets	Do not protect updates
Lists	Public unless gathering competitive intelligence
Profile	Always public
Favorites	Always public

PERFORM YOUR JOB SEARCH ON THE BIG 3 SITES

The second part of the 6Ps system covers the fourth "P"—performance—the core of the 6Ps system. The chapter is long but divided into three sections, one dedicated to each of the Big 3 sites.

CHAPTER 4

Performance

PERFORMANCE OVER PRESENCE

AFTER completing part 1 of the 6Ps system, you will have a *presence* on the Big 3 sites. But, a mere presence is not enough to succeed in your job search. As we saw in the Premise, it was President Obama's and Senator Brown's *performance*, not their mere presence, on social networking sites that distinguished them from other candidates using social networking and made social networking a winning piece of their political campaigns.

CAP YOUR PERFORMANCE

The second part of the 6Ps system focuses on job seekers' performance, the fourth "P" and an essential piece of a successful job search campaign. You must complete three steps on each of the Big 3 social networking sites in order to maximize or CAP your performance. The three steps include:

1. ***Step 1 - Connect.*** Connect to the right people, including contacts who will refer you jobs (or refer you for positions) and contacts who are potential employers or hold some hiring authority.

   Most job seekers using the Big 3 sites complete this step, but few advance to steps 2 and 3. Moreover, many job seekers connect with the wrong people.

   Levels of Scrutiny. When choosing your connections on the Big 3 sites, follow a three-tiered analysis, similar to the three-tiered equal protection analysis you learned in Constitutional Law: strict scrutiny, intermediate scrutiny, and minimum (or rational basis) scrutiny. The three levels of scrutiny are described in detail throughout this chapter and summarized in Table 4.1.

Table 4.1 - Three-Tiered Analysis to Determine Connections on Big 3 Sites

	Level of Scrutiny	Rule
Facebook Profile (Majority View)	Strict Scrutiny	Home Invitation Rule
LinkedIn	Intermediate Scrutiny	Business Card Rule
Twitter	Rational Basis	Cocktail Party Rule

2. *Step 2 - Assimilate.* Once you are connected to your referral sources and potential employers, you can learn about specific openings, potential openings, and specific firms or attorneys to target. You can also gain information from the Big 3 sites that will help prepare you for job interviews. Some, but not all, job seekers complete this level.

3. *Step 3 - Participate.* To fully benefit from the Big 3 sites you must participate. Remember, it's called social networking. If you don't socialize and engage with your network, you will never receive all the benefits the Big 3 social networking sites offer. Moreover, it's your participation that keeps you on your contacts' radar screens. Very few law students and lawyers currently complete this step, but as more attorney job seekers complete this step, more success stories regarding social networking in the legal job search will be reported.

Remember, the three CAP steps must be followed on each of the Big 3 sites to reach maximum performance level. This chapter is divided into three sections and analyzes the CAP steps for each of the Big 3 sites.

Section 1 - Facebook

Facebook is an effective tool for keeping in touch with friends and family, and you may already use Facebook for this reason. Facebook, however, can be just as powerful for professional networking. Your best friend from high school may be married to the general counsel of a Fortune 500 company. Or, your college roommate's mother may be the hiring partner in a law firm. Your Facebook friends list probably includes several friends who have contacts in some hiring capacity at law firms or corporations.

Therefore, your use of Facebook will be professional to some degree. Your performance on Facebook in your job search campaign should correspond to the degree of professionalism for Facebook. If you follow the Majority View (defined in Chapter 1), for example, 5-40% of the content you share or the time you spend on Facebook may be professional in nature.

You performance on Facebook will consist of the CAP steps discussed on page 113. To incorporate Facebook into your job search campaign, you will connect, assimilate, and participate. Finally, you will perform these steps on both your individual profile page and various Facebook fan pages and groups.

STEP 1: CONNECT

You will find that connecting with friends, fan pages, and groups on Facebook can help in your job search. Only the friends you connect with through your profile page can see the information you share on your profile page. The people affiliated with the fan pages or groups will not see your own profile page information, unless you choose to become friends with each person or share your profile information with everyone.

Connecting with people, pages, or groups on Facebook involves two steps:

1. **Who** – determining your Facebook Connections
2. **How** – learning the various connection methods so you do not overlook one

Profile Page

Who: Level of Scrutiny to Connect with Friends

Because of the significant amount of personal information that is shared through your Facebook profile, it is imperative to establish boundaries before connecting with friends through your personal profile page.

Majority View: Strict Scrutiny

As noted on page 113, choosing your connections on the Big 3 sites requires a three-tiered analysis, similar to the three-tiered equal protection analysis you learned in Constitutional Law: strict scrutiny, intermediate scrutiny, and minimum (or rational basis) scrutiny. Because of the significant amount of personal information that is shared through your Facebook profile, I recommend a strict scrutiny analysis, the most selective, in determining your Facebook connections.

Home Invitation Rule

To apply the strict scrutiny analysis, follow the **Home Invitation Rule**: only accept a person as a Facebook friend if the person is someone you would invite into your home now or at any time in my past. If you follow the Home Invitation Rule, your Facebook friends will include childhood friends, family friends, relatives, former classmates, and even professional colleagues you socialize with outside the office. The friends in this category are people who know, like, and trust you and probably the first people in your network to introduce you to one of their contacts (if you ask) or refer you for a job because they have known you for some period of time.

How: Connection Methods

There are six ways to connect with other individuals through your Facebook profile page:

1. ***E-mail Contacts:*** Upload your e-mail address book to Facebook and invite your existing contacts to connect with you.

2. ***Facebook Suggestions:*** Once you are connected to a certain number of people, Facebook will suggest people you may know. Review these suggestions and determine whether you want to connect with them.

   To view the people Facebook suggested for you, look at the upper right section of your Facebook home page and you will find a section called **"Suggestions."**

   As you can see in Image 4.1, Facebook suggested that I become friends with Mike and informed me that Mike and I share 27 connections. Facebook thinks Mike and I might know each other as well. If so, I could invite Mike to connect on Facebook by clicking **"Add as a friend."**

Image 4.1

To view other friend suggestions by Facebook, click "**See All**" and Facebook will list other people you might know.

3. *Search for People.* When you click the "See All" tab in the **Suggestions** area of your home page (see Image 4.1), there's a section at the bottom of the page called **Search for People**. Enter a single name or e-mail address.

    Facebook can also find former classmates and colleagues if you entered your education and work information in your profile (Chapter 2). As shown in Image 4.2, there are links to click to find your classmates and colleagues.

Image 4.2

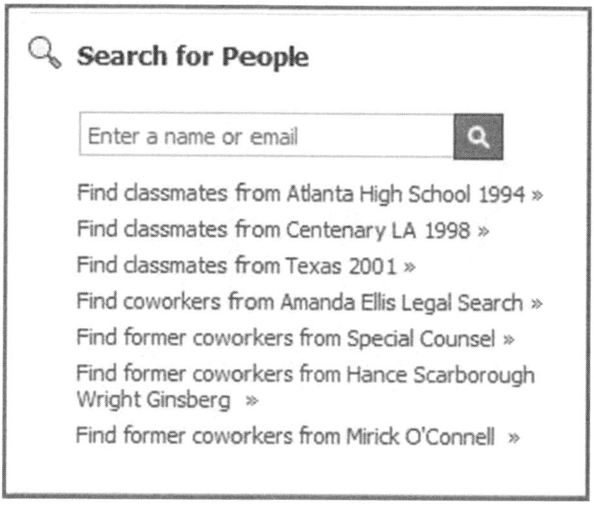

> 🔍 **Search for People**
>
> | Enter a name or email | 🔍 |
>
> Find classmates from Atlanta High School 1994 »
> Find classmates from Centenary LA 1998 »
> Find classmates from Texas 2001 »
> Find coworkers from Amanda Ellis Legal Search »
> Find former coworkers from Special Counsel »
> Find former coworkers from Hance Scarborough
> Wright Ginsberg »
> Find former coworkers from Mirick O'Connell »

4. *News Feed.* Monitor your news feed to see who your friends become friends with on Facebook. If you know the other people, you may want to connect as well. For example, the fourth entry in my news feed in Image 4.3 is an alert that my friend David became friends with Courtney and seven other people. I can check to see if I know these people and want to connect with them.

Image 4.3

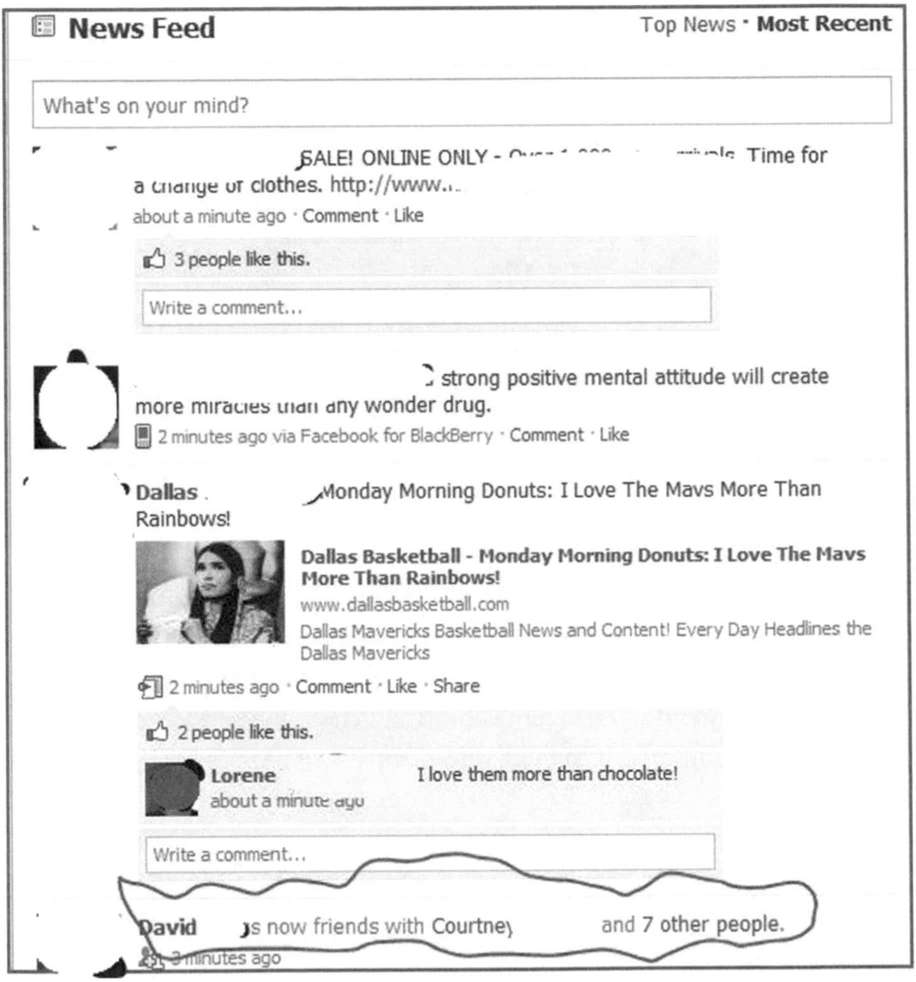

5. *Friend Suggestions.* Your friends may suggest people for you to become friends with. Monitor the "**Requests**" section in the upper right corner of your home page.

Image 4.4

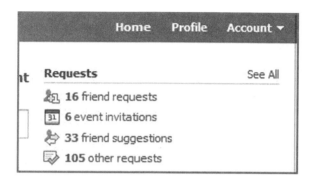

Click on **Friend Suggestions** to see which friends have suggested new friends for you.

In Image 4.5, my friend Lee suggested I add John as a friend. I can tell from the information in Image 4.5 that John and I share 11 mutual friends. I can also click through John's name to read more about his profile if I feel I need more information before adding John as a friend.

Image 4.5

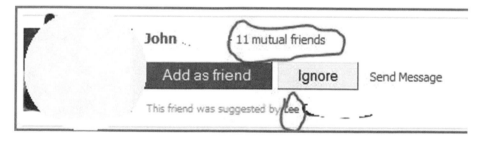

6. *Fan Pages & Groups.* As you interact on Facebook fan pages and groups, you may find people you know and want to add as a Facebook friend. For example, you may read your law school alumni page and read a comment by a classmate you lost contact with three years ago. You may want to send a friend request to the former classmate.

Fan Pages & Groups

In addition to connecting with friends on Facebook, you'll also want to identify and connect with certain Facebook fan pages and groups since many law school groups and law firms have a page or group.

Who: Level of Scrutiny to connect with Pages/Groups

If your privacy settings are set to Friends Only, your Facebook personal profile remains private to other users on the fan pages and groups when you connect with these pages. The only information that is visible to other contacts on fan pages and groups is your profile picture, as discussed in Chapter 2. Therefore, there is little risk at exposing too much information, assuming you follow the Office Desk Photo Rule (Chapter 2) when selecting a profile picture.

Minimum (Rational Basis) Scrutiny

Because there is little personal information to reveal, you don't need to follow the strict scrutiny analysis and Home Invitation Rule as you did with your individual Facebook profile page. Instead, you can apply minimum, or rational basis, scrutiny. Join as many Facebook groups and "like" as many Facebook pages as you want as long as you don't mind your picture being associated with the name or title of the page or group.

How: Connection Methods

There are six ways to connect with Facebook fan pages and groups.

1. *Specific Search.* If you are a law student, look for your law school, your law school career services office, other law schools' career services offices (if business pages or open group pages, you can still connect), bar associations (state and local), and other professional organizations.

   Go to the search bar across the main menu bar and enter the relevant key words.

Image 4.6

For example, if you are a law student attending Case Western School of Law, you may want to check to see if your career services office has a Facebook page. You would type "Case Western Law Career" in the search bar. As you can see in Image 4.7, the law school's career office has a fan page which you can "like."

Image 4.7

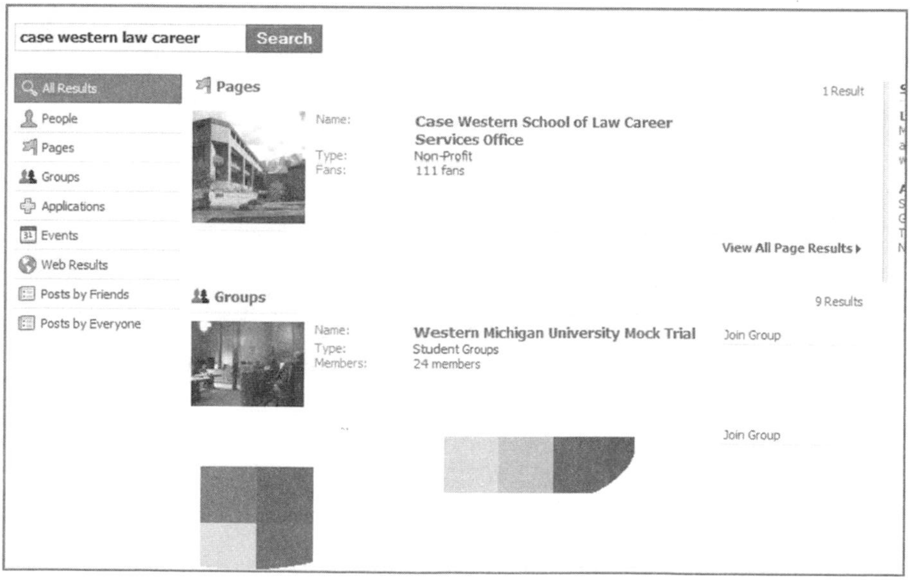

case western law career	Search			
All Results	**Pages**			1 Result
People		Name:	Case Western School of Law Career Services Office	
Pages		Type:	Non-Profit	
Groups		Fans:	111 fans	
Applications				
Events				View All Page Results ▶
Web Results				
Posts by Friends	**Groups**			9 Results
Posts by Everyone		Name:	Western Michigan University Mock Trial	Join Group
		Type:	Student Groups	
		Members:	24 members	
				Join Group

If you are a practicing attorney job seeker who graduated from the University of Texas School of Law, you may want to find out if your school has an alumni page. You could enter "University of Texas Law" in the search and find the results shown in Image 4.8.

Image 4.8

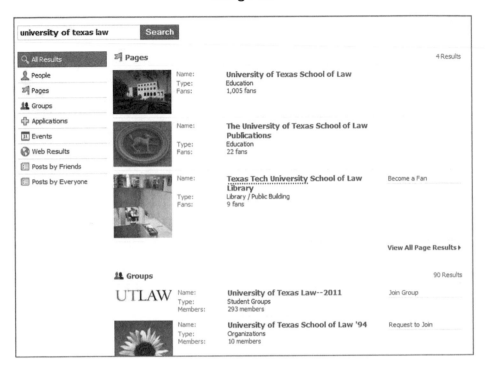

As you can see in the search results in Image 4.8, the law school has a Facebook fan page. The search results also reveal a page for the law school's publications and various group pages such as groups for certain graduating classes.

2. *Invitations.* Friends may send you invitations to become a fan of a page or join a group; accepting these invitations is another way to connect with groups and fan pages.

3. *News Feed Notifications.* You may also see notifications in your news feed when friends "like" a page or join a group. The particular fan page or group may be of interest to you as well and you can click the link to learn more about the page or group.

4. *Appendix A.* **Appendix A** at the end of the book lists law school career services offices with Facebook fan pages or groups.

5. ***Appendix B.*** **Appendix B** at the end of the book lists law firm career/ recruiting departments with Facebook fan pages.

6. ***Law Firm Facebook Pages.*** While most large firms don't have Facebook pages specifically for their career/recruiting departments, many have a firm Facebook page. You can search for large firms on Facebook by entering the firm's name in the search bar. There are also many smaller firms that have Facebook pages. JD Supra compiled a list of lawyers and law firms with Facebook fan pages, and you can find many smaller firms on this list.[28] http://scoop.jdsupra.com/2009/07/articles/law-firm-marketing/ lawyers-and-law-firms-on-facebook/.

7. ***Key Word Search.*** Another way to identify law firms and law school career services pages is to perform a key word search in the Facebook search bar. Rather than searching for a specific firm or law school, search for key words like "law" and "firm" or "law" and "career."

STEP 2: ASSIMILATE

The second step in performing your job search on Facebook is to assimilate—gather information that may assist your job search, including specific job openings, potential openings, networking events, and information that will help prepare you for interviews. There are nine ways you may gather this information.

(1) Review Friends' Status Updates

Review your friends' status updates. If your friends are in a hiring role, they may post job openings. Or, friends might announce when their company is hiring, as in the example in Image 4.9.

Image 4.9

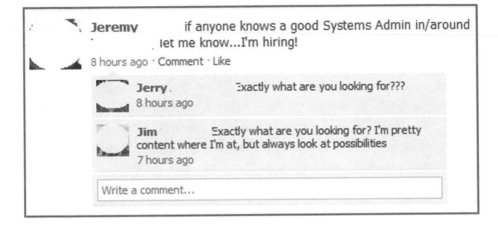

(2) Review Friends' Wall Posts & Notes

Status updates are limited to 420 characters, so check your friends' wall posts and notes for job leads, too. Some friends might include a detailed job description and tag friends in a Facebook note. If you are friends with the person who posted the note, you'll see the activity in your news feed. Plus, if you are friends with people who are tagged in the note, you'll see the activity in your news feed. Thus, you don't need to be connected to the person who posted the position if he or she tags one of your other friends. Image 4.10 is an example of a Facebook note containing a job posting.

Image 4.10

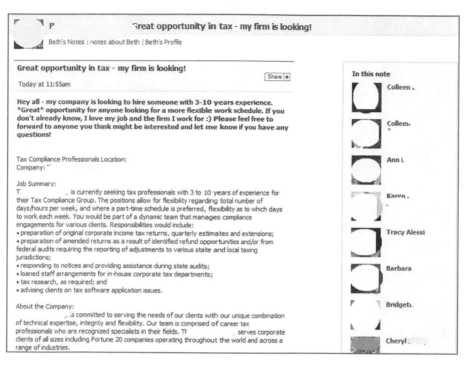

(3) Review Events in News Feed

Monitor your news feed for networking events. Some, such as the example in Image 4.11, might be events for the legal community only, while others might be events for the community at large.

Image 4.11

Click on the event link to gather more information, including a list of attendees. If the attendees are people who might help in your job search, consider attending.

(4) Search BranchOut

BranchOut launched in July 2010, and the Facebook application allows you to see where your Facebook friends (and, your friends' friends) work or previously worked. You can use the application when identifying law firms to target in your search and preparing for interviews. For example, enter the name of the firm where you are interviewing, and BranchOut identifies your Facebook friends (and friends' friends) who currently work at the firm and previously worked at the firm.

Image 4.12 shows the results BranchOut generated when I searched for the firm Vinson & Elkins. As you can see, one of my Facebook friends currently works at Vinson & Elkins and another one of my friends, Ashley Hunter, has a friend who works at Vinson & Elkins. If I want to learn more about Vinson & Elkins to prepare for an interview, I can reach out to my friend who works there or my friend who knows someone who works there.

Image 4.12

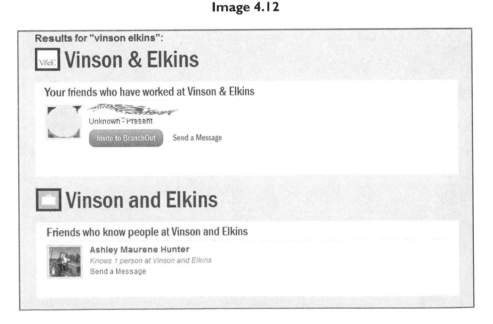

Caveat: As noted in Chapter 2, BranchOut only identifies friends if they include their work information on their Facebook profiles.

You should also note that BranchOut has a job board where you can view positions posted by your Facebook friends.

(5) Search Marketplace

Another place to gather job search information on Facebook is the Marketplace tab in the menu to the left of your news feed, as shown in Image 4.13.

Image 4.13

As the name implies, the Marketplace section is like your Facebook classifieds. You'll find houses to rent, cars for sale, and even jobs. While I wouldn't focus my energy on this section of few listed legal jobs, I would put this section on my radar. I suspect more firms—especially smaller firms—may begin to use it.

Create an account and you can receive weekly updates. For example, a recent update I received contained an associate position with a Chicago law firm, as shown in Image 4.14.

Image 4.14

From:	Marketplace [apps+mwkwmbrx@facebookappmail.com]
To:	Amanda Ellis
Cc:	
Subject:	...just posted in Facebook Marketplace

Hi Amanda,

Here is your weekly summary of Friend activity in Facebook Marketplace

Friends-of-Friends : **246 new postings**

Penny

See Postings Now!

Latest postings in your Social Circle

1999 Volkswagon Beetle for $3,800
posted by   friend Scott . ...

1999 VW Beetle (101k miles) One Owner Non-Smoking 6 Disc CD Changer Regularly Serviced

Mobile, AL - 3 hours ago

Commercial Litigation Attorney
posted by   's friend Ginger ....

NO THUMBNAIL AVAILABLE

Mid-sized Chicago Loop law firm is seeking a senior associate to join its busy commercial litigation practice. Qualified candidates should have experience drafting pleading...

Chicago, IL - 3 hours ago

(6) Review Firm Pages for Practice Area Insight

Monitor law firms' Facebook pages to learn about hot issues of certain practice areas. This information may be helpful in interviews, and some information may predict future hiring trends. For example, the update in Image 4.15, posted on a law firm's business page, discusses the increased mortgage litigation and may indicate increased hiring in this practice area.

Image 4.15

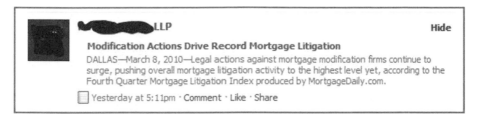

(7) Review Job Postings on Firm Pages

Look for specific job opportunities. In Image 4.16, the law firm posted an opening on its Facebook business page.

Image 4.16

(8) Review Career-Related Articles on Law Schools' Career Pages

Many law schools' career pages and groups on Facebook contain general job search advice that might help a first-time job seeker or a person who hasn't had to look for a job in several years. For example, in the posting in Image 4.17, Tulane Law School's Career Development Office posted a link to an article about succeeding in lunch interviews, a common practice for first-time job seekers and lateral attorneys.

Image 4.17

(9) Search Community Pages to Learn About Firms

Facebook added Community Pages in April 2010. The Community Pages are similar to Wikipedia pages for Facebook fan pages. They pull information that other Facebook users are saying about a topic or business and display it on one page.

You may want to consider Facebook Community Pages as another tool to help prepare for interviews, especially if you are interviewing with larger firms. For example, I entered the name of a large firm in my Facebook search bar and the first result was a link to the firm's Community Page, as shown in Image 4.18.

Image 4.18

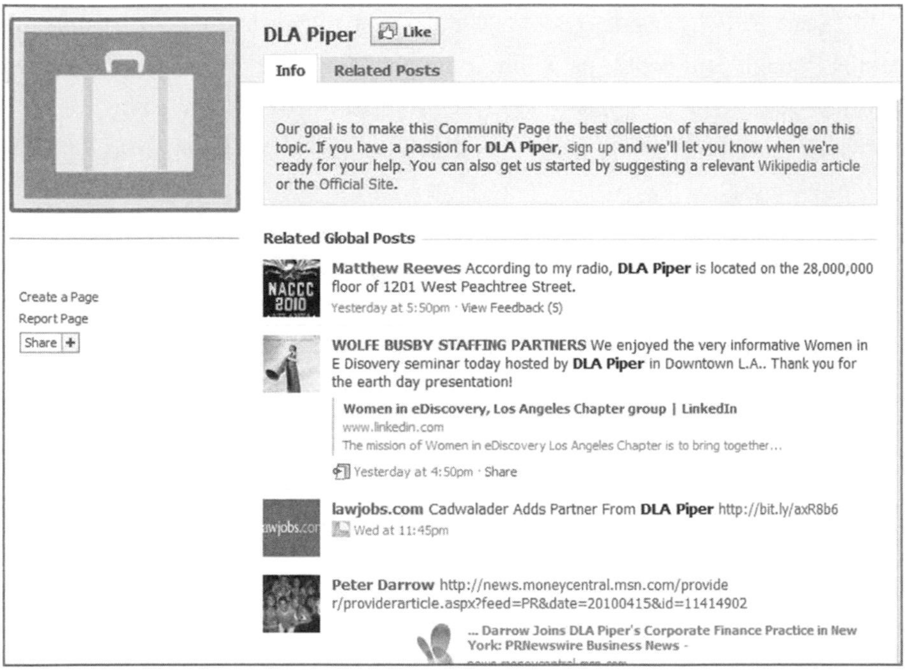

The Community Page pulled updates where other Facebook users mentioned the firm's name. From reading this page, you would learn that the firm recently hosted a Women in eDiscovery Seminar in its LA office, lost a partner to another firm, and added an attorney to the firm's Corporate Finance Practice in NYC.

Be alert to all news on Facebook. Even though the primary purpose or use is to communicate with close friends and family, you can also learn information which might assist you in your job search.

STEP 3: PARTICIPATE

If you currently use Facebook, you are probably connected to friends and family through your profile page. These are people who know, like, and trust you and probably the first people in your network to introduce you to one of their contacts (if you ask) or refer you for a job because they have known you for some period of time.

In order to gain an introduction to your friends' contacts or a referral for a position, it is necessary for you to let your friends know what you do and what you hope to find. For Facebook to be effective in generating introductions and referrals you must participate on the site—socialize and talk about what you do. If you don't share information with others and only check Facebook once a month, you'll fall off of your Facebook friends' radar screens and they won't remember to refer you if they hear of an opportunity (or if they are personally hiring).

There are 14 ways you can remain on your friends' radar screens by participating in activities such as updating your status, posting and sharing professional links, and commenting on friends' pages.

(1) Update your Status with Personal Updates

One feature on Facebook is the ability to update your status or respond to the prompt, "what's on your mind?" The status update is one of the most effective means of communication because (1) you can update multiple friends and family members at one time with a single message/status update; and (2) many Facebook users access Facebook from their phones and will see new updates even if they don't log onto Facebook from their computers.

Since most people use Facebook to communicate with friends and family, most of the updates are personal in nature. You still remain on your friends' radar screens by sharing personal status updates, such as:

Travel
- ***Off to Hong Kong for a day before heading to Vegas for CES.***

Life (in general)
- ***Facebooking from home until I get that new phone (this time with the extended warranty).***

Life Events (births, deaths, marriages)
- ***Uh...how is it possible that the wedding is only 3 months away?!?!?***

Sports
- ***LGA to Burbank, CA tomorrow. Section 5, Row 6. Hook'em!***

(2) Post Status Updates about your Job Search

You can share information about your job search in a status update. It is important, however, that you don't repeat the same "I'm looking for a job" update. People will grow tired of the same update. Not to mention, people need more information to help you with your job search.

If you are a law student, you may share information about your job search as well as law school in general to remind your friends and family that you are in law school, about to graduate, and in search of a job. Some examples of status updates for law students include the following:

- First week back in classes since the holiday break
- Attending a resume and cover letter writing workshop at the law school tonight – do any of my lawyer friends have tips to share?
- At Starbucks working on my *Law Review* note re 1st Amendment issues – think I might be interested in this area of practice
- On Campus Interviews start this week – I'm interviewing with Law Firm XYZ and Law Firm ABC - any friends with connections to these firms?
- Still no word from the firms I interviewed with last month – any friends know of any job openings for new lawyers?

If you are a practicing attorney looking for a new job, you can combine information about your practice plus your job search.

- Moving from NY to TX in two months; I welcome any and all job leads. 3 years experience representing creditors in commercial bankruptcy matters.
- Approx 10 hours of brief writing stand between me and Philly Girls Weekend 2010.
- Successful road trip. In Philly. :-)
- Lawyer-types: Nashville Young Lawyer Mentoring program is this Thursday 2/2 at 4PM. Please join us and/or pass the invite to your newer colleagues!
- Heading to Dallas for Spring Break to visit family, search for apartment. One interview scheduled – would love more if you know of opportunities in commercial bankruptcy.

(3) Market your Expertise in your Status Updates

If you are a practicing attorney, you may not want your current employers to know that you are looking for a new position. You must be careful not to risk leaking this information in a Facebook status update or wall post. The best option, in this case, is to avoid talking about your job search directly on Facebook. One other option is to use the List function discussed in Chapter 3 and create a professional list of your work colleagues. Then, exclude that list from viewing your job search related updates.

Moreover, you can update your status with statements that market you indirectly. You can talk about what you do—perhaps as part of your business development strategy. However, the updates might present new career opportunities as well if you consistently post updates about what you do.

For example, the updates in Images 4.19 through 4.22 are from a Dallas appellate attorney, Chad Ruback; if Chad consistently posts updates about his work projects and successes, his Facebook friends will take note. If one of his friends is a hiring authority in a firm, the person might contact Chad if the firm needs to hire an appellate attorney. Or, Chad's Facebook friends may hear of an appellate position, and they may refer Chad for that opportunity. Thus, Chad's posts about his work may lead to other career opportunities even though he doesn't explicitly state that he's looking for a new job.

Image 4.19

Chad Ruback will be speaking tomorrow at the Dallas Bar Association's North Dallas CLE meeting. My topic: What must be done in the trial court to preserve error for appeal?
February 11 at 5:25pm · Comment · Like

Image 4.20

Chad Ruback did not speak at the Dallas Bar Association's North Dallas CLE meeting scheduled for today. Thankfully, the meeting was rescheduled to April. Hopefully, the weather will be better by then. . .
February 12 at 2:57pm · Comment · Like

Image 4.21

Chad Ruback is getting ready for an oral argument in the Fort Worth Court of Appeals.
Mon at 12:34pm · Comment · Like

Image 4.22

Chad Ruback was recently hired to draft a motion for new trial. It's nice to be retained this early-on in the appellate process.
Yesterday at 3:42pm · Comment · Like

---

(4) Tag Friends in Status Updates

Another way to remain on your network's radar screen is to tag your friends in the status updates you post. For example, when asking a question about interviewing in Dallas, tag some Dallas friends who work in the legal field so they don't overlook your update. By tagging them, they will receive an alert about your status.

To tag someone in an update, begin typing your update and type the @ symbol before typing your friend's name. Facebook will retrieve a list of possible friends from which you can select the one that should be tagged.

Image 4.23

I would select Ashley Maurene Hunter if my update is directed to her or about her, as follows:

Image 4.24

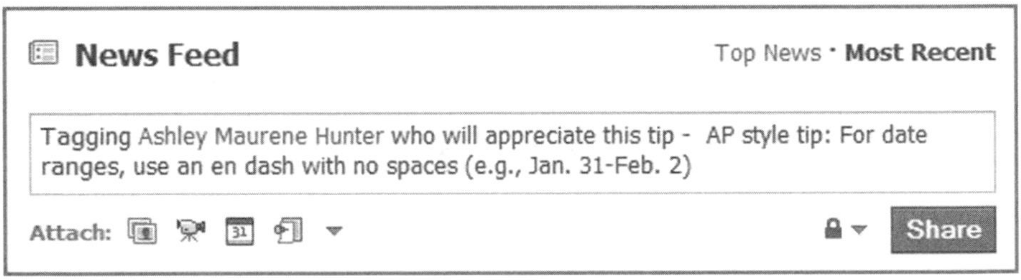

(5) Share Articles Reflective of your Practice Area

Consider posting links to articles or blogs that are professional in nature and reflective of your area of practice or expertise.

In Image 4.25, Jennifer Taddeo, an estate planning attorney in the Boston area, linked to an article about placing assets in joint names. The comments from readers of the article reflect an obvious appeal to many of the attorney's Facebook friends.

Image 4.25

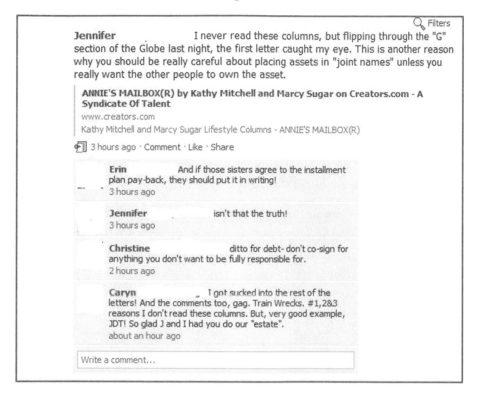

Q Filters

Jennifer I never read these columns, but flipping through the "G" section of the Globe last night, the first letter caught my eye. This is another reason why you should be really careful about placing assets in "joint names" unless you really want the other people to own the asset.

ANNIE'S MAILBOX(R) by Kathy Mitchell and Marcy Sugar on Creators.com - A Syndicate Of Talent
www.creators.com
Kathy Mitchell and Marcy Sugar Lifestyle Columns - ANNIE'S MAILBOX(R)

3 hours ago · Comment · Like · Share

> **Erin** And if those sisters agree to the installment plan pay-back, they should put it in writing!
> 3 hours ago
>
> **Jennifer** isn't that the truth!
> 3 hours ago
>
> **Christine** ditto for debt- don't co-sign for anything you don't want to be fully responsible for.
> 2 hours ago
>
> **Caryn** I got sucked into the rest of the letters! And the comments too, gag. Train Wrecks. #1,2&3 reasons I don't read these columns. But, very good example, JDT! So glad J and I had you do our "estate".
> about an hour ago

Write a comment...

The example in Image 4.25 is exactly the type of article or blog to share with friends and family on Facebook because it reminds the attorney's contacts of the type of law she practices. It also helps that the topic was of interest to several of the attorney's friends.

(6) Share Legal News

Post links to articles about hiring trends in the legal field, news about your law school, or events you are involved with in law school to remind your network of your profession.

Image 4.26

(7) Share Posts & Tag Friends

Facebook allows you to share links that others post, including links posted by fan pages or groups. And, you can tag friends in your commentary to a link. For example, the *Austin Business Journal* posted the article in Image 4.27 about an Austin condo development. I "shared" the article to my personal profile page and mentioned or "tagged" Ashley Maurene Hunter, one of my friends in Austin who insures real estate developers and would find the article interesting. Sharing a post and tagging your friend is like forwarding an article of interest to a friend via e-mail and another way to remain on your network's radar screen.

Image 4.27

(8) Leave Note after Networking

If you meet someone at a networking event, you can write a note on the person's Facebook wall as a follow-up to the initial meeting to stabilize the new friendship. In Image 4.28, Etan Tepperman, a first-year law student at Texas Wesleyan School of Law, followed up with an attorney he met at a networking event by writing a note on the attorney's Facebook wall.

Image 4.28

> **Etan Tepperman** It was nice meeting you last week at the tweetup. Let me know if you ever get to Denton, I'll set up lunch with Karl.
> February 14 at 7:01pm · Comment · Like · See Wall-to-Wall

(9) Wish Friends 'Good Luck' on Professional Endeavors

If one of your friends is the managing partner of a small firm and posts a status update that she is speaking at an event, you may choose to comment on that status and wish her good luck for a successful presentation.

(10) Congratulate Friends on Personal Achievements

You can even comment on non-professional updates and still remain on your friends' radar screens. For example, if one of your friends, who also happens to be the hiring partner at a firm, recently had a baby and posted pictures on Facebook, you can comment on the picture.

(11) Happy Birthday!

One of my favorite Facebook features is the birthday calendar. Midway down the right side of your home page you will find the birthday alerts. You can then click on the name of your friend celebrating a birthday and write a short greeting on the honoree's wall.

Image 4.29

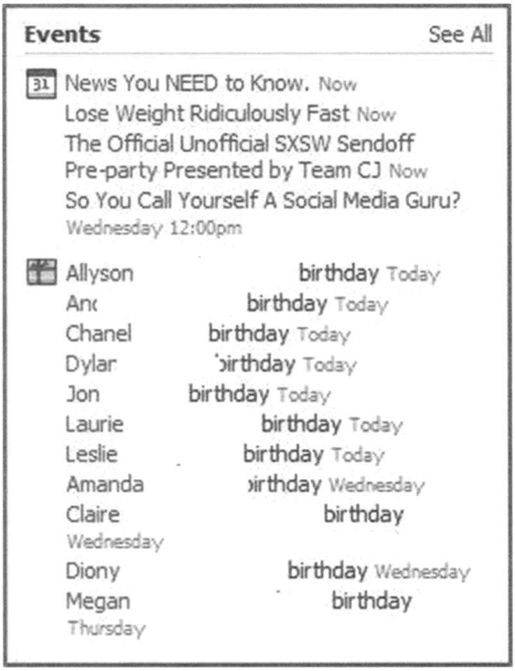

Events   See All

31 News You NEED to Know. Now
    Lose Weight Ridiculously Fast Now
    The Official Unofficial SXSW Sendoff
    Pre-party Presented by Team CJ Now
    So You Call Yourself A Social Media Guru?
    Wednesday 12:00pm

    Allyson   birthday Today
    An(birthday Today
    Chanel   birthday Today
    Dylar   'irthday Today
    Jon   birthday Today
    Laurie   birthday Today
    Leslie   birthday Today
    Amanda   )irthday Wednesday
    Claire   birthday
    Wednesday
    Diony   birthday Wednesday
    Megan   birthday
    Thursday

(12) Like (Thumbs Up) your Friends' Content

Perhaps you spend only 5-6 minutes on Facebook each day (yes, it's possible) and, therefore, don't have time to comment. You can "like" a friend's comment, post, or picture instead with the click of your mouse. A thumbs up symbol will appear below the update, post, or picture along with your name, as shown in Image 4.30. Thus, you remain on your friend's radar screen with only minimal attention and interaction.

Image 4.30

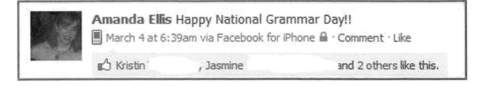

Amanda Ellis Happy National Grammar Day!!
March 4 at 6:39am via Facebook for iPhone · Comment · Like

👍 Kristin   , Jasmine   and 2 others like this.

Caveat: Remember that a single comment probably won't land you a job. Achieving that goal will require developing a relationship with your Facebook friends and remaining on their radar screens. The relationships are built over time and through consistent communication, not just a single Facebook comment.

(13) Comment on Target Firms' Pages

Interact on the law firm fan pages and groups, especially with the law firms that are your potential targets. You can add your own thoughts to a law firm's Facebook posting as shown in the example in Image 4.31; or, you can ask questions about the information posted or congratulate the firm or a particular attorney in the firm if the article or update describes a significant accomplishment.

Image 4.31

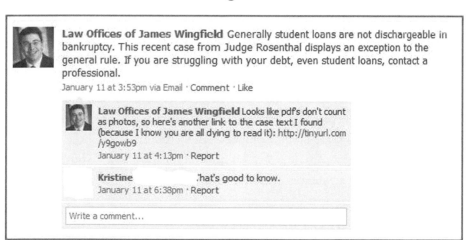

(14) Like (Thumbs Up) Firms' Content

The thumbs up or "like" feature is available on fan pages, too. If you don't have time or don't want to leave a comment on a firm's fan page, you can always "like" a posting or update and remain on the firm's radar.

Image 4.32

Law Offices of James Wingfield My newest Blawg entry on the Law Offices of James Wingfield Bankruptcy Blawg is up now. http://wingfieldlaw.blogspot.com /2010/02/famous-bankruptcy-filers.html

Law Offices of James Wingfield's Bankruptcy Blawg: Famous Bankruptcy Filers
wingfieldlaw.blogspot.com
Very often my new clients tell me or otherwise let me know that they are ashamed that they are even thinking of filing bankruptcy. Amazingly, many of those clients have those feelings reinforced by comments …

February 23 at 10:38pm · Comment · Like · Share

Terry   likes this.

Once you interact, the owner of the page receives notification—you are on the owner's radar screen. Moreover, other Facebook users who read the page will see your comment. The more consistent you are with your comments, the more you brand yourself as someone with a genuine interest in a particular topic, as discussed in Chapter 6 Protocol.

> ***Caveat about engaging on group and business pages:*** Remember that your profile picture will appear next to any comments or questions you make. As discussed in Chapter 2, it's critical to keep your Facebook profile picture clean. It doesn't have to be a professional picture, but it should comply with the Office Desk Photo Rule discussed in Chapter 2. It shouldn't embarrass you if your mother, boss, or a potential employer were to see it.

Section 2 - LinkedIn

Most people know that LinkedIn is a professional social networking site, and many lawyers now have a LinkedIn profile. In fact, the number of legal professionals using LinkedIn nearly quadrupled between June 2008 (216,000) to June 2009 (840,000),[29] and the number of lawyers with LinkedIn profiles crossed over the 1 million mark at some point in fall 2009 (1,359,590).[30] But, remember the mere presence is not enough get hired through social networking sites.

To see optimum results, you must follow the CAP analysis discussed on page 113. You must connect, assimilate, and participate.

STEP 1: CONNECT

The more people you are connected to on LinkedIn, the more you will find LinkedIn helpful in your job search because LinkedIn's power lies in the ability to access your connections' connections.

LinkedIn tells you if you are connected to another LinkedIn user directly (1st degree contact—your connections) or through another LinkedIn user (2nd or 3rd degree—your connections' connections). Each blue circle with the numbers 1, 2, or 3 in the middle indicates the degree of connection that person has to you. Thus, the more 1st degree connections you have, the more 2nd and 3rd degree connections you have and the wider your LinkedIn network which you may tap in your job search.

To successfully connect with contacts on LinkedIn, you must:

- Determine the level of scrutiny to apply when selecting 1st degree connection
- Grow your 1st degree connections
- Write an introduction to your 1st degree connections
- Ask for introductions to connect to your 2nd and 3rd degree connections
- Join LinkedIn Groups and identify new contacts in the Groups

Who: Level of Scrutiny to Connect with Contacts

In the Facebook section, I recommended the Home Invitation Rule, a strict level of scrutiny, for choosing your Facebook connections because much of the information shared is personal in nature.

Intermediate Scrutiny

With LinkedIn, however, the information shared is professional, so you can connect with a wider range of people. If you choose to follow the three-tiered analysis for determining your contacts on the Big 3 sites, intermediate scrutiny is the appropriate level for choosing your LinkedIn connections—a level more lenient than Facebook's strict scrutiny but not as lenient as Twitter.

Business Card Rule

To apply an intermediate scrutiny analysis, I recommend the **Business Card Rule** to determine your LinkedIn connections. This rule, simply stated, suggests you connect with people on LinkedIn if the person is someone with whom you would exchange business cards.

You may connect with people you've never met in person but who are in the same industry or field as you. The key to successfully connecting with people you haven't met in person is making sure you identify yourself in your invitation to connect and avoid the generic invitations. Keep this in mind because you'll want to use Method 6 below (page 149) to connect with these "warm" contacts.

Possible Connections

Some examples of people with whom job seekers may connect include:

- High school friends
- College friends
- Law school friends
- Former colleagues
- Friends from professional organizations
- Anyone in your e-mail address book
- People you've interviewed with in the past
- Opposing counsel from cases you handled
- People you meet at conferences or job related events
- Reporters
- Holiday card list

How: Grow Your 1ˢᵗ Degree Connections

To begin adding contacts, go to the Add Connections tab in the top menu bar.

Image 4.33

There are six ways to connect with your contacts. As noted above, Method 6 is preferred once you get started because it allows you to customize your invitations. However, you may want to consider some of the other methods to get started.

1. ***Classmates***. If you included your education history in your LinkedIn profile, LinkedIn will pull people you graduated with or people who attended a school during the same years you attended. If you recognize the classmates LinkedIn recommends, then you click the "send invitation" button. Many LinkedIn users begin with Classmates as a point of entry for this network.

2. ***Colleagues***. If you included your work history in your LinkedIn profile, LinkedIn will pull people you worked with at your places of employment. If you recognize the colleagues LinkedIn recommends, then you click the "send invitation" button. Following up with colleagues LinkedIn suggests is another method of building a sizeable cache of new contacts.

3. ***Web-based e-mail***. LinkedIn will search the address book of your web-based e-mail such as Gmail, Hotmail, or Yahoo. Simply enter your e-mail address in the "See who you Already Know on LinkedIn" box.

Image 4.34

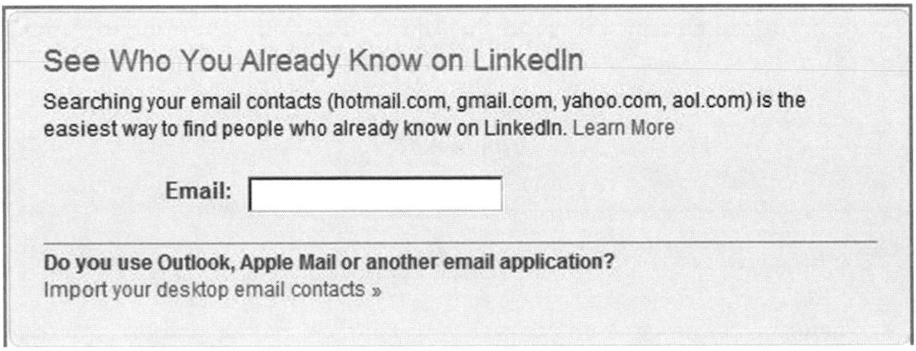

See Who You Already Know on LinkedIn

Searching your email contacts (hotmail.com, gmail.com, yahoo.com, aol.com) is the easiest way to find people who already know on LinkedIn. Learn More

Email:

Do you use Outlook, Apple Mail or another email application?
Import your desktop email contacts »

LinkedIn then generates contacts from your e-mail address book and will indicate if these contacts already have a LinkedIn account. You may choose to send invitations to all or some of them.

Image 4.35

Invite 4 Contacts to Connect

You have **4** contacts that can be invited and **1** is already using Linkedin. Select which contacts you wish to invite to connect.

☑ Select all

☑ **Jennifer**
   Member sin.   .gust 2007 | 63 connections

☑   @gmail.com

☑   ;   ,@gmail.com

☑   @gmail.com

[Send Invitations] or Cancel

If you click "Send Invitations," LinkedIn will send a *generic* invitation. For example, if I were to invite a contact named Jennifer, the subject line of the e-mail would say, "Amanda Ellis wants to stay in touch on LinkedIn" and the message would look like the example in Image 4.36.

Image 4.36

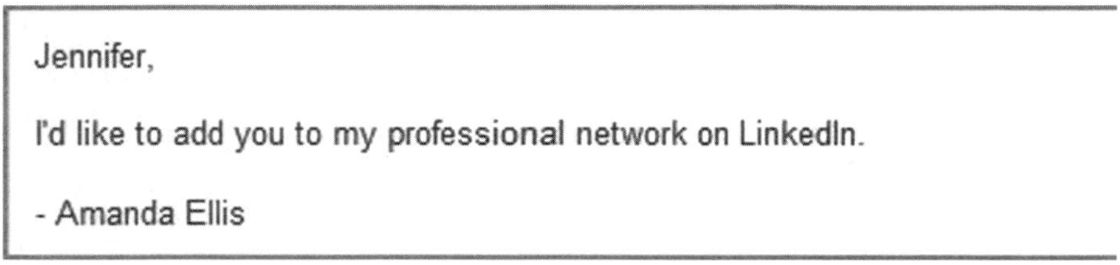

Jennifer,

I'd like to add you to my professional network on LinkedIn.

- Amanda Ellis

4. *E-mail Applications.* You can import your address book from Outlook or another e-mail application. LinkedIn then sends an invitation to your contacts. The link for this task is also in the **See Who You Already Know on LinkedIn** box. That information is at the bottom of the box.

Image 4.37

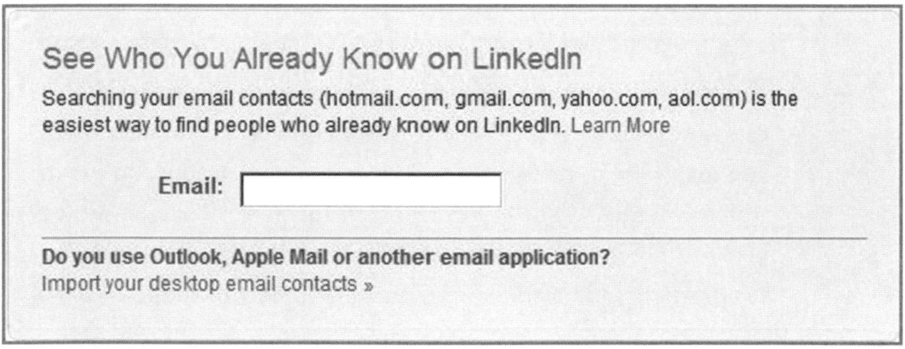

See Who You Already Know on LinkedIn

Searching your email contacts (hotmail.com, gmail.com, yahoo.com, aol.com) is the easiest way to find people who already know on LinkedIn. Learn More

Email: [   ]

Do you use Outlook, Apple Mail or another email application?
Import your desktop email contacts »

You click on **Import Your Desktop E-mail Contacts** to add these people to those you already have.

5. *Individual E-mail.* You may type a person's e-mail address and invite the person to connect with you.

6. *Existing LinkedIn Users.* You can invite people who already have a LinkedIn account. Several situations may cause this opportunity to arise.

a. *Business Card Rule.* The previous section discussed using the Business Card Rule to determine your LinkedIn connections. Practice it. When you attended a networking event and receive three business cards, enter the names into LinkedIn to see if the contacts have LinkedIn profiles. If the contacts have LinkedIn profiles, select "Add ___ to your Network" from the right menu, as shown in Image 4.38.

Image 4.38

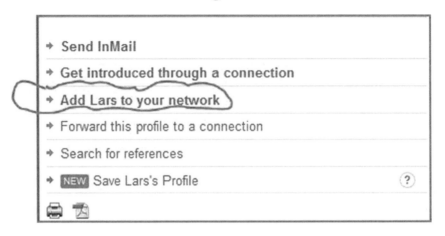

You have the ability to personalize the invitation as well as indicate how you know the contact. For a contact you recently met, you may want to refresh his or her memory about the context in which you met. While the example in Image 4.39 doesn't show a personal note, the next section, Writing Introductions to 1st Degree Connections, addresses how to customize your introduction.

Image 4.39

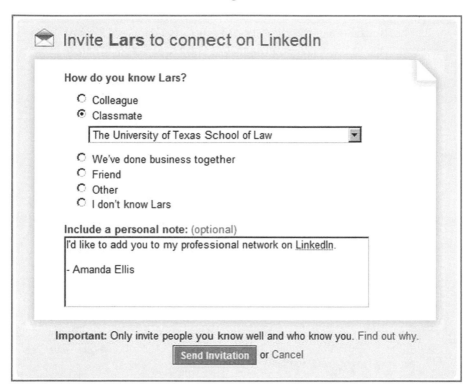

Practice Pointer

Note that one choice as to how you know the person is "I do not know." I try to refrain from using this one. The choice I tend to use as a default is the one about doing business at one of my previous companies. Even if you didn't do business with the named person, the contact might be someone you met while in that role or position

b. *Network Updates*. Monitor your LinkedIn news feed or weekly update digest to see your connections' new connections. You, too, may know these new connections and want to send an invitation to connect. Follow the steps for Method (6)(a) to send these contacts a personalized invitation.

c. ***People you may know.*** LinkedIn also recommends existing users to you, based on mutual connections. The recommendations are found in a box in the upper right corner of your home page and labeled, "People You May Know." Some of them you will know, while others may be strangers to you. Follow the steps for Method (6)(a) to send these contacts a personalized invitation.

Image 4.40

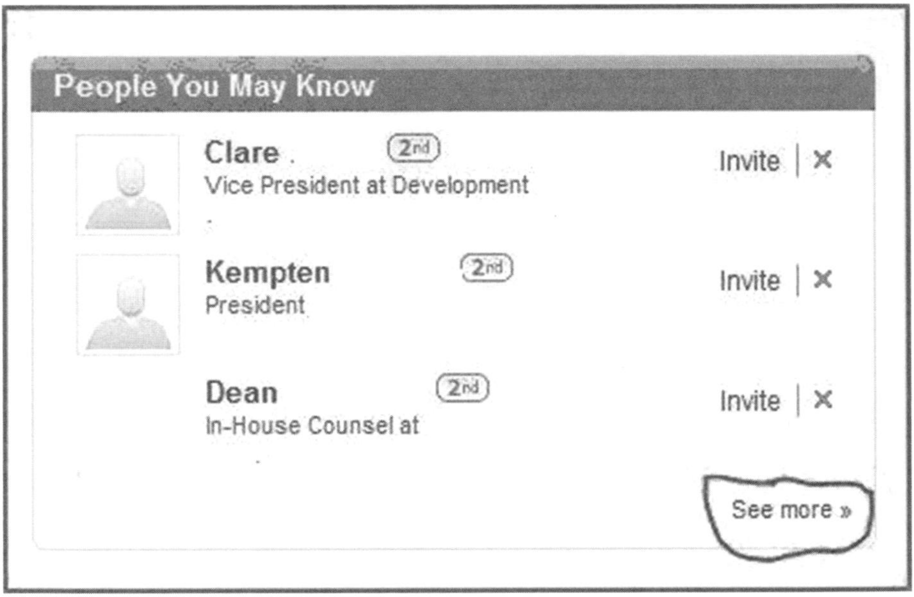

Write Introduction to 1st Degree Connections

I strongly urge you to send personalized invitations available in Method 6 (Images 4.38 and 4.39) over the generic LinkedIn invitation. Your personal note doesn't need to be long. You should, however, remind the contact of your connection, relationship, or commonality. Review the following examples:

Scenario: Connecting with law school classmate that you haven't seen or talked to since graduation

Invitation:

> Hi, Joe –
>
> Good to see you on here—I didn't realize you were in Dallas. I've been in Dallas since 2005 after practicing bankruptcy law for 4 years in MA. I stopped practicing in 2006 and started recruiting, which I continue to do. Perhaps we'll run into each other at a DAYL event in the future.
>
> Amanda

Scenario: Law student who recently completed on-campus interviews and received business cards from recruiters and interviewing partners. [NOTE: the note in your LinkedIn invitation does not substitute the thank you note required following an interview]

Invitation:

> Hi, Ashley –
>
> It was nice to meet you during OCI week at UT Law. I'd love to connect on LinkedIn so we can remain in touch as I proceed through law school.
>
> Amanda

Scenario: You read an article, Googled the author, and found the author's LinkedIn profile. You want to send a note, letting him know how much you enjoyed the article.

Invitation:

Image 4.41

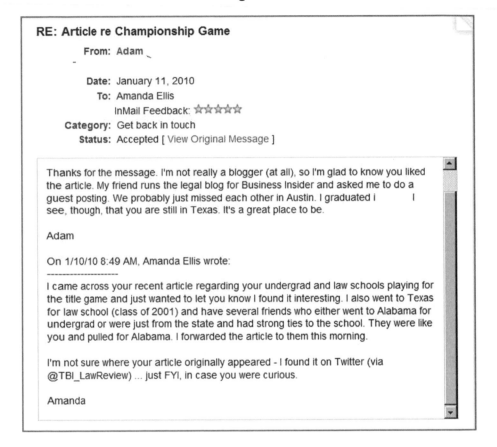

RE: Article re Championship Game

From: Adam

Date: January 11, 2010
To: Amanda Ellis
InMail Feedback: ☆☆☆☆☆
Category: Get back in touch
Status: Accepted [View Original Message]

Thanks for the message. I'm not really a blogger (at all), so I'm glad to know you liked the article. My friend runs the legal blog for Business Insider and asked me to do a guest posting. We probably just missed each other in Austin. I graduated i   I see, though, that you are still in Texas. It's a great place to be.

Adam

On 1/10/10 8:49 AM, Amanda Ellis wrote:

I came across your recent article regarding your undergrad and law schools playing for the title game and just wanted to let you know I found it interesting. I also went to Texas for law school (class of 2001) and have several friends who either went to Alabama for undergrad or were just from the state and had strong ties to the school. They were like you and pulled for Alabama. I forwarded the article to them this morning.

I'm not sure where your article originally appeared - I found it on Twitter (via @TBI_LawReview) ... just FYI, in case you were curious.

Amanda

Scenario: Former client or colleague that you haven't talked to in several years

Invitation:

Image 4.42

Amanda,

Greetings,

Catching up on my social networking. Shall we connect on LinkedIn? I'm still living in Acton, MA, and practicing IP law (trademarks, domain names, patents) in Maynard. Hope all is well with you!

Regards,

Ask for Introductions to 2nd & 3rd Degree Contacts

As you establish 1st degree contacts, your 2nd and 3rd degree contacts will grow. You may want to tap your 1st degree contacts for introductions to your 2nd and 3rd degree contacts.

You can write a note or introduction to your 2nd or 3rd degree contact you wish to connect with, and LinkedIn sends the note to your mutual contact. The mutual contact will decide whether to forward it to your 2nd or 3rd degree contact. Essentially, it's a virtual introduction. Instead of one of your contacts introducing you to one of his contacts at a cocktail party or business meeting, the introduction takes place via LinkedIn.

In order to get introduced to a 2nd or 3rd degree contact through a mutual connection, the 2nd or 3rd degree contact must have indicated in her Contact Settings that she'll accept Introductions.

Image 4.43

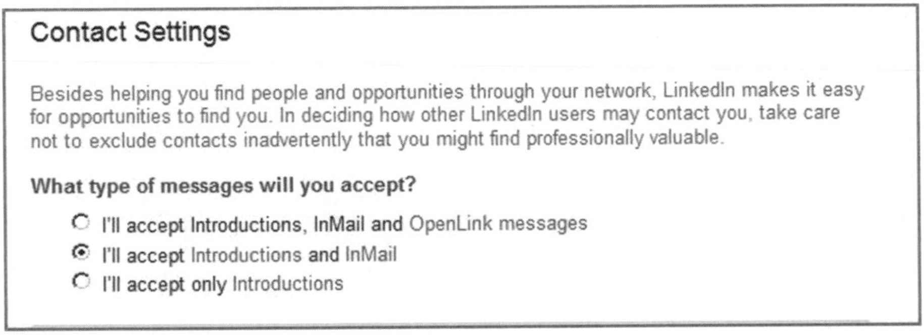

Contact Settings

Besides helping you find people and opportunities through your network, LinkedIn makes it easy for opportunities to find you. In deciding how other LinkedIn users may contact you, take care not to exclude contacts inadvertently that you might find professionally valuable.

What type of messages will you accept?

- ○ I'll accept Introductions, InMail and OpenLink messages
- ◉ I'll accept Introductions and InMail
- ○ I'll accept only Introductions

1. Check the profile page of your 2nd or 3rd degree contact—the person you want to meet. Scroll down to the bottom of the page to the **Contact Settings**. If your target is open to introductions, the link "**Get introduced through a connection**" will appear, as shown in Image 4.44. Click the link to compose your introduction.

Image 4.44

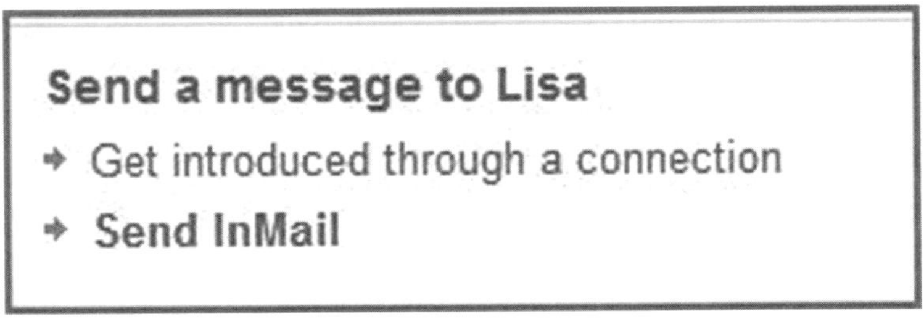

Send a message to Lisa

→ Get introduced through a connection

→ Send InMail

2. If you and the 2nd or 3rd degree connection share multiple mutual connections, you must indicate which connection you want to introduce you to the 2nd or 3rd degree person.

Image 4.45

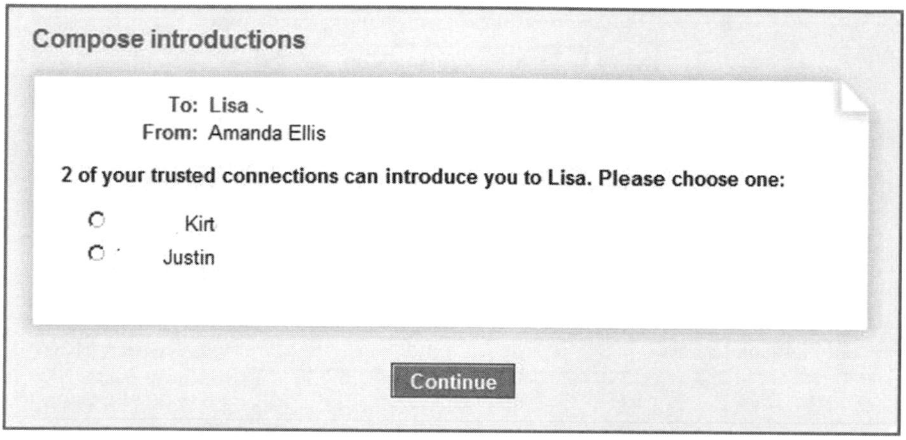

Compose introductions

To: Lisa
From: Amanda Ellis

2 of your trusted connections can introduce you to Lisa. Please choose one:

○   Kirt

○   Justin

[Continue]

---

3. Next, compose your introduction. Note that you can write a note to your target contact—the 2nd or 3rd degree connection—and to your mutual connection (perhaps explaining why you'd like to meet Lisa).

Image 4.46

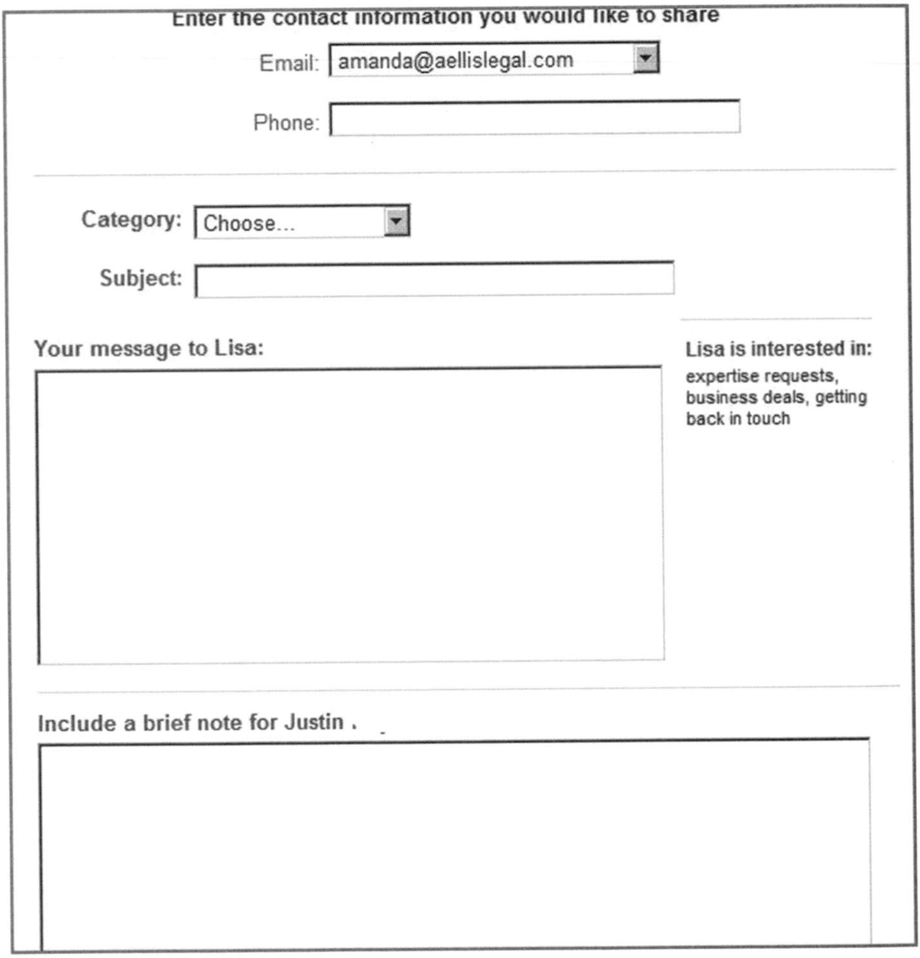

Enter the contact information you would like to share

Email: amanda@aellislegal.com

Phone:

Category: Choose...

Subject:

Your message to Lisa:

Lisa is interested in:
expertise requests,
business deals, getting
back in touch

Include a brief note for Justin .

Caveat: Chapter 6 addresses the protocol for sending introductions, including why law students should refrain from sending introduction requests to their law school career counselors.

STEP 2: ASSIMILATE

The second step in performing your job search on LinkedIn is to gather information that will help you identify firms, attorneys, job openings, and networking events (the "*Identification Phase*") and prepare for interviews (the "*Interview Phase*"). There are 12 ways to gather this information.

(1) Search Companies (Firms)

LinkedIn is one tool that helps lawyers and law students identify smaller firms, gather information about the firms to determine whether the firms are "targets" as potential employers, and identify hiring contacts at the firms. Additionally, the information obtained from LinkedIn company profiles can help job seekers prepare for interviews.

1. From the main menu across your LinkedIn home page, click on "**More**" and then "**Companies.**"

Image 4.47

2. *Identification Phase.* If you are at the beginning of your job search and searching for target firms, enter a zip code for your target market. *Interview Phase.* If you are in the interview phase of your job search, enter the name of the firm(s) where you are interviewing in the "Company Name" box, and then skip to Step 5.

Image 4.48

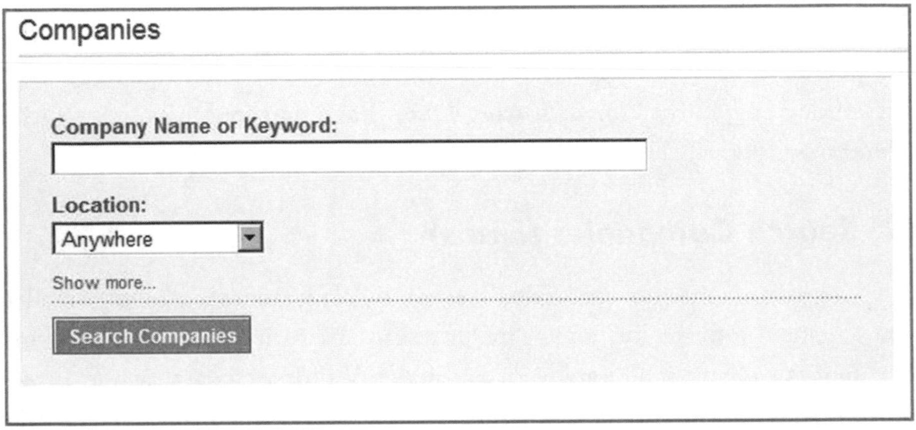

3. *Identification Phase.* LinkedIn displays all companies with LinkedIn profiles in the market you selected. In the example in Image 4.49, I searched for companies in a Dallas, TX zip code and found over 9,000 Dallas companies with LinkedIn profiles.

Image 4.49

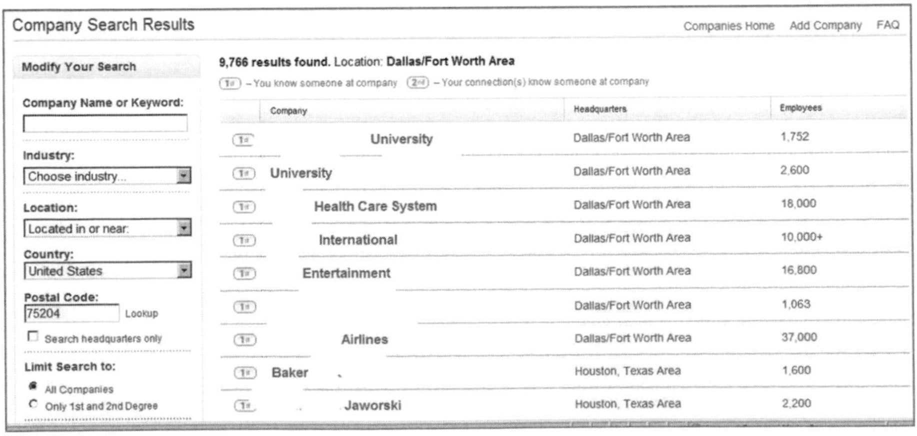

4. *Identification Phase.* You can narrow your search to speed the identification process—for example, you can narrow the results to only law firms, or only law firms with a particular practice area or of a particular size.

To narrow this list of companies to law firms in the Dallas area with fewer than 50 employees, click the drop down menu below **Industry** and select **Law Practice**. Check the box under **Company Size** for 11-50 employees. Your results will include a narrower list of smaller law firms in the Dallas area.

Image 4.50

Law Practice				
	(1st) Underwood, Perkins & Ralston, P.C.		Dallas/Fort Worth Area	11-50
Related Industries:	(1st) . ⌐ Cox, LLP		Dallas/Fort Worth Area	11-50
☐ Legal Services				
☐ Judiciary	(1st) Stevens, LLP		Dallas/Fort Worth Area	11-50
☐ Financial Services				
☐ Banking	(1st) .. ⌐ LLP		Dallas/Fort Worth Area	12
☐ Real Estate				
	(1st) Wright G,. .,		Dallas/Fort Worth Area	20
	(2nd) Addison Law Firm		Dallas/Fort Worth Area	11-50
Location:	(2nd) Bennett, ,. ,. .		Dallas/Fort Worth Area	11-50
Located in or near:	(2nd) Brown		Dallas/Fort Worth Area	11-50
Country:				
United States	(2nd) . Perrin, P.C.		Dallas/Fort Worth Area	11-50
Postal Code:				
75204 Lookup	(2nd) Clouse .		Dallas/Fort Worth Area	25
☐ Search headquarters only	(2nd) Hitt (		Dallas/Fort Worth Area	11-50
Limit Search to:	(2nd) . Clemons, PLLC		Dallas/Fort Worth Area	11-50
⦿ All Companies				
○ Only 1st and 2nd Degree	(2nd) Firm		Dallas/Fort Worth Area	11-50
Company Size:	(2nd) Group		Dallas/Fort Worth Area	11-50
☐ 1-10 ☐ 501-1000				
☑ 11-50 ☐ 1001-5000	(2nd) Stewart .		Dallas/Fort Worth Area	11-50

Alternative Career Path: If you are seeking to leave the practice of law completely, you can still use this search method to search target companies in your desired industry.

5. *Identification Phase.* You can view a firm's profile by clicking on a firm's name from the search results in Image 4.50.

Interview Phase. If you entered a firm's name in Step 2 in Image 4.48, LinkedIn displays the firm's company profile.

Images 4.51 and 4.52 contain the company profile for a Texas-based law firm.

Image 4.51

Last edited by Marketing Manager   Companies Home   Add Company   FAQ

Munson Hardt, a commercial law firm, provides the highest quality legal
service ... to companies and individuals of all
... rowing company seeking cost-effective results -
Mu... Now.® Our practice groups include all aspects of
Business Litigation; Corporate & Securities;... see more

Related Companies

Career path for Munson Hardt Kopf & Harr, P.C. employees
... after:
• ... • W...
• ...PC

See more »

Specialties

Commerical law including all aspects of Business Litigation; Corporate & Securities; Energy &
Environmental; Finance; Insolvency, Restructuring & Creditors' Rights; Intellectual Property; Real
Estate and Tax.

Key Statistics

Top Locations
• Dallas/Fort Worth Area (116)
• Houston, Texas Area (17)
• Austin, Texas Area (11)
▸ Headquarters Address

Current Employees (144 total, 50 in your network)

(1st) b... ..., Director of Employee Relations & Recruiting
(2nd) M'...dell, Attorney/Shareholder
through An...
(3rd) ...ka, Paralegal
th... Stutsman
(2nd) ...ni, Paralegal - Business Organizations
through ...
(2nd) V...z, Associate
through Oliver ...man, and 1 others

See more »

HQ Region	Dallas/Fort Worth Area
Industry	Law Practice
Type	Privately Held
Status	Operating
Company Size	215 employees

Image 4.52

See more »

Founded 1985
Websi'

Former Employees

(1st) ...n, Campus Recruiting Manager at BDO
Attorney Recruiting & Development Coordinator (to February 2010)
(1st) ...k, Attorney at Wright ...w P.C.
Associate (to April 2002)
(2nd) ...n, Founder at Green Squared
Attorney (to January 1997)
through Kevi...gh
(2nd) Robert ...vel, Attorney ...
Summer Associate (to August 2008)
through Erica ...n, Be...n
(2nd) B...mi, Legal Assistant at ... LLP
Executive Legal Secretary (to 2009)
through ...

New Hires

(2nd) M...m, Associate Attorney
was Assistant Counsel at HKS, Inc. - 2 months ago
...ggoner, and 3 others

Popular Profiles

(2nd) ...cka, Paralegal
... Attorney
... an & CEO
(...) ...Attorney
Sally ...wer, Shareholder

Common Job Titles		
	Attorney	27%
	Shareholder	25%
	Associate	10%
	Legal Secretary	7%
Top Schools	Southern Methodist Univ. Dedman School of Law	10%
	The Univ. of Texas at Austin	8%
	The Univ. of Texas School of Law	8%
	Texas A&M Univ.	5%
	Texas Tech Univ. School of Law	4%
Median Age	40 years	
Gender	Male	60%
	Female	40%

Estimated based on LinkedIn Data

A firm's company profile provides the following information that is
helpful for job seekers in both the identification and interview stages.

- *Current Employees.* LinkedIn identifies current employees at
  the firm who are in your network—that includes your 1st degree
  connections as well as your 2nd and 3rd degree contacts. Pay

attention to the current employees. If you are connected to an employee directly (1st degree), perhaps you want to contact that person for more information about the firm. If you are connected to a current employee in the 2nd or 3rd degree, perhaps you can ask your mutual connections for an introduction (discussed on page 155) and then learn more about the firm.

- *Former Employees.* LinkedIn also identifies employees who previously worked at the firm and indicates how you are connected to them. Perhaps you want to contact former employees to see what they liked and disliked about the firm.

- *New Hires.* Perhaps you want to talk to people who were recently hired by the firm and learn more about their experience interviewing with the firm. You can check the new hires section to see if you know any of the new hires directly (1st degree) or indirectly (2nd or 3rd degree). The new hires section might also indicate if someone at your level of experience was recently hired. Such information might indicate if the firm has a need for someone at your level.

- *Popular Profiles.* If you are looking for the name of a particular hiring contact, you might want to review the popular profiles section. The popular profiles section lists the employee profiles with the most views. Frequently, employees in the human resources section or recruiting department are the most viewed and included in this section.

- *Job Openings.* The law firm profile in Images 4.51 and 4.52 does not include a section for job openings. However, if the firm had a job opening listed on LinkedIn, the position would appear on the firm's company profile in a section labeled job openings. This section often appears to the right of the popular profiles section.

- *Firm Statistics.* LinkedIn provides statistics about firms such as the law schools attended by a significant number of the firm's attorneys.

- *Follow Company.* A new LinkedIn feature allows you to follow companies or firms, and information about the companies or firms—such as new hires, recent departures, and job openings—appears in your LinkedIn news feed, as shown in Image 4.53.

Image 4.53

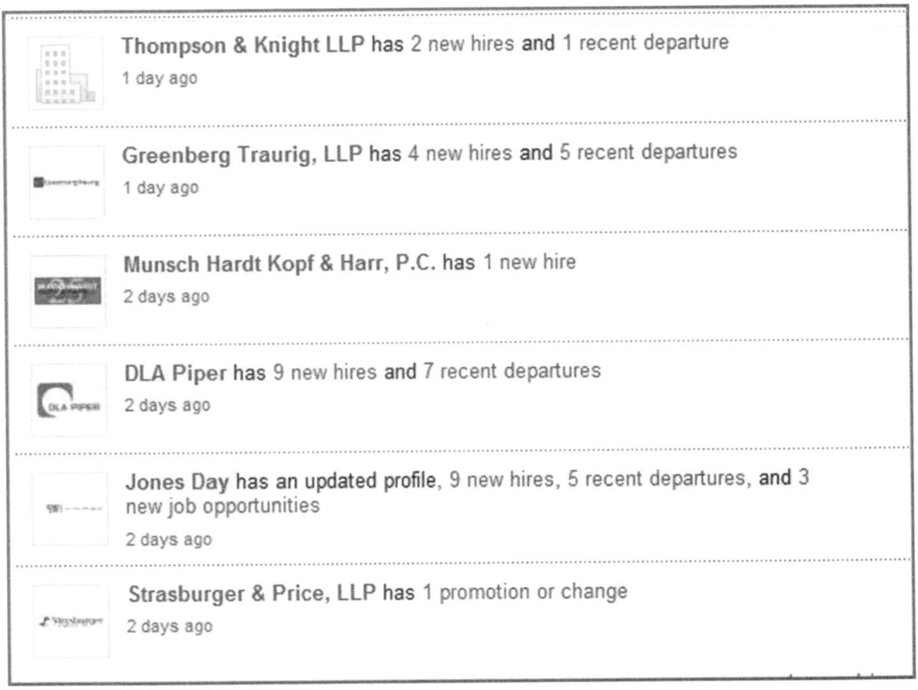

	Thompson & Knight LLP has 2 new hires and 1 recent departure 1 day ago
	Greenberg Traurig, LLP has 4 new hires and 5 recent departures 1 day ago
	Munsch Hardt Kopf & Harr, P.C. has 1 new hire 2 days ago
	DLA Piper has 9 new hires and 7 recent departures 2 days ago
	Jones Day has an updated profile, 9 new hires, 5 recent departures, and 3 new job opportunities 2 days ago
	Strasburger & Price, LLP has 1 promotion or change 2 days ago

To follow a company or firm, click on "Follow company," as shown in Image 4.54. I recommend following firms or companies after you identify them as potential targets.

Image 4.54

Companies Home   Add Company   FAQ

☆ **Follow company** *NEW*

- *Related Companies.* The related companies section outlines comparable firms by telling you several firms where many of the current firm's employees worked before joining the firm and after leaving the firm. Thus, you can gain some insight into the career path of an attorney at the given firm. The related companies information can also serve as a checklist or a reminder to see if you have considered potential opportunities with the related firms.

- **Public Companies.** If your goal is to work in the legal department of a corporation, you can learn even more information from the corporation's LinkedIn profile.

    - **Corporate Structure.** In addition to providing career paths of employees, the related companies section provides information about the companies' divisions, subsidiaries, and acquisitions.

Image 4.55

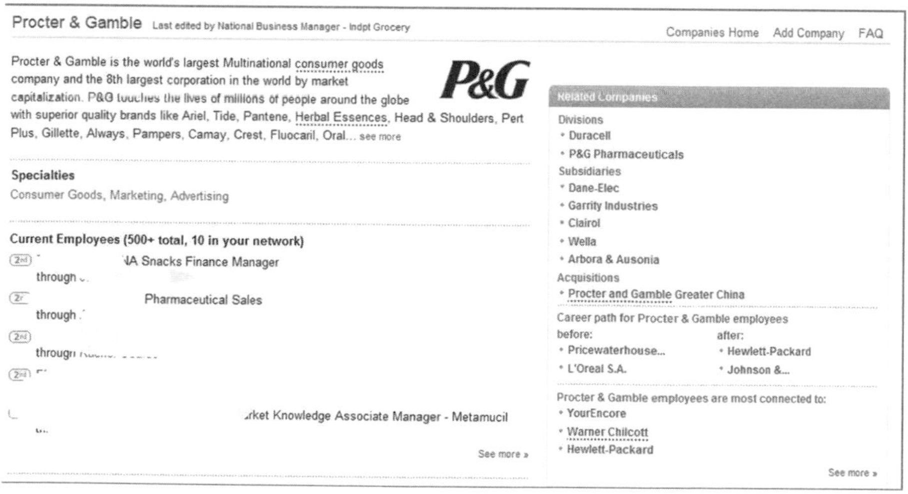

- **Stock Information.** A public company's LinkedIn profile will also include stock information.

Image 4.56

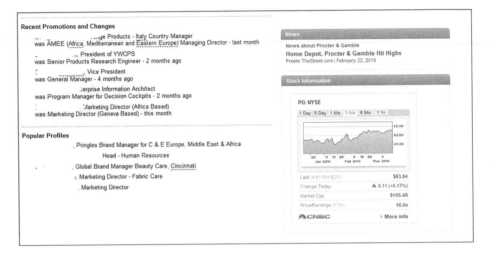

(2) Search People (Attorneys)

You can also use the people search function of LinkedIn to identify firms and prepare you for interviews. The people search function allows you to search for attorneys with certain characteristics. For example, you may want to identify firms with attorneys who are alumni of your law school or college or who practice a certain area of the law or who practice in a certain geographical market.

Identification Phase. Use the **Advanced** search function in the upper right hand corner of your homepage, as shown in Image 4.57

Image 4.57

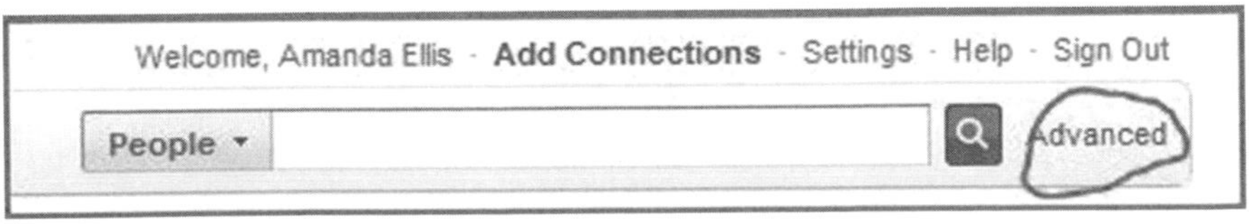

Then, fill in the characteristics of the attorneys you seek to find. Include information such as the geographical area, practice area (you would include this under keywords), or the law school attended.

Image 4.58

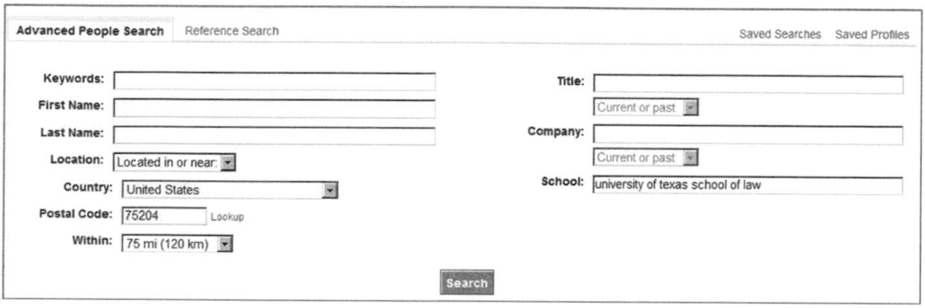

Image 4.59 shows the results of a people search in the Dallas market for attorneys who attended the University of Texas School of Law. The search generated over 3,000 results.

Image 4.59

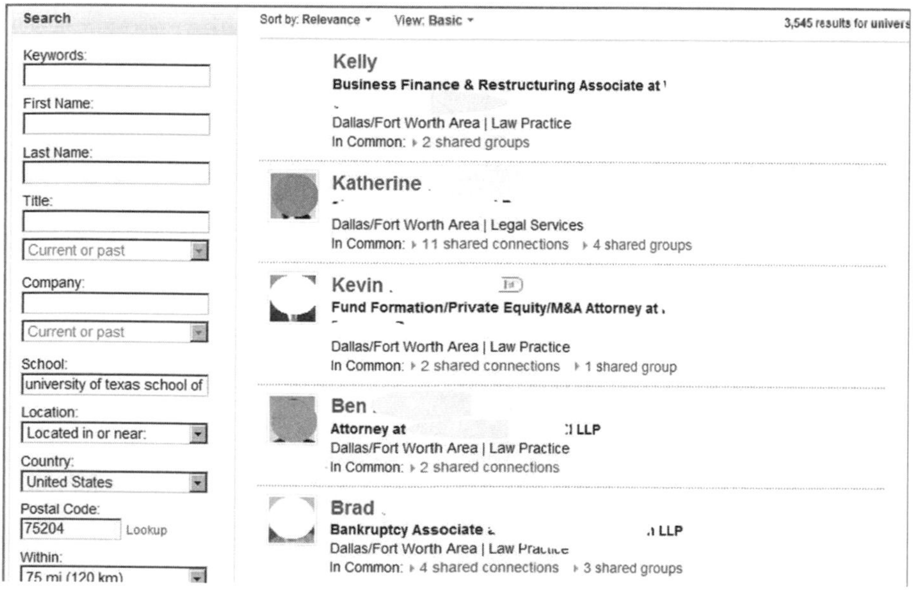

A few things to note about the search results:

1. LinkedIn displays your 1st degree connections at the top of your search results so all of the people you are connected to who fit the criteria appear first.
2. LinkedIn tells you how many shared connections and shared groups

you have with each result. By clicking on shared connections or shared groups, you'll see the specific names. This is more helpful with your 2nd and 3rd degree connections when you might need an introduction through your mutual connection(s).

3. You can narrow your search results. For example, you may want to limit your search to just litigation attorneys. You can type litigation in the keywords box to narrow the results.

Interview Phase. You can also use the people search when preparing for an interview. If you know in advance the names of the attorneys you will be meeting, type each attorney's name into LinkedIn to see if he or she has a LinkedIn profile.

For example, suppose you are interviewing with an attorney named Evan Fogelman. You can type Evan's name in the people search bar in the main menu in Image 4.60.

Image 4.60

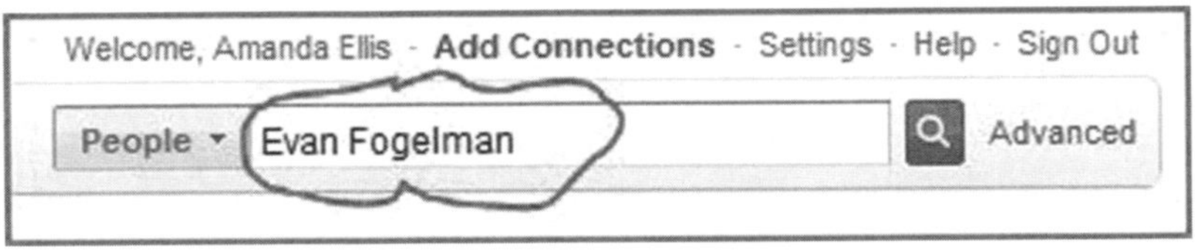

Then, glimpse at the snapshot of Evan's profile.

Image 4.61

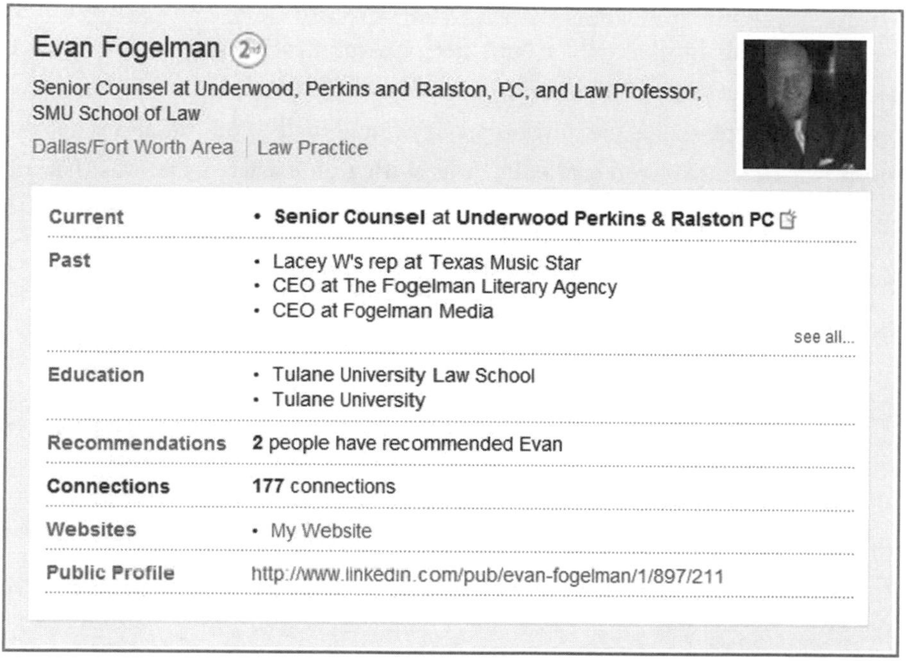

You will see that Evan is a 2nd degree connection, so you will scroll down the page to see your mutual connections. Then, you may decide to contact one of those mutual connections to learn more about Evan or the firm. You may also want to review Evan's complete profile to see if there is information on his LinkedIn profile that is not on his firm bio.

Don't invite him or her to connect at this point—you are in your information gathering stage. You can, however, connect following the interview.

(3) Search Job Board

Job seekers can use the job search function on LinkedIn to search for job openings in the legal industry. The job search function is similar to many of the popular job boards serving the legal industry. But, it offers some additional features and benefits.

As you can see in Image 4.62, if the person who posted the job opening on behalf of the firm also has a LinkedIn account, the person's name will appear in the "Posted By" column. Moreover, the circle with the level of connection will also appear, and you can click on it to see how you are connected to this hiring contact. This method is much better than sending your resume to a generic inbox for a position. You can actually contact a human, and you can find out more about that hiring contact (and perhaps the firm) through your mutual contacts. You can then send a note to the person you know, requesting an introduction to the person at the job you are seeking. Finally, you can also see if the job is listed exclusively on LinkedIn. Jobs with a blue asterisk are jobs that are exclusive to LinkedIn.

Image 4.62

Job Search Results

We found 4 jobs matching these criteria:
• Job Function: Legal • Located within: 50 mi (80 km) of 75204, United States • Sorted by: Date posted

▸ refine search results

LinkedIn Jobs | The Web

✻ — Jobs available exclusively on LinkedIn   Send us your feedback on these results

Title	Company	Location	Date			Posted By
Strategic Sourcing Contracts Manager - FNC Mid-Senior level, Full-time		Dallas, US-TX	12/03/2009			
Associate General Counsel, Single Family Mortgage, Litigation Director, Full-time		Dallas, TX	12/02/2009	(3ᵈ)		Lauri . Company HR
Solution Consultant-Dallas Associate, Full-time		Dallas, Texas	11/25/2009	(3ᵈ)		Stephanie . Company HR
Corporate Counsel Mid-Senior level, Full-time		TX, Dallas	11/13/2009			

Practice Pointer

Use the advanced search feature and select two industry labels when searching for legal jobs – law practice and legal services.

(4) Identify Lost Contacts through Group Search

The groups on LinkedIn vary and range from law school classes and alumni groups to practice area groups and professional development groups. I recommend joining, at a minimum, alumni groups for each school you attended. Some law firms even have alumni groups for former attorneys. The alumni groups serve as a great resource for identifying attorneys with whom you have some overlooked connection. Use the groups to find and identify these contacts and then connect with them through your personal LinkedIn page.

For example, assume you graduated from the University of Texas School of Law and are a member of the group, University of Texas School of Law Alumni. You go to the group's LinkedIn page and see the following:

Image 4.63

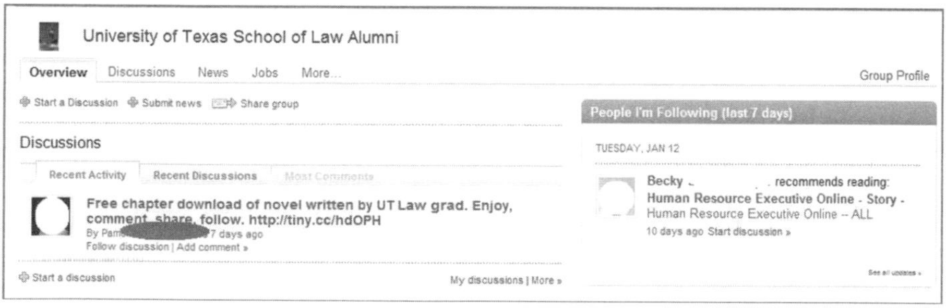

You recognize the attorney to the right, Becky, who recommended an article for reading. You believe the attorney previously practiced at your firm. However, you are not connected to this attorney. Click on the attorney's LinkedIn profile and send her a personalized invitation to connect by following **Connection Method 6** discussed in the **Step 1: Connect** section.

(5) Identify Firms/Attorneys in Target Practice Area through Group Search

If you are a law student interested in a particular area of law or if you are currently practicing in a particular area, join several groups that are specifically designed for your practice area. Monitor the attorneys who actively post information in the groups and then see where they practice. Are these firms on your target list? If not, add them.

(6) Search Group Job Openings

Each group on LinkedIn has the option of a job board. Some groups have active job boards, while some groups omit them. Make sure you check to see about the job boards in your groups. In the example below, you'll note that there are five jobs posted in the Leadership for Lawyers group.

Image 4.64

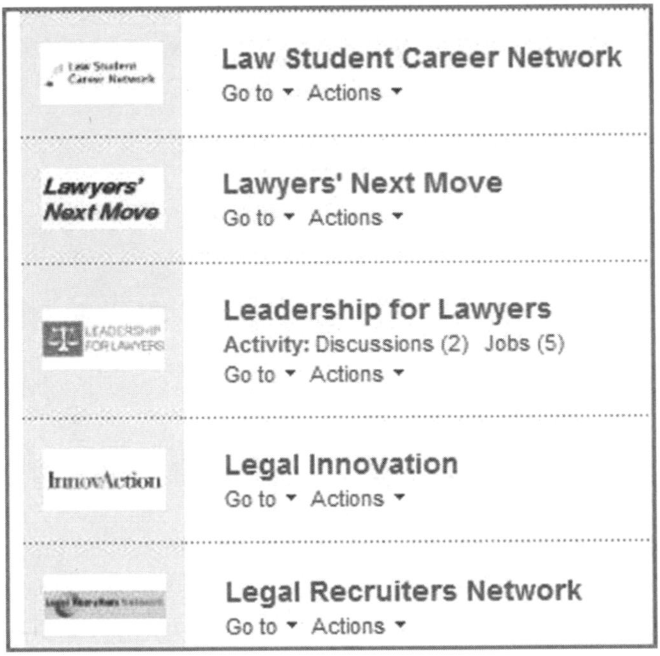

Law Student Career Network
Go to ▾ Actions ▾

Lawyers' Next Move
Go to ▾ Actions ▾

Leadership for Lawyers
Activity: Discussions (2)   Jobs (5)
Go to ▾ Actions ▾

Legal Innovation
Go to ▾ Actions ▾

Legal Recruiters Network
Go to ▾ Actions ▾

Practice Pointer

You don't have to look at each group to which you belong to see if the group has a job posted. Rather, go to "My Groups" under the Groups tab from the main menu toolbar. It will list all of your groups and any activity in the groups, including job postings.

(7) Discover Interview Talking Points through Group Search

Review LinkedIn groups, especially those in your practice area, when preparing for interviews. Note which topics are being discussed. How can you incorporate these topics into the questions you raise during your interview or into the comments you make in response to the interview questions? For example, in the Bankruptcy Lawyers group in Image 4.65 you'll see that an attorney member posted a discussion topic, iPhone Apps for Bankruptcy Lawyers.

Image 4.65

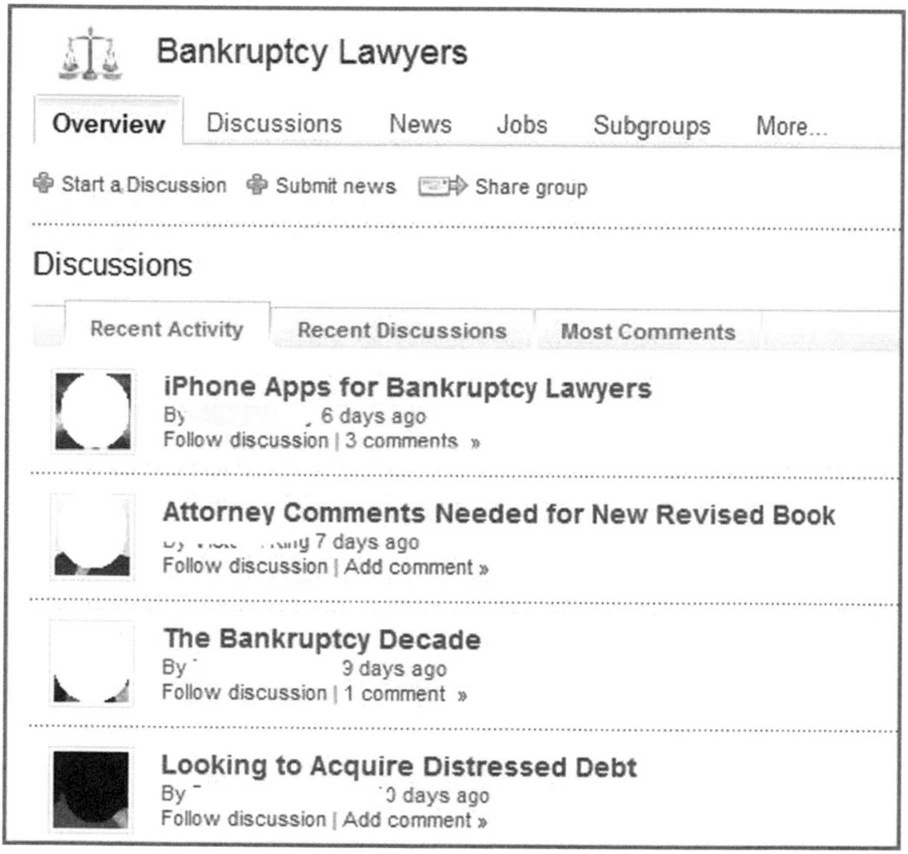

This topic sounds like a cutting-edge topic so you review it. If you are interviewing with a bankruptcy firm, perhaps you can incorporate this topic in your interview discussion.

Practice Pointer

One benefit of using the groups on LinkedIn is that you gain access to contacts outside of your network. For example, I might do a search on LinkedIn to determine all the bankruptcy attorneys within a 75 mile radius of Dallas, TX. However, that search only pulls attorneys that I'm connected to in the 1st, 2nd, and 3rd degrees. By joining a bankruptcy related group on LinkedIn, however, I might find ten other local bankruptcy attorneys and gain the ability to engage and connect with them.

(8) Review Status Updates for Job Leads

You can learn about job opportunities by reading other LinkedIn users' status updates. For example, Kathleen Pearson, Director of Professional Recruiting at Waller Lansden Dortch & Davis, posted the status update in Image 4.66 when conducting a real estate associate search for her firm's Nashville office.

Image 4.66

Kathleen Pearson is accepting resumes for a real estate associate in Nashville, TN. Candidates ONLY please send resumes to my attention.
1 hour ago · Reply privately · Add comment

In addition to viewing status updates in your news feed, you may also consider performing a LinkedIn people search (discussed on page 166) to identify law firm recruiters and hiring personnel on LinkedIn. Then, bookmark their profiles and review them on a regular basis to see if the recruiters post job openings in their status updates. I don't recommend connecting with all of these people, but I do suggest that you monitor the information displayed in their status updates.

(9) Review Profile Updates for Job Leads

The Profile Updates section tells you when a contact joins a new firm (*i.e.*, Ashley is now a Litigation Associate at XYZ Law Firm) or changes her title to a new role (*i.e.*, Regina has updated her current title to Partner at ABC Law Firm). This information can provide three clues to job seekers:

Potential Opening at Old Firm: Now that Ashley joined XYZ Law Firm, perhaps there's an opening at Ashley's old firm. Do you and Ashley practice in the same area? If so, inquire about this potential opportunity—don't wait until you find a job posting advertising the position.

Possible Elimination: If you, too, applied for the position at XYZ Law Firm, the update will let you know the position has been filled. Knowing this outcome helps you prioritize your job search. You can now move on and pursue other opportunities.

Potential Opening Resulting from New Role: If one of your contacts was promoted to a new role or position, perhaps the contact's old position needs to be filled. If you are qualified, inquire about the opportunity. Again, don't wait for the position to be advertised.

(10) Find Networking Events to Attend

Watch for events that your contacts are attending. You may find networking events worth attending, especially if a target contact is attending.

(11) Monitor Application Updates

Your news feed alerts you when your contacts install or update an application. Some application updates are helpful. For example, TripIt informs you when contacts are leaving for trips and identifies the market. For example, if I were in Boston and saw the update in Image 4.67 from my contact Kathryn, I might try to coordinate a meeting with her during her Boston visit.

Image 4.67

> **Kathryn Moran** is planning a trip to Boston, MA in February 2010 using My Travel by TripIt.
> 1 day ago · 2 comments

(12) Learn about Practice Areas through Legal Updates by JD Supra JD

Supra is a repository of legal articles, newsletters, cases, and more. You can add JD Supra's LinkedIn application, Legal Updates, so that certain legal articles appear in your news feed.

You can receive updates from the practice areas shown in Image 4.68.

Image 4.68

Subjects You May Like	
Subjects	
General Business Law	+ Add
Labor & Employment Law	+ Add
Finance & Banking	+ Add
Intellectual Property	+ Add
Bankruptcy	+ Add
Taxation	+ Add
Real Estate	+ Add
Securities Law	+ Add
Immigration Law	+ Add
Insurance	+ Add
Communications & Media Law	+ Add
Antitrust & Trade Regulation	+ Add
Environmental Law	+ Add
Consumer Protection	+ Add
Privacy	+ Add
See All Subjects »	

For example, if you are a law student interested in employment law, you can use the Legal Updates application to deliver employment law articles and updates, information that will help prepare you for interviews, to your LinkedIn news feed, as shown in Image 4.69.

Image 4.69

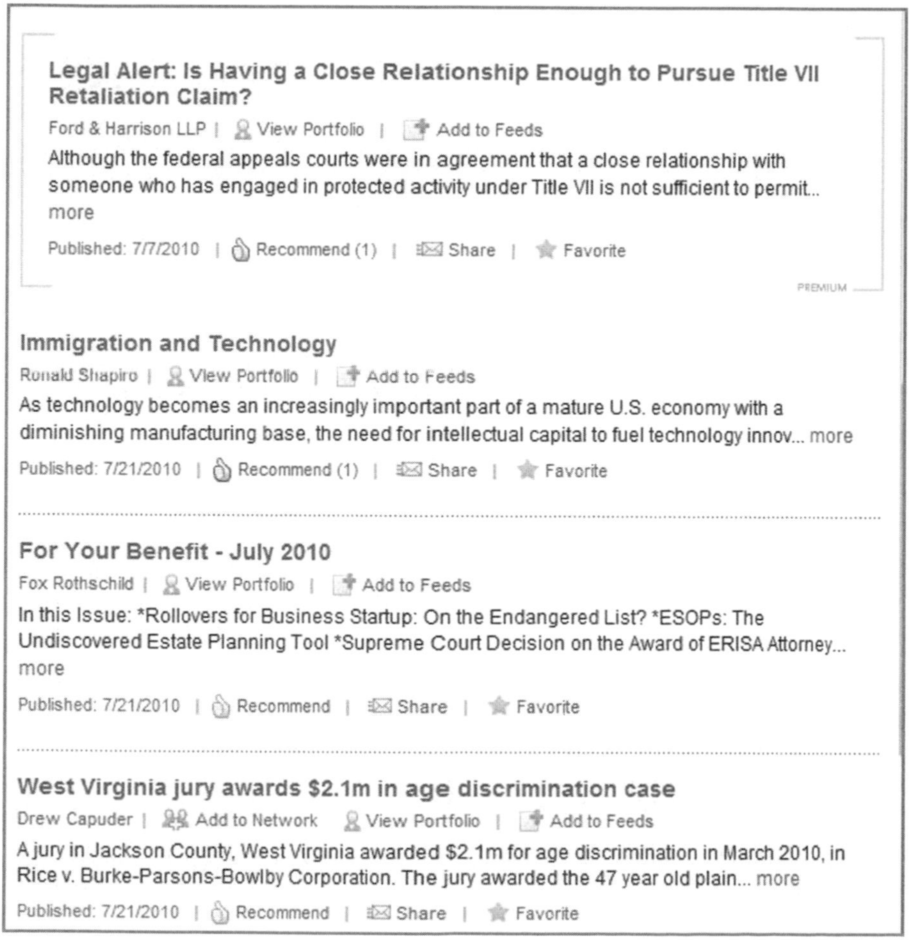

You may also use Legal Updates to get topic ideas when writing notes, articles, and papers.

STEP 3: PARTICIPATE

Now that you know how to connect with people on LinkedIn and how you can use various LinkedIn functions to identify target firms, people, or jobs or gather information to help you prepare for interviews, you now need to know how to participate with these contacts to remain on their radar screens.

While there is certainly not as much participation on LinkedIn as there is on Facebook and Twitter, there are nine ways for you to participate on LinkedIn.

(1) Update your Status

Use the status update to alert your contacts or network about your job search and your professional life.

- <u>Law students</u>. Talk about activities at the law school and articles you are writing, share information about your job search, including the geographical markets you are considering, and ask for feedback from your contacts or network.
- <u>Practicing attorneys</u>. Talk about seminars at which you'll be speaking, projects on which you are working, or articles in which you were quoted.

<u>Examples of professional status updates include:</u>

- I will be a panelist at ____ event (include a link with more information about the event)
- I recently started a new career as _____; my new contact information is _____.
- Looking for a legal receptionist
- Preparing for a call with counsel for ____ in order to have my clients retained as postpetition professionals.
- Preparing presentations on _____
- Reviewing FL law regarding formation of non-profit organizations
- Seeking clerkship for summer 2010
- Looking for summer job for summer 2010
- Creating new blog on networking for the SBA
- Attending session on mock trial competition

Practice Pointers

(1) Don't let your status update become stale. Change your status at least once a week. You don't want new contacts to connect with you and see a status update that is a month or three months old.

(2) Don't write the same update each time you change it. Mix it up. You can share professional information without stating that you are "searching for job" in each status update.

(3) *Number of connections is important.* You are wasting your time if you write status updates but don't have many LinkedIn connections.

(2) Comment on your Contacts' Status Updates

In addition to sharing your own status updates, you can also comment on other users' updates. Commenting is one way to remain on the radar of your network so they remember you if they are hiring or they hear of a position. If someone announces a new job, congratulate that person. If the status asks a question and you prefer not to make a public comment with your answer, you can always comment that you'll send an e-mail with an answer, as shown in Image 4.70, or reply privately.

Image 4.70

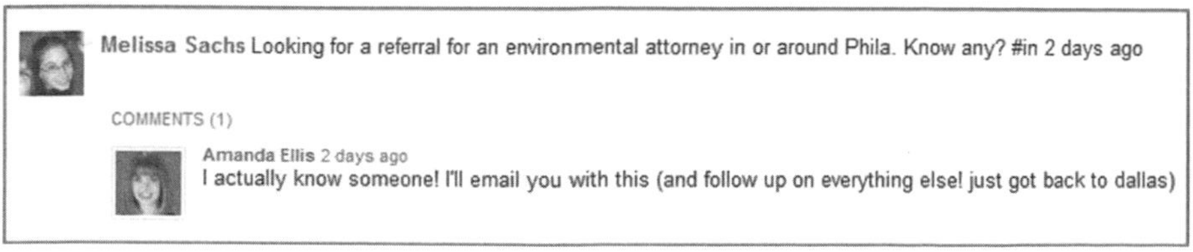

Melissa Sachs Looking for a referral for an environmental attorney in or around Phila. Know any? #in 2 days ago

COMMENTS (1)

Amanda Ellis 2 days ago
I actually know someone! I'll email you with this (and follow up on everything else! just got back to dallas)

(3) Like (Thumbs Up) your Contacts' Updates

You can also "like" a status update, similar to the like feature on Facebook which displays a thumbs-up sign next to the update, as shown in Image 4.71

Image 4.71

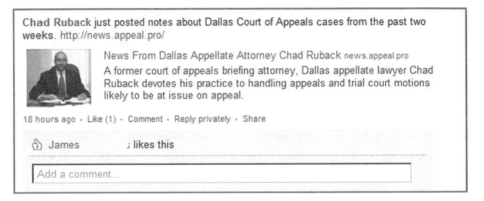

(4) Share your Contacts' Links to Articles/Posts

Some updates contain links to articles or blogs, such as the update in Image 4.71. You can also share links posted by one of your contacts so that it appears on your profile.

(5) Share Articles with Group(s)

By joining groups on LinkedIn, you can communicate with other members within that group even if you aren't connected to them individually. In this way, job seekers can catch the attention of attorneys in similar practice areas, even if they aren't connected and don't know each other.

The example in Image 4.72 is from a women lawyers group on LinkedIn. You will note that one group member posted a link to an article about a law firm teaching its female associates to communicate 'powerfully' with clients and colleagues. Several other members commented on the article, resulting in a discussion via the LinkedIn group.

Image 4.72

> **~~...~~y is to teach female associates to communicate 'powerfully' with clients and colleagues - a patronising stigmatisation of women in the profession or a much-needed initiative?**
>
> http://www.thelawyer.com/story.aspx?
> storycode=1001924&PageNo=2&SortOrder=dateadded&PageSize=10#comments
>
> ---
>
> Posted 14 days ago | Reply Privately

Comments (3)

(6) Initiate or Participate in Group Discussion

Image 4.73 is from a group of bankruptcy attorneys on LinkedIn. One of the members initiated a discussion by asking for referrals for a bankruptcy attorney in Denver.

Image 4.73

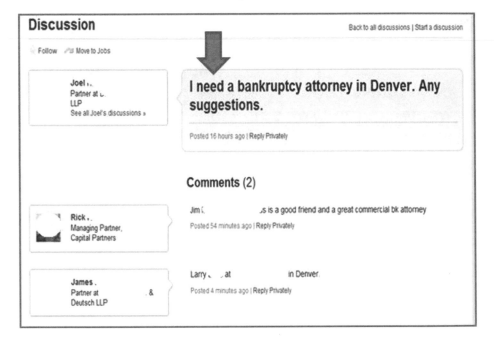

Image 4.74 shows how a law student initiated a discussion in the Law Student Career Network, a LinkedIn group for law students seeking employment in both the public and private sectors. Ellen Faba, a student at the University of Detroit Mercy School of Law, posted a question about preparing for on-campus interviews. Ellen's question generated five responses, including the two visible in Image 4.74 by Philip Guzman, Director of Public Service Programs at North Carolina Central University School of Law, and Drew Carls, the On-Campus Interview Coordinator at the University of Texas School of Law.

Image 4.74

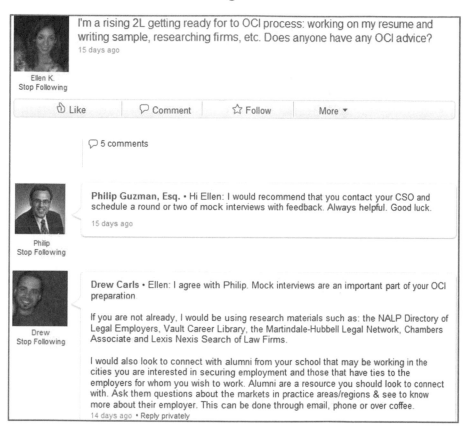

I'm a rising 2L getting ready for to OCI process: working on my resume and writing sample, researching firms, etc. Does anyone have any OCI advice?
15 days ago

Ellen K.
Stop Following

👍 Like   💬 Comment   ☆ Follow   More ▾

💬 5 comments

Philip Guzman, Esq. • Hi Ellen: I would recommend that you contact your CSO and schedule a round or two of mock interviews with feedback. Always helpful. Good luck.
15 days ago

Philip
Stop Following

Drew Carls • Ellen: I agree with Philip. Mock interviews are an important part of your OCI preparation.

If you are not already, I would be using research materials such as: the NALP Directory of Legal Employers, Vault Career Library, the Martindale-Hubbell Legal Network, Chambers Associate and Lexis Nexis Search of Law Firms.

I would also look to connect with alumni from your school that may be working in the cities you are interested in securing employment and those that have ties to the employers for whom you wish to work. Alumni are a resource you should look to connect with. Ask them questions about the markets in practice areas/regions & see to know more about their employer. This can be done through email, phone or over coffee.
14 days ago • Reply privately

Drew
Stop Following

(7) Market Yourself to a Group

Image 4.75 shows a creative attorney job seeker who posted a note about his job search in the discussion section of a bar association's LinkedIn group.

Image 4.75

Anyone looking for an experienced IP litigator with 5 + years experience and someone who was named a 2009 Rising Star in IP lit?

I am a patent litigator with 5+ years experience, mainly in semiconductor and software cases, have worked at elite firms such as ⌐   ., worked on federal court as well as ITC cases, and was named a 2009 Rising Star in IP litigation by Northern California Super Lawyers Magazine. I have been finding it very difficult to secure interviews despite a great resume and enthusiasm for a new position. I am open to just about anywhere in the US (but prefer Texas, especially Dallas ⌐   ⌐ :
⌐   ▶), and can be admitted on motion to many jurisdictions in the US by virtue of having the MO bar as well as the CA bar. You can call my patent lit partner ⌐¯ ¯ .   ¯ ¯ ⌐ to get a sense of what I can do for you. Please contact me if you are interested or know of someone who might be. My resume, transcript, writing sample, and references are available upon request. Thank you very much and I look forward to getting some feedback soon!

Posted 1 month ago | Reply Privately

Caveat: Chapter 6 addresses etiquette and protocol issues regarding posting information in LinkedIn Groups.

(8) Update your Profile Information

Your network is alerted any time you change or update any section on your profile. When you change your status, register to attend an event through LinkedIn, or update any of your applications (see Chapter 2), your network will know. Thus, if you upload a new article to your LinkedIn profile, your network will know. Or, if you are leaving for a trip that is scheduled on Tripit, your network will know. Again, all of these updates are just another way to help you stay on your network's radar.

(9) Send a LinkedIn Message

Periodically, send a LinkedIn message to drive traffic to your LinkedIn profile. For example, perhaps you read about one of your LinkedIn contacts receiving an award. Instead of sending a regular e-mail to congratulate the contact, send a message through LinkedIn. There's nothing wrong with sending a regular e-mail, but there's a significant chance the recipient will review your LinkedIn profile if you send a LinkedIn message.

Assuming you have a complete profile, the recipient can view your recent career changes, accomplishments, and speaking engagements. He or she might also click to read your blog, recent articles, or presentations. If the recipient (or his or her firm) is in the position to hire, you just made a positive impression.

SECTION 3 - TWITTER

When you think of Twitter, you may think of Oprah, Ashton or Ellen—some of the celebrities known for their large following on Twitter. But, Twitter is so much more than following your favorite celebrity. Twitter is about conversations with anyone, including professionals, which lead to offline professional relationships. As you'll see in Chapter 7, these relationships built on Twitter can lead to jobs for young lawyers.

To perform on Twitter, you will follow the same CAP steps discussed on page 113—connect, assimilate, participate—as you did with Facebook and LinkedIn. But, you'll connect with more people, learn more about the legal profession, and build relationships with new legal professionals.

Moreover, while Twitter is primarily professional, you will also share some personal content though not as much as you share on Facebook.

STEP 1: CONNECT

Your Twitter experience is defined by the people with whom you connect. If you connect with interesting people, you will learn about the legal profession and build new relationships. This section examines how to choose your Twitter connections and how to connect, including where to find legal professionals with whom you may want to connect.

Who: Level of Scrutiny to Connect with Followers

Minimum (Rational Basis) Scrutiny

Because the purpose of Twitter is to build relationships with new contacts, you want to be able to connect with most people. Therefore, you may apply the lowest level of scrutiny in determining who to follow on Twitter—minimum (or rational basis) scrutiny.

Cocktail Party Rule

I recommend the **Cocktail Party Rule** for applying the rational basis scrutiny analysis. Many people equate Twitter with an online cocktail party where you can jump in and out of conversations. When choosing your contacts on Twitter, accept most people unless you would not talk to them at a cocktail party.

By applying the Cocktail Party Rule, you may connect with legal professionals as well as professionals outside your industry, celebrities, and local businesses. The only people to avoid are those you would be embarrassed to be seen with at a cocktail party. For example, I avoid following people on Twitter if they only tweet about "making money online" or "getting more followers."

How: Connection Process

You connect with other people on Twitter by clicking the follow link below the user's profile picture, as shown in Image 4.76.

Image 4.76

Other people will connect with you by following you. As noted in Chapter 3, the majority of people on Twitter do not restrict the privacy of their profiles so you can see most users' tweets and determine whether they look interesting and worth following before clicking the follow button. Moreover, there is no connection approval process like on Facebook and LinkedIn unless the person's tweets are protected. Once you click follow, you are connected to the other user.

How: Find Legal Professionals

You should follow people who are likely to provide job leads. This could include law school career counselors or the law school career services offices, practicing attorneys—especially attorneys in your target market and practice area, third-party recruiters (headhunters), law firm recruiters, law firm marketing professionals, legal news outlets, job boards, career experts, and practice area and professional organizations.

Remember the primary purpose of Twitter discussed in Chapter 1—to connect with people you don't know. Thus, it's okay to follow people you don't know, especially career professionals and attorneys in your target practice area or industry.

There are multiple ways to find these unknown but helpful people on Twitter. I recommend trying several of the following methods because no single method will find all the Twitter users you want to identify.

1. Published legal listings
2. Search tools
3. Other users
4. Job boards
5. Directories

Published Legal Listings

Some legal professionals have done the work for you and published listings of other legal professionals on Twitter. I recommend starting with these lists to find legal professionals to follow. Such listings include:

1. ***AmLaw Tweeple:*** Melissa Sachs, founder of RecruiterEsq.com, created a list of legal professionals at AmLaw firms who use Twitter. The list is coded for each professional's role in the firm—*i.e.,* marketing, recruiting, attorney. Visit Melissa's website, www.recruiteresq.com, to access the list.[31]

2. ***145 Lawyers (and Legal Professionals) to Follow on Twitter:*** This is the list I used when I got started on Twitter in September 2008. Adrian Laussen of JD Supra compiled the list which initially had only 145 legal professionals; the list has grown to over 750 legal professionals.[32] The list contains the professionals' usernames as well as a short bio. http://scoop.jdsupra.com/2008/09/articles/law-firm-marketing/145-lawyers-and-legal-professionals-to-follow-on-twitter/

3. ***Texas Lawyers to Follow on Twitter:*** Todd Smith, an appellate specialist based in Austin, published a blog post in December 2008 that listed over 20 Texas lawyers on Twitter.[33] The list can be found http://www.texasappellatelawblog.com/2008/12/articles/technology/texas-lawyers-to-follow-on-twitter/.

4. ***Minnesota Legal Professionals to Follow on Twitter:*** The Minnesota

Bar Association maintains a directory of Minnesota legal professionals on Twitter. The directory can be found http://www.practicelaw. org/161.[34]

5. **LexTweet:** LexTweet, created by LexBlog, is a community of legal professionals using Twitter. You can add yourself to the listing by visiting the website, www.lextweet.com.[35]

6. **Legal Birds:** Justia.com tracks legal professionals on Twitter. You can add yourself to the list by visiting the website, http://legalbirds.justia. com/.[36]

7. **Tweet Law:** TweetLaw is a Twitter application designed for legal professionals. TweetLaw contains over 40 categories of legal professionals so you can search by the categories that interest you.[37] http:// tweetlaw.com/

8. **15 People All Securities and Corporate Litigators Should Follow on Twitter:** Bruce Carton, President of Docket Media LLC and editor of *Securities Docket*, compiled a list of users who routinely tweet about corporate and securities litigation matters.[38] http://www.complianceweek.com/blog/carton/2010/02/17/ updating-my-15-must-follows-on-twitter/

9. **CLE Resources**: Mandatory CLE Unplugged maintains a Twitter Directory of providers, associations, and all things related to continuing legal education.[39] http://www.umcle.com/socialmedia/twitter/

10. **Law School Career Offices:** **Appendix A** contains a list of law school career services offices with Twitter accounts.

11. **22 Tweets (@22twts):** Lance Godard, an international legal business development and marketing consultant, interviews practicing attorneys who tweet. Follow the twitter handle @22twts to follow the live interviews. Or, visit the 22 Tweets blog, www.22tweets.com, to review past interviews with attorneys and learn about upcoming interviews.[40]

Search Tools

You should be familiar with three ways to use search tools to identify people to follow on Twitter:

1. Find People
2. Tweep Search
3. Twitter Search

Find People

Find People is a search feature on the Twitter website in the upper right-hand tool bar.

Image 4.77

Home
Profile
Find People
Settings
Help
Sign out

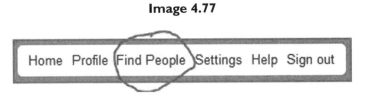

You simply type in a user's full name in the box "Who are you looking for?"

Image 4.78

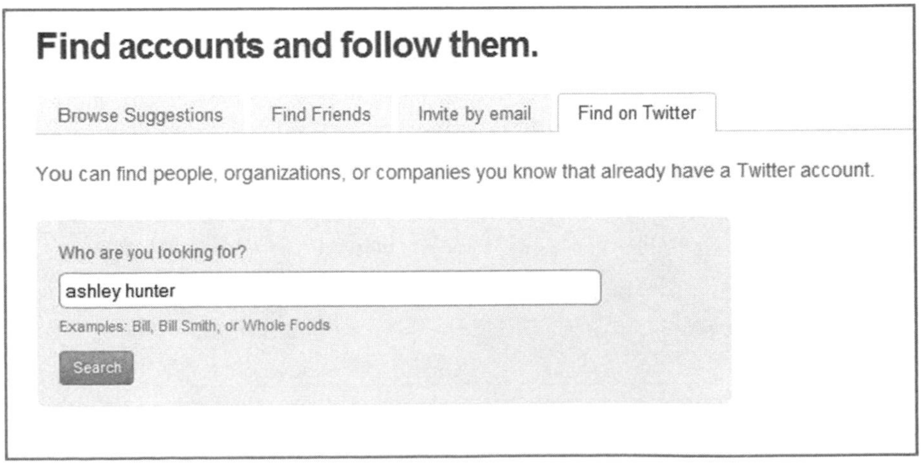

Find accounts and follow them.
Browse Suggestions
Find Friends
Invite by email
Find on Twitter
You can find people, organizations, or companies you know that already have a Twitter account.
Who are you looking for?
ashley hunter
Examples: Bill, Bill Smith, or Whole Foods
Search

Twitter lists users with the name you entered. In Image 4.79, the Ashley Hunter I'm searching for is the first user mentioned in the search results.

Image 4.79

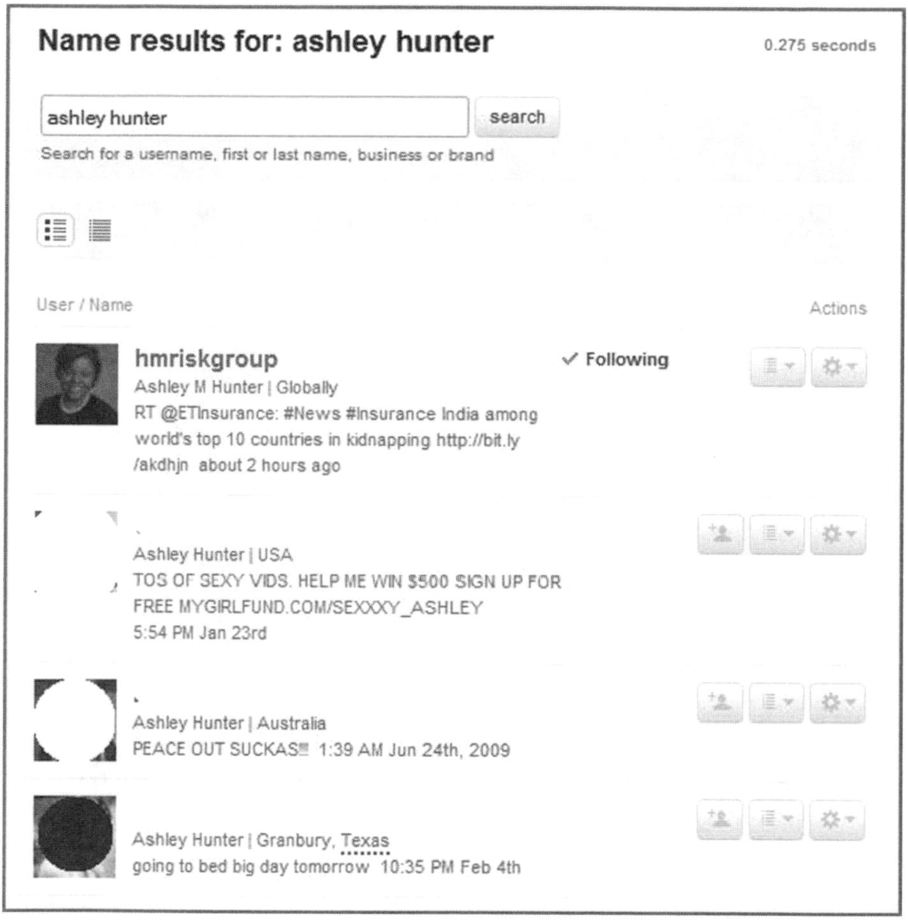

Name results for: ashley hunter

0.275 seconds

ashley hunter	search

Search for a username, first or last name, business or brand

User / Name   Actions

hmriskgroup ✓ Following
Ashley M Hunter | Globally
RT @ETInsurance: #News #Insurance India among
world's top 10 countries in kidnapping http://bit.ly
/akdhjn about 2 hours ago

Ashley Hunter | USA
TOS OF SEXY VIDS. HELP ME WIN $500 SIGN UP FOR
FREE MYGIRLFUND.COM/SEXXXY_ASHLEY
5:54 PM Jan 23rd

Ashley Hunter | Australia
PEACE OUT SUCKAS!!! 1:39 AM Jun 24th, 2009

Ashley Hunter | Granbury, Texas
going to bed big day tomorrow 10:35 PM Feb 4th

One problem with this tool is that many users do not identify their full name in their Twitter profiles so they may not be found in a Find People Search. For example, I searched for Evan Fogelman, a person whom I know has a Twitter account. But, as Image 4.80 indicates, Twitter couldn't find anyone named Evan Fogelman.

Image 4.80

Name results for: evan fogelman

| evan fogelman | search |

Search for a username, first or last name, business or brand

We couldn't find anyone named evan fogelman.

Twitter couldn't find Evan because, as you can see below, Evan did not list his full name in his Twitter profile. Rather, Evan listed his Twitter *username* in the name section of his Twitter profile.

Image 4.81

efogelman

Name efogelman
Location UT:
32.972128,-96.80288

513   50   0
following followers listed

Tweets   11

✓ Following   ☰ Lists ▾   ☼ ▾

Favorites

Another problem with Find People is that you often don't know the name of a specific person you want to follow; rather, you are looking to follow other law students, law school career counselors, job resources, and leads you don't yet know by name. I use TweepSearch to find categories of people.

TweepSearch

TweepSearch is a third party site that can be found at www.tweepsearch.com.

Image 4.82

TweepSearch searches the bio section of other Twitter users' profiles. Thus, you can search for key words based on the type of people you are searching for on Twitter.

For example, if you enter "law school career," TweepSearch finds over 20 profiles with the words "law school career" in their bio.

Image 4.83

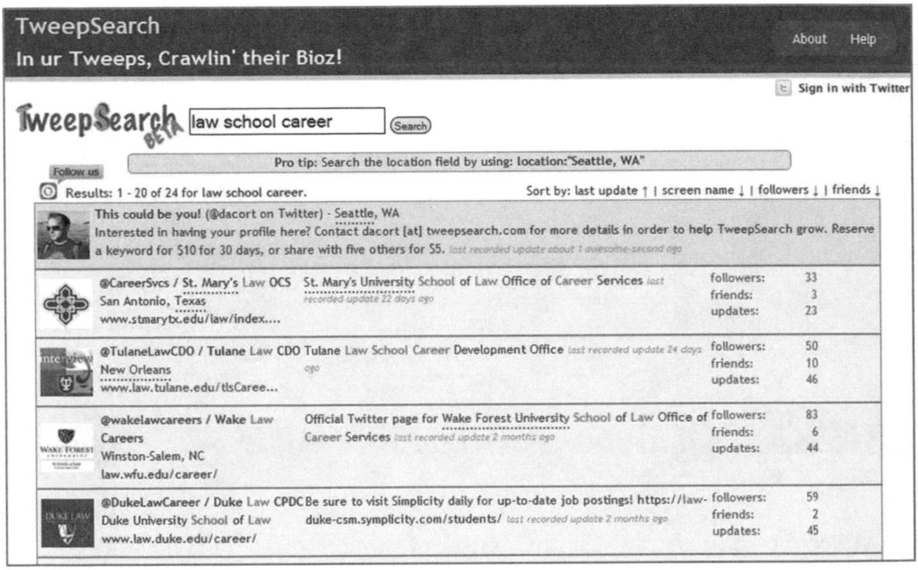

You can refine the results by including a specific geographical region in your search.

Practice Pointer

LocaFollow.com is another third-party site that allows you to search Twitter users' bios. www.locafollow.com

Twitter Search

The third search tool is the Twitter Search function which is found on your home page on the Twitter website, as shown in Image 4.84.

Image 4.84

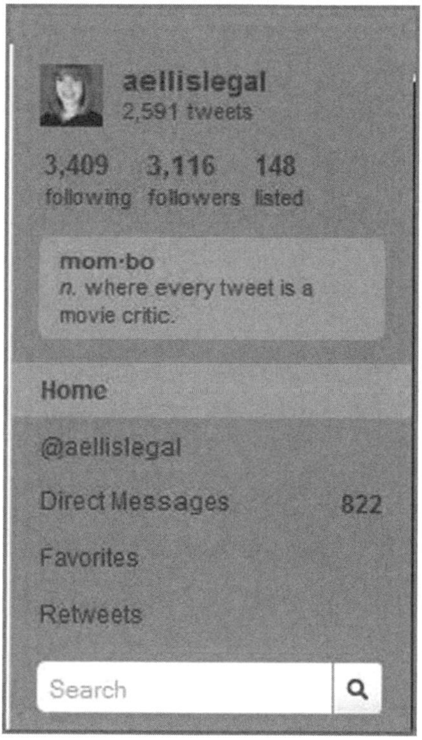

The Twitter Search function only searches tweets, not users' bios. Thus, the Twitter Search function is helpful for finding conversations about particular topics while TweepSearch is better for finding titles.

However, searching for conversations in Twitter Search can lead you to find Twitter users who tweet about the topic of interest. For example, if you are a bankruptcy lawyer or one who is interested in practicing in this area, you might search for "bankruptcy." The following search results contain the word bankruptcy.

Image 4.85

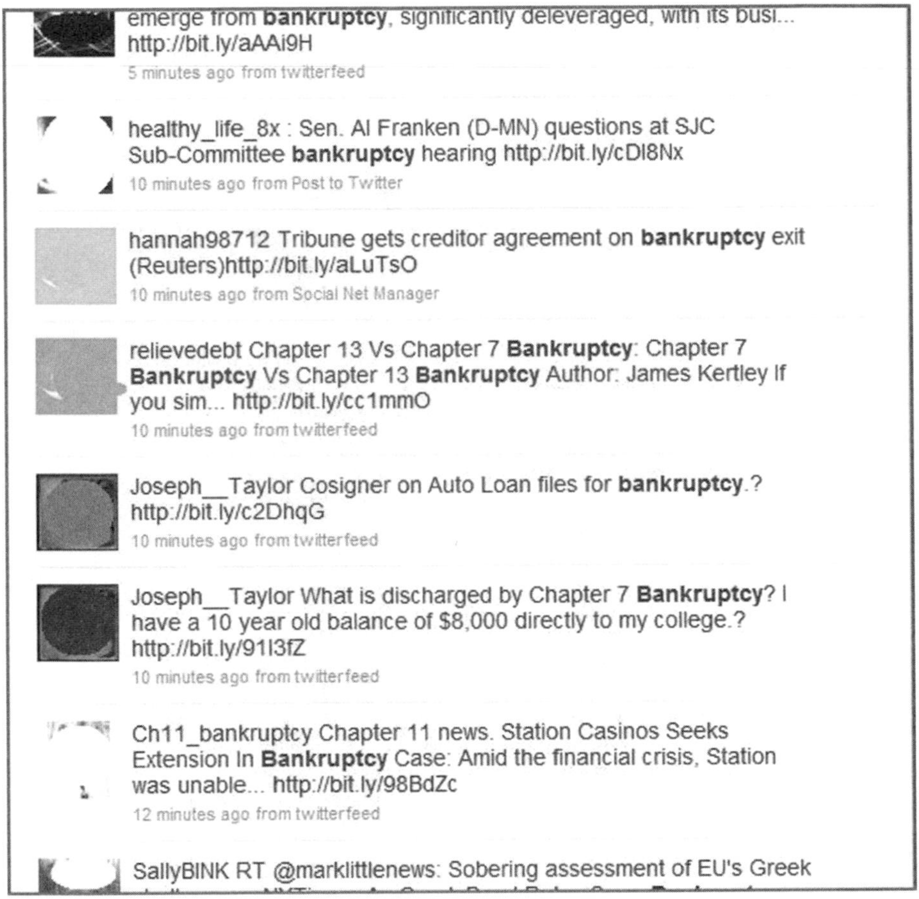

You can click on the users who tweeted interesting information about bankruptcy and decide if they are users that you want to follow.

Other Users

As you begin following people, you will discover additional Twitter users you may want to follow through other users' conversations, Follow Friday recommendations, and Twitter Lists.

1. *Conversations:* As you read the updates of the people you follow, you might observe a conversation between the person you follow and another Twitter user you don't follow. For example, the tweet below is

by Melissa Sachs. I follow Melissa, the former recruiter and founder of RecruiterEsq.com, and she frequently tweets about career issues. Since the conversation below is about resumes, I might check to see if I'm following the other users mentioned in the tweet—@fishdogs and @ Keppie_Careers.

Image 4.86

RT @Keppie_Careers: Resumes from the recruiter's ☆
perspective:The Best Format for your Resume (...not .PDF) by
@Fishdogs http://bit.ly/aqVIDs
1:12 PM Feb 2nd from web

2. *Follow Friday:* Fridays on Twitter are designated as Follow Friday and users recommend other users to follow. They label their tweets with #FF or #FollowFriday and then list the usernames of the people they recommend following. Thus, you can find new people to follow by monitoring the Follow Friday recommendations.

Image 4.87

#ff @jjlevin @FraudAttorney @DrLizH @Chicagogirl27 @aellislegal
@nassefi Follow Friday
9:22 AM Jan 22nd from web

3. *Twitter Lists:* The Twitter List feature allows you to group people you follow and then read all of the tweets by group members at one time. For example, you might create groups for local attorneys, law school career-related accounts, and law students. You are allowed 20 lists and 500 people on each list. You can also place one person on multiple lists.

The List feature is helpful for job seekers because it's a quick way to find other people to follow. As you follow new legal professionals, check their profiles to see if they created Twitter lists—especially lists of people of interest to you. For example, we know that Melissa Sachs, founder of RecruiterEsq.com, tweets about careers, so let's see if she has a Twitter List for career people.

Image 4.88

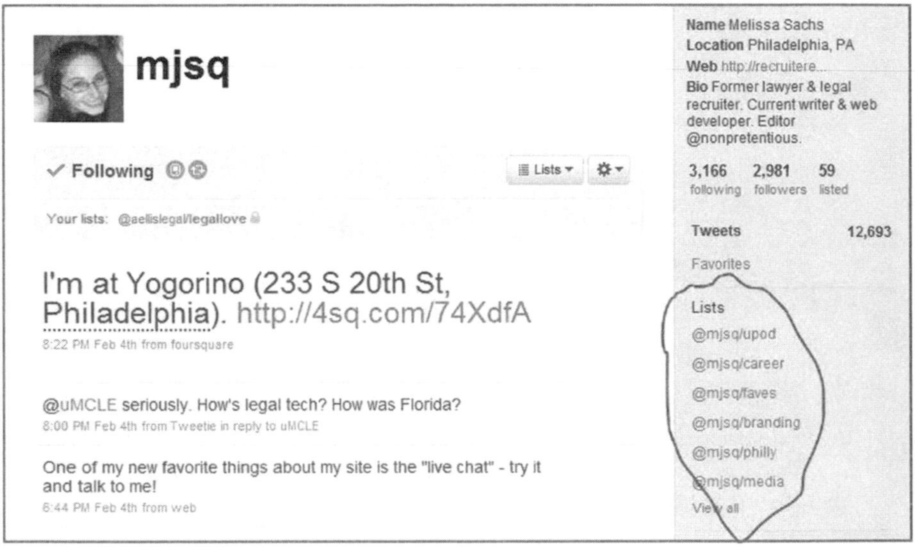

As you can see in Image 4.88, Melissa has a list for "career." Another user could view the list and then determine if he or she wanted to follow Melissa's Career List. To follow the list, simply click "Follow this list," as shown in Image 4.89.

Image 4.89

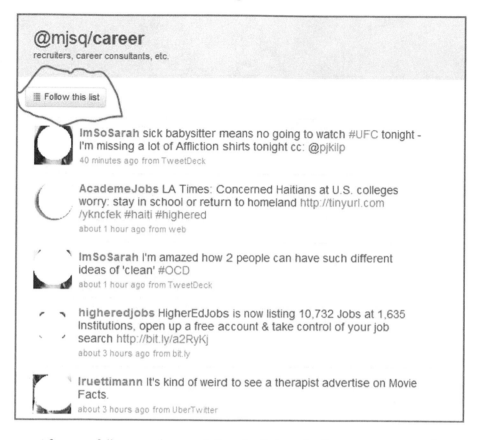

After you follow another user's list, the link to the list appears on your home page and you can view the list at any time from your page, as shown in Image 4.90.

Image 4.90

Job Boards

Finally, many job boards have their own Twitter profiles that you may follow. I've compiled a list of over 30 job boards for the legal industry and listed them in **Appendix C** in the following categories: national legal job boards, regional legal job boards, international legal job boards, and practice area/industry specific legal job boards.

Directories

There are third-party directories that list a variety of people on Twitter— legal and non-legal professionals. The one thing to note about these directories is that users must list themselves in the directories, so don't expect to find everyone on Twitter in these directories. The directories are helpful in finding non-legal professionals on Twitter. As you learned in Chapter 1, you should follow 80% legal professionals and 20% non-legal professionals. Your non-legal professionals may include business professionals, media professionals, celebrities, politicians,

or local restaurants. Some of the directories to help you identify non-legal professionals include:

1. WeFollow - http://wefollow.com/
2. Twellow - http://www.twellow.com/
3. ExecTweets - http://exectweets.com/
4. MediaOnTwitter - http://www.mediaontwitter.com/
5. SocialBrandIndex - http://www.socialbrandindex.com/
6. GovTwit - http://govtwit.com/
7. Tweet Congress - http://tweetcongress.org/
8. Muck Rack - http://muckrack.com/

STEP 2: ASSIMILATE

After connecting with legal professionals, you will begin to learn from their
tweets. You will assimilate information that will alert you of job opportunities,
prepare you for interviews, and advance your career. Consider the following 11
ways you can assimilate information from Twitter.

(1) Monitor your Contacts' Tweets for Job Openings

Lawyers, law school career counselors, recruiters, and the job boards listed
in **Appendix C** frequently tweet job openings. As mentioned in the previous
section, your Twitter experience is defined by the people with whom you connect.
If you are connected to the right lawyers, law school career counselors, recruiters,
and job boards, you'll receive tweets from lawyers looking to hire law students to
work as interns/clerks, as shown in Images 4.91 and 4.92.

Image 4.91

BOSTON AREA LAW STUDENTS: RT @jessicaafoley I'm looking
for a law clerk.
5:53 PM May 24th via web

Image 4.92

LAW STUDENTS - 2Ls: RT @fredabramson I am looking for a 2L
Law Intern with an entrepreneurial bent.
8:51 AM May 10th via web

Some attorneys share other firms' or companies' job openings. The attorney in Image 4.93 shared a job opening with Google.

Image 4.93

marciahofmann Google looking to hire telecom policy counsel
based in DC. http://bit.ly/SKSNL
1:37 PM Jun 30th from web

Law school career counselors frequently tweet about jobs in multiple regions of the country—not just the region in which they are located. For example, Marina Feehan, Assistant Director of the Office of Career Planning at the University of San Francisco School of Law, tweeted the two job openings in Images 4.94 and 4.95, one opening in New Jersey and one opening in California.

Image 4.94

Sr. Associate - Litigation: Bonner Kiernan Trebach & Crociata,
Parsippany, NJ http://bit.ly/9iMW5d #attorney #lawyer #lawjob
Monday, July 19, 2010 7:10:24 PM via TweetDeck

Image 4.95

JOB: Alt Legal Career: Director – Sydney Irmas Housing Project:
LA, CA http://bit.ly/94QWV2 #attorney #lawyer
12:23 PM Jun 3rd via TweetDeck

Finally, don't forget to follow job boards for your region or practice area such as Lawyer Jobs Houston if you are seeking positions in the Houston region. Regional job boards are listed in **Appendix C**.

Image 4.96

> **LawyerJobsHOU** Hiring a Senior Legal Counsel - Trading at Shell
> Oil Company (Houston, TX) http://bit.ly/b0l1TW #jobs #shjobs
>
> sin⸮⸮⸮ ᵉᵈ about 12 hours ago via twitterfeed

Practice Pointer

Use the Twitter List feature to help you organize your contacts. Group your contacts who tweet about jobs in lists and check those daily. Image 4.97 shows an attorney who created lists for job boards, law firm recruiters, law school career counselor, and lawyers by markets and practice area.

Image 4.97

(2) Discover Job Opportunities through Twitter Search

As mentioned on page 195, the Twitter search function is helpful when looking for discussions or tweets on a particular topic. I noted that you could type in key words to find legal contacts on Twitter. You can also type in key words to find job openings. For example, a search for "law" and "job" yields the results shown in Image 4.98.

Image 4.98

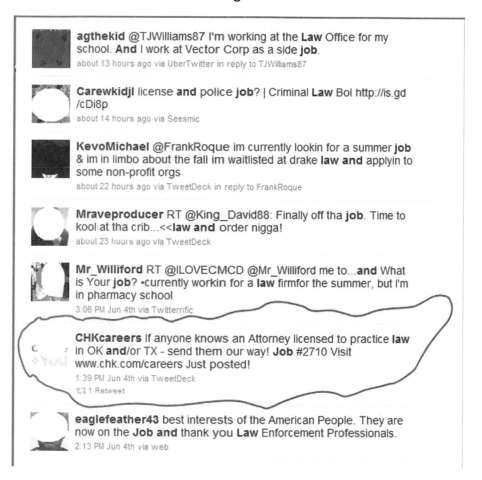

agthekid @TJWilliams87 I'm working at the **Law** Office for my school. **And** I work at Vector Corp as a side **job**.
about 13 hours ago via UberTwitter in reply to TJWilliams87

Carewkidjl license **and** police **job**? | Criminal **Law** Boi http://is.gd /cDi8p
about 14 hours ago via Seesmic

KevoMichael @FrankRoque im currently lookin for a summer **job** & im in limbo about the fall im waitlisted at drake **law and** applyin to some non-profit orgs
about 22 hours ago via TweetDeck in reply to FrankRoque

Mraveproducer RT @King_David88: Finally off tha **job**. Time to kool at tha crib...<<**law and** order nigga!
about 23 hours ago via TweetDeck

Mr_Williford RT @ILOVECMCD @Mr_Williford me to...**and** What is Your **job**? •currently workin for a **law** firmfor the summer, but I'm in pharmacy school
3:06 PM Jun 4th via Twitterrific

CHKcareers If anyone knows an Attorney licensed to practice **law** in OK **and**/or TX - send them our way! **Job** #2710 Visit www.chk.com/careers Just posted!
1:39 PM Jun 4th via TweetDeck
♺ 1 Retweet

eaglefeather43 best interests of the American People. They are now on the **Job and** thank you **Law** Enforcement Professionals.
2:13 PM Jun 4th via web

Note the posting by Chesapeake (@CHKcareers), an energy company, seeking an attorney. If you are only following legal professionals on Twitter, you might have missed this tweet/job posting. But, the Twitter search led you to the tweet by using the right key words.

(3) Search for Job Opportunities on TwitJobSearch.com

Another way to find job opportunities is to perform a search on www.
TwitJobSearch.com, a third-party job search engine for Twitter.   Search by
keywords such as legal, lawyer, attorney, or counsel.   Your results will include
legal job postings on non-legal job boards that might be off your radar.   In the
example below, you'll see that I searched with the keyword "counsel" and the
search generated two postings for corporate counsel positions on two non-legal
job boards—@zulujobsil and @execjobsla.

Image 4.99

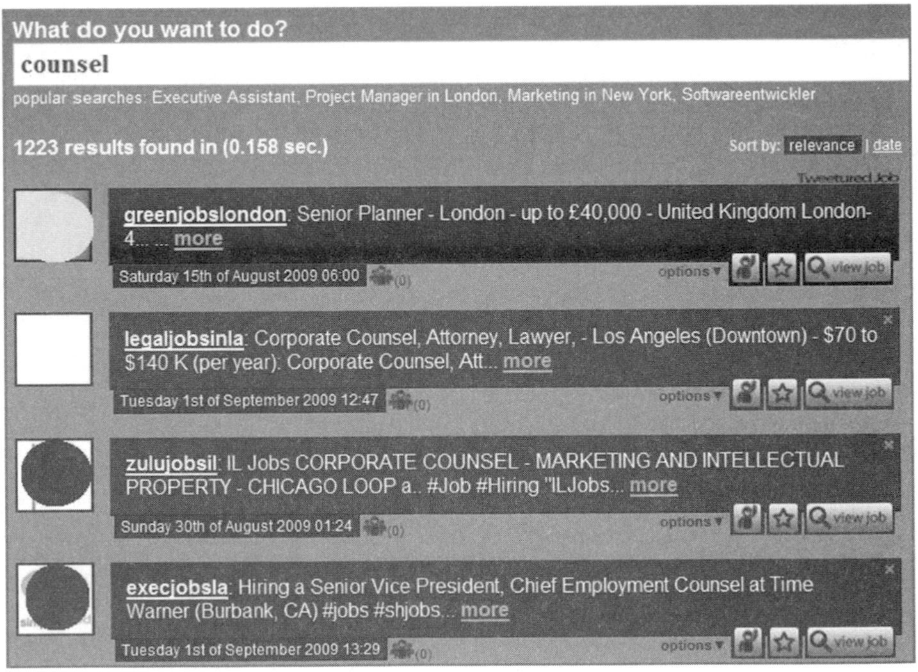

(4) Monitor your Contacts' Tweets for Potential Job Openings

In addition to specific job openings, watch for potential openings. For example, Image 4.100 is a tweet from the *ABA Journal* announcing that the DOJ *plans* to hire 50 more lawyers.

Image 4.100

> **ABAJournal** DOJ to Hire 50 More Lawyers, Gear Up for Civil Rights Enforcement Drive http://bit.ly/okKzv
> about 13 hours ago from twitterfeed

And, Image 4.101 is a tweet and link to an article regarding a practice area that continues to boom—e-discovery—discussing how many firms have created the position of e-discovery attorney. If you have an IT background, you could use this information to market yourself as an e-discovery attorney to firms potentially looking.

Image 4.101

> **PivotalD** RT @DigitalCrimeInv @IntegreonEDD: The Growing Role of the E-Discovery Attorney http://om.ly/IppQ | Texas Bar Journal
> 9 minutes ago from otweet

(5) Prepare for Interviews by Searching Firms

Enter the firm's name where you are interviewing into Twitter Search to find recent tweets about the firm. For example, if you are interviewing at Duane Morris in Philadelphia and enter Duane Morris in the search bar, you will find, among others, the tweets in Image 4.102. You will learn that the firm recently hired a Nuclear Law Attorney for its DC office and named a chair of the corporate department. You will also find several cases with which the firm is involved.

Image 4.102

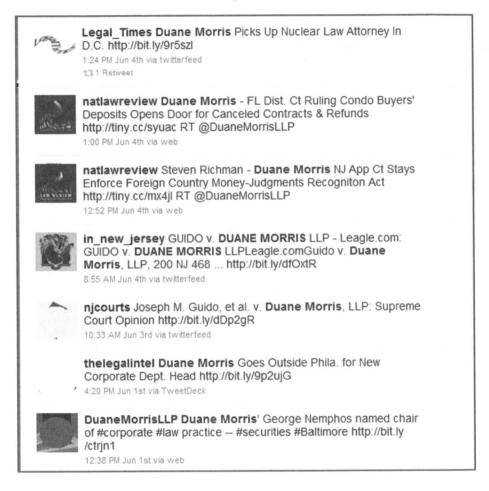

Legal_Times Duane Morris Picks Up Nuclear Law Attorney In
D.C. http://bit.ly/9r5szl
1:24 PM Jun 4th via twitterfeed
↺ 1 Retweet

natlawreview Duane Morris - FL Dist. Ct Ruling Condo Buyers'
Deposits Opens Door for Canceled Contracts & Refunds
http://tiny.cc/syuac RT @DuaneMorrisLLP
1:00 PM Jun 4th via web

natlawreview Steven Richman - **Duane Morris** NJ App Ct Stays
Enforce Foreign Country Money-Judgments Recogniton Act
http://tiny.cc/mx4jl RT @DuaneMorrisLLP
12:52 PM Jun 4th via web

in_new_jersey GUIDO v. **DUANE MORRIS** LLP - Leagle.com:
GUIDO v. **DUANE MORRIS** LLPLeagle.comGuido v. **Duane
Morris**, LLP, 200 NJ 468 ... http://bit.ly/dfOxtR
8:55 AM Jun 4th via twitterfeed

njcourts Joseph M. Guido, et al. v. **Duane Morris**, LLP: Supreme
Court Opinion http://bit.ly/dDp2gR
10:33 AM Jun 3rd via twitterfeed

thelegalintel Duane Morris Goes Outside Phila. for New
Corporate Dept. Head http://bit.ly/9p2ujG
4:20 PM Jun 1st via TweetDeck

DuaneMorrisLLP Duane Morris' George Nemphos named chair
of #corporate #law practice -- #securities #Baltimore http://bit.ly
/ctrjn1
12:38 PM Jun 1st via web

(6) Prepare for Interviews by Searching Attorneys

Enter the names of the attorneys with whom you are interviewing into Find People to see if they have a Twitter profile. For example, if you are interviewing with Michael Maslanka, an employment law partner at Ford & Harrison, you will click on Find People in the main menu and enter the attorney's name. You will then find the following Twitter profile for the partner and gather information about the partner that is not listed on his firm bio, such as his recommendation of a particular book about human decision-making.

Image 4.103

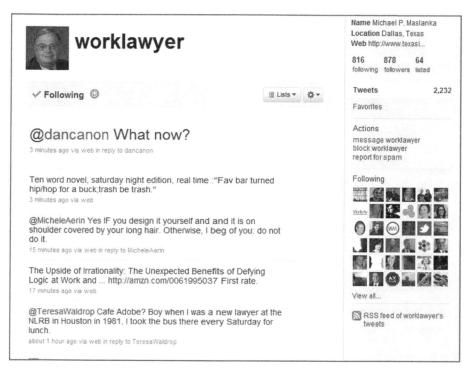

(7) Research Practice Areas

Conduct a Twitter search on Google for the practice area in which you are interested. For example, if you are interested in finding tweets about employment law or accounts that tweet about employment law, enter the following in the Google search bar: site:twitter.com "employment law"

Image 4.104

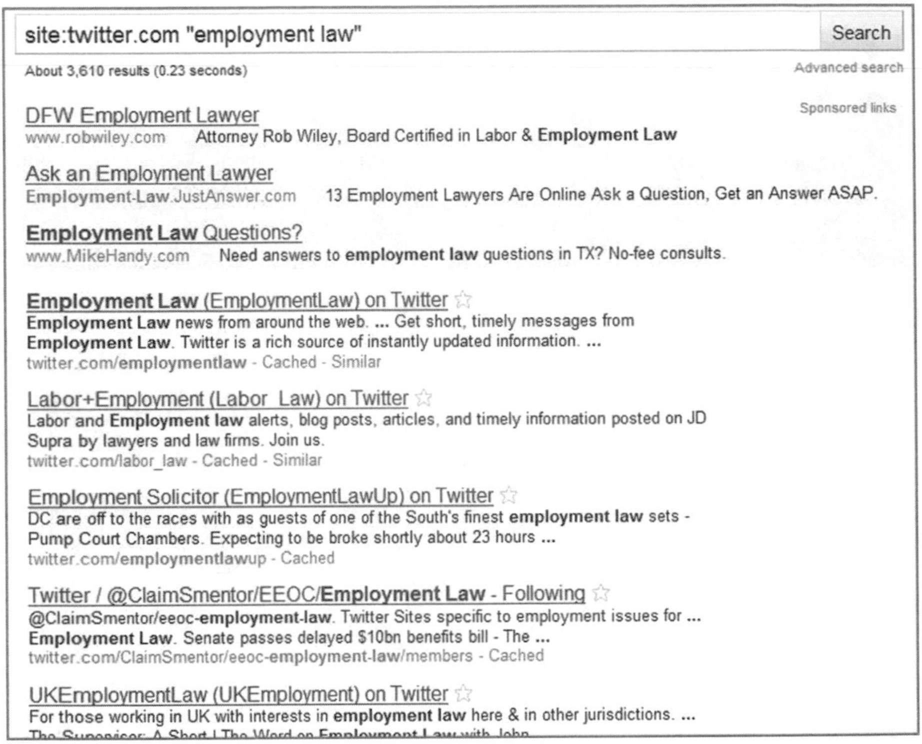

If you click on the first search result, you'll see that it's a Twitter feed for employment law news around the web (see Image 4.105) and perhaps a helpful site to review to prepare you for the latest employment law topics.

Image 4.105

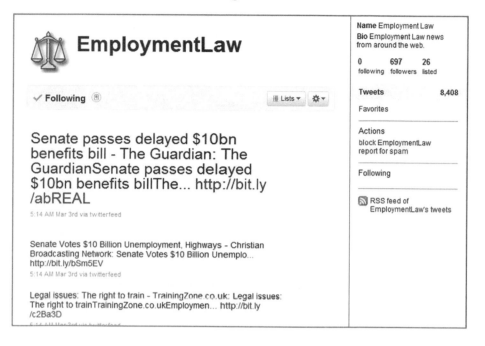

(8) Identify Media Opportunities

As you'll learn in Chapter 7, a recent law school graduate obtained her job after a reporter she met on Twitter wrote an article about the new lawyer's use of social networking in her job search. You should watch for opportunities for you to interact with the media. Such opportunities can help not only your job search but also your legal career. You will find such opportunities on Twitter; reporters frequently post if they are looking for a particular type of person for a story.

For example, the reporter in Image 4.106 was looking to speak to people, including lawyers, who had been laid off for four months or longer.

Image 4.106

LAID-OFF LAWYERS: CLeor~~~~~g looking to interview
people who have been unemployed for four months or longer/via
@helpareporter
3:54 PM Jun 4th via web

In Image 4.107, the reporter with the *Wall Street Journal* was looking for
people who failed at one career but ended up doing something better.

Image 4.107

LAWYERS (for WSJ): Did you "fail" at dream career only to end up
doing something better? E-mail ~~~~~~~~~~~~~~ (via
@alevit)
5:06 PM May 21st via web

To celebrate its 25th Anniversary, the *Texas Lawyer* announced in the blog
post in Image 4.108 that it was seeking input from Texas lawyers regarding
predictions on the next 25 years of the practice of law in Texas.

Image 4.108

TX LAWYERS: Opportunity to share ideas, get mentioned/quoted in
TX Lawyer (@TexParteBlog) http://bit.ly/99anGr
5:27 AM May 18th via web

(9) Identify Writing/Speaking Opportunities

Watch for writing and speaking opportunities, such as the examples in Images 4.109 through 4.111. Evaluate whether they would help your job search or career advancement and pursue them accordingly.

Image 4.109

LAW STUDENTS: @cbsandrewcohen is looking for law student interested in horse racing for research, writing on law of same (via @profjonathan)
9:08 AM Jun 4th via web

Image 4.110

LAW STUDENT BLOGGERS: Want your blog featured on The Weekly Law School Roundup? Here's how (via @eschaeff): http://bit.ly/a8LuD4
9:41 AM May 10th via Facebook

Image 4.111

LAW STUDENTS: Interested in part time job w/ LexBlog assisting in Tweeting selected legal blog posts/news? (via @kevinokeefe - reply to him)
1:10 PM Apr 30th via web

You will also find tips on how to improve your writing or speaking, such as the example in 4.112.

Image 4.112

Presenting? Tell your audience ONE thing http://bit.ly/bsXihy (via @LawWriting)
8:31 AM May 27th via web

(10) Identify Conference Opportunities

You will learn about a variety of legal conferences on Twitter. You may wish to attend some in person. Or, you may wish to follow the designated conference hashtag and review the tweets from or about the conference.

Image 4.113

> **chiyounglawyer** Can't make it to Philly for the ABA WILL
> Conference? Listen @ your desk to its 4pm ET program, Advice
> from the Bench www.abanet.org/women
> 6:42 AM Apr 29th via Twitter for BlackBerry®
> Retweeted by you and 1 other

You will also learn of webinars that other Twitter users host, such as the webinar about alternative legal fees in Image 4.114. Many of these webinars are free and might be worth attending. Or, you might find value in sharing the information about the webinar with another contact.

Image 4.114

> LAWYERS: 3/31 webinar on alternative fees led by in-house GC of
> VC firm (via @rocketmatter) http://bit.ly/9t1hZo
> 2:48 PM Mar 29th via Facebook

(11) Obtain Legal News & Developments

Finally, you will learn of developments and news in the legal industry.

Some news related updates might help you in your job search, such as the tweet in Image 4.115 by the Pace Law School Center for Career Development.

Image 4.115

LAW STUDENTS RT @PaceLawCCD New Job Search videos on
NYSBA website: http://www.totalwebcasting.com/view/?id=nysbarlit
7:33 PM Mar 25th via web

Other tweets will keep you informed on the state of the legal market such as the number of minority partner promotions in 2009 (Image 4.116) or the income of lawyers from regional law schools (Image 4.117).

Image 4.116

eicdocket RT @marinafeehan: RT @MCCA_Brandon: Which
minorities made partner in 2009? Check out MCCA's list!
http://tiny.cc/mfcii #attorney #news #law
1:34 PM Mar 29th via TweetDeck
Retweeted by you

Image 4.117

Regional Law Schools & Lawyer Income http://bit.ly/czzzuL
9:47 AM Mar 29th via Facebook

STEP 3: PARTICIPATE

After connecting with legal professionals and gathering information from their tweets, you will then participate on Twitter. There are at least 11 ways you can participate on Twitter.

(1) Tweet about your job search

Let your followers know you are looking for a full-time position or clerk-ship/internship. Image 4.118 contains a tweet from a first-year law student who is looking for a clerkship. The tweet is not directed to anyone specific; anyone reading the student's news feed would see the tweet.

Image 4.118

> Who wants to recommend/give this fabulous, hardworking, conscientious 1L a summer legal internship/clerkship???
>
> about 17 hours ago via web

You can include a link to your LinkedIn profile in your tweet so potential employers can learn more about your background and experience. Image 4.119 contains a tweet from Jerry Levine, a tech savvy attorney seeking a new associate position. Jerry specified his interests and directed readers to his LinkedIn profile to learn more about his background and experience.

Image 4.119

> Is your #law #firm looking for a new #associate? 3 yrs exp (inc. clerkship). Interests: #gaming #media #tech. LinkedIn: http://j.mp /9w4ZgK
>
> 7:28 AM Jun 4th via web

Compare the tweets in Images 4.118 and 4.119 to the example in Image 4.120 where Rachel London, a law student at Brooklyn Law School, directed her tweet to @bunyan71, another Twitter user and the music manager known for his association with hip hop artists Eminem, Three 6 Mafia, The Knux, and pop punk band Blink-182.[41] The tweet in Image 4.120 is an **@reply** or **mention**; it is directed to another Twitter user, @bunyan71, because Rachel loves Eminem and would love to work for his manager. When @bunyan71 checks his @replies, he'll see the following tweet. Thus, using the @reply captures another user's attention. The tweet is visible to Rachel's other followers as well.

Image 4.120

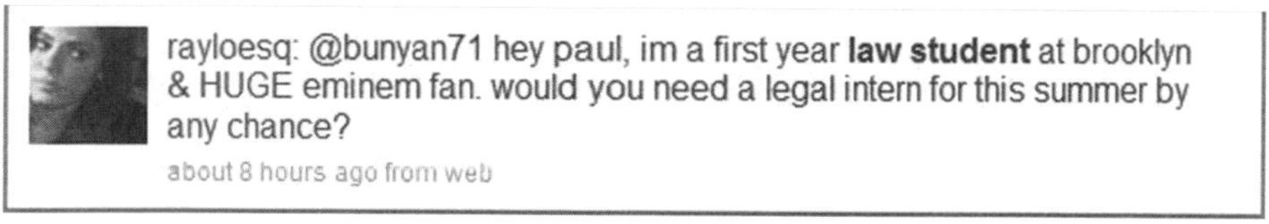

rayloesq: @bunyan71 hey paul, im a first year **law student** at brooklyn & HUGE eminem fan. would you need a legal intern for this summer by any chance?

about 8 hours ago from web

Checking @replies/mentions

To check your @replies, click on @username in the profile section of your Twitter home page. For example, I would click on **@aellislegal** in Image 4.120(a), to see:

1. What other users have said to me;
2. What other users have said about me; and
3. Manual retweets about me.

IMAGE 4.120(a)

The tweet in Image 4.121 is another @reply. Note that the tweets in Images 4.120 and 4.121 are both @replies targeted to specific users and specific areas of the law. While you don't want to preclude opportunities, it does help to have a focus in your job search; it shows a sincere interest rather than a desperate plea for *any* job.

Image 4.121

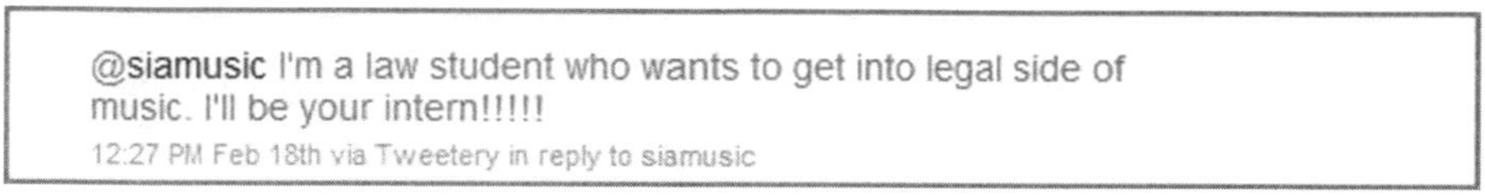

> @siamusic I'm a law student who wants to get into legal side of music. I'll be your intern!!!!!
> 12:27 PM Feb 18th via Tweetery in reply to siamusic

(2) Tweet about your practice

Practicing attorneys who don't want to risk losing their current jobs may not want to tweet about their job search. However, they can tweet about their practice and area of expertise without revealing confidential client or job search information. If done consistently, tweets about your practice or expertise market you to other legal professionals on Twitter, and they may approach you about other career opportunities.

For example, the tweets in Images 4.122 through 4.124 are from Todd Smith, an Austin attorney, over a three-day period. You can infer from the tweets that Todd focuses on appellate law. The tweets market Todd's area of expertise and may lead potential clients or employers to contact Todd if they were impressed with his tweets. You want to be in demand—by clients and potential employers. The contents of your tweets can lead to such demand.

Image 4.122

Really enjoy the consulting work I do for trial lawyers. Love being able to make a difference in a case before an appeal.
11:23 AM Jun 4th via Ping.fm

Image 4.123

Heading to annual SCOTX Briefing & Staff Attorney Breakfast. Always fun to catch up with current and former justices, staff, and clerks.
7:49 AM Jun 5th via Ping.fm

Image 4.124

Lineup finalized for SBOT Appellate Section seminar geared toward in-house counsel. E-brochure at http://bit.ly/bNM7I8.
1:00 PM Jun 3rd via TweetDeck

(3) Share Links to Articles/Blog Posts

As shown in Image 4.124 above, you can share links to articles, blogs, or brochures in your tweets to market yourself. Images 4.125 and 4.126 are additional examples of attorneys sharing their own blog posts on Twitter.

Image 4.125 – User's Blog Post

New post: My Take on American Needle v. NFL http://bit.ly/aIqTfQ (more personal than substantive) #antitrust #law #scotus
12:16 PM May 24th via TweetDeck

Image 4.126 – User's Blog Post

How Will Proposed New Taxes On S Corporation Shareholders Affect... http://lnkd.in/sdXKdt
1:02 PM Jun 6th via LinkedIn

You can also share articles mentioning or quoting you or your firm, as shown in Images 4.127 and 4.128.

Image 4.127 – Quoting Attorney

Rich Vetstein quoted in tomorrow's Banker Tradesman re. new
Fannie last minute credit report rules http://ow.ly/1UH6t
8:50 AM Jun 6th via HootSuite

Image 4.128 – Mentioning Firm

King & Spalding Establishes Office in
Geneva http://bit.ly/ajBAgs
about 4 hours ago via TweetDeck

Or, you can share links about the legal profession, your practice area, or
current events, as shown in Images 4.129 through 4.131.

Image 4.129 – Legal Profession

http://ow.ly/2iSoB 2011 Looking Better for Summer Associates
#lawstudent #lawschool

Image 4.130 – Practice Area

Chapter 11 news. Bankruptcy Judge Keeps Aug. 4 As Date For
Auction Of MLB Rangers: SportsBusiness Daily (subscript...
http://bit.ly/92evsx
1:44 PM Jul 23rd via twitterfeed

Image 4.131 – Current Events

Facebook Reaches 500 Million Users - http://bit.ly/a2ezRd
9:06 AM Jul 19th via TweetDeck

If you are a law student, you can also share news and information about your
law school. In Image 4.132, Luke Gilman, a May 2010 graduate of the University
of Houston Law Center, shared an article about the law school's Immigration
Clinic winning a unanimous Supreme Court decision.

Image 4.132 – Law School News

> @UHLAW Immigration Clinic earns unanimous decision from U.S.
> Supreme Court on deportation case. http://tinyurl.com/2fqopzm
> Monday, June 14, 2010 5:22:26 PM via Twitterrific

Short URLs: Note that the links in Images 4.127 through 4.132 are from bit.ly, ow.ly, or tinyurl.com. Bit.ly, ow.ly, and tinyurl.com are examples of URL shortening services which reduce the length of a web link or URL. You want to reduce URLs on Twitter because you are only allowed 140 characters for your entire tweet.

To reduce a URL, go to the bit.ly, ow.ly, or tinyurl.com site and paste a link to your original URL. The shortening services generate a short URL which you may use in Twitter or other documents.

For example:

http://bit.ly/dfGVX7

instead of

http://www.6psbig3.com/blog/index.php/2010/06/13/
law-school-career-offices-on-facebook-twitter/

(4) Retweet

At some point, you have probably forwarded an e-mail. When you receive an e-mail with an article attached from a friend that is relevant to wider group of friends, you forward the article. You can also forward tweets you find helpful by retweeting them.

There are two ways to retweet:

1.   Auto retweet; and
2.   Manual retweet.

Auto Retweet

When you want to retweet a tweet, hover your mouse over the lower right corner of the tweet until you see the words reply and retweet.

Image 4.133

Click on Retweet, and a new box will appear asking you to confirm that you wish to retweet the tweet.

Image 4.134

Once you retweet a tweet, the tweet appears in your Twitter stream for all of your followers to see. However, credit is given to the person who posted the original tweet. In Image 4.135, you see the name of the person who posted the original tweet next to the tweet. The box with up and down arrows indicates the tweet was retweeted.

Image 4.135

Manual Retweet

Another way to retweet is to copy and paste another user's tweet and add "RT" plus the user's username at the beginning of the tweet. For example, if I want to retweet the following tweet by @hmriskgroup about an event, I will first copy the tweet.

Image 4.136

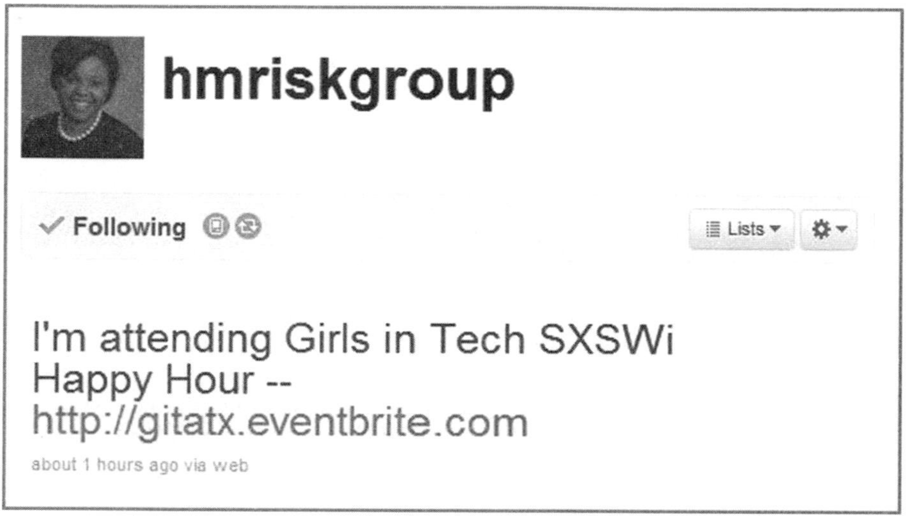

Then, paste the tweet in the "what's happening?" box in Image 4.137.

Image 4.137

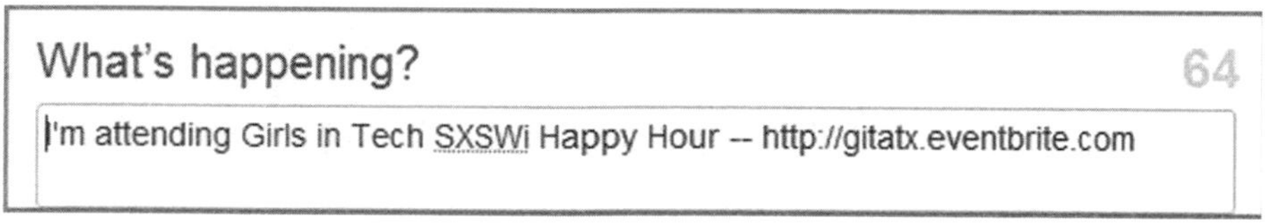

Before updating, add "RT" and the username of the person who posted the original tweet—@hmriskgroup.

Image 4.138

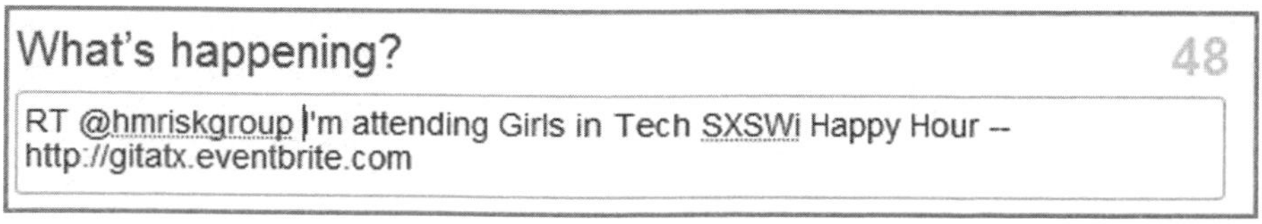

Then, click update, and your tweet appears, as shown in Image 4.139.

Image 4.139

RT @hmriskgroup I'm attending Girls
in Tech SXSWi Happy Hour --
http://gitatx.eventbrite.com

less than a minute ago via web

Reason for Manual Retweeting

Why would you go through the steps to copy, paste, and add RT + username? If you want to add a comment to the original tweet—perhaps your thought or reaction to the tweet—you would have to use the second method. At this time, you can't add your own comment to auto retweets.

For example, in Image 4.140, I retweeted another user's tweet about the increased hiring of social media directors by corporations. Before I retweeted the link to the article, I added my own comments to direct social savvy, job-seeking lawyers to the article.

Image 4.140

JOB OPP for social savvy law grads: RT @kcgrammargirl:
corporate America rushing to hire SM directors http://bit.ly/bKuFVn

8:55 AM Jul 19th via TweetDeck

Benefit of Retweeting

Users can check to see when other users retweet their tweets. Thus, re-tweeting is another way to get or remain on someone's radar screen. Retweeting is especially helpful if you want someone who is not following you to notice you.

(5) Respond to @replies/Mentions, Retweets

One easy way to engage with your followers is to see who is talking to you and respond accordingly. Other users might have mentioned you in a tweet, directed a question to you, or commented on something you previously tweeted.

<u>Checking @replies/mentions, retweets</u>

To check your @replies, click on @username in the profile section of your Twitter home page. For example, I would click on **@aellislegal** in Image 4.120(a), to see:

1. What other users have said to me;
2. What other users have said about me; and
3. *Manual retweets* about me.

Image 4.120 (a)

To check your **auto retweets**, click on the Retweets link in the profile section of your Twitter home page, as shown in Image 4.120 (a).

If you see a question directed to you, engage with the user by responding. For example, in Image 4.141, Ashley Clark, a law student at Elon University School of Law, tweeted a question about jury consultants. Ashley directed the question to me. I noticed the question when I checked my @replies/mentions, and I engaged by responding.

Image 4.141

ashleyc433 @aellislegal are you familiar with any jury selection consultants by chance? my office is looking to get in touch and price a few. thanks!
about 20 hours ago via web

(6) Comment on Other Users' Links

You can engage by commenting on a link posted by another user. For example, in Image 4.142, I shared a link to a video about associate business development.

Image 4.142

YOUNG LAWYERS/LAW STUDENTS: a must see video re Associate Business Development (via @riskin) http://youtu.be /vtuXGprQWyA
12:11 PM Jun 6th via TweetDeck

One of my followers, @jkhoey, watched the video and engaged by sharing her thoughts about the video.

Image 4.143

jkhoey @aellislegal start building those rel'shps early and building those BD muscles!!!
12:16 PM Jun 6th via UberTwitter in reply to aellislegal

(7) Ask Job Search Questions

One form of engagement that is a little bolder than a response to another user is to ask your own questions. Ask questions about your job search. For example, the tweets in Image 4.144 are from Sohana Barot, a law student at Rutgers School of Law-Camden, who asked for advice about her interview with a bankruptcy judge.

Image 4.144

> Nervous for my interview tomorrow!! Any advice from the #lawschool people? It's with a bankruptcy judge
> 6:59 PM Feb 4th from Echofon
>
> Interview Friday with Federal Bankruptcy Judge
> 12:32 PM Feb 3rd from Echofon

In Image 4.145, Jason Tenenbaum, a law student at Hofstra University School of Law, tweeted a question about which blogs to follow to learn more about his desired area of practice.

Image 4.145

> Can anyone suggest some good Labor & Employment law blogs to follow. 2L interested in the field.
> about 20 hours ago via Socialite.app

In Image 4.146 Laura McWilliams, a law student at Suffolk Law, asked whether it was proper to include her blog on her resume. As you can see in Images 4.147 through 4.152, Laura's question generated eight replies, and the majority favored including the blog on the resume.

Image 4.146 - Question by Laura McWilliams,
Law Student at Suffolk Law:

lawyer/ law student friends: I want to work in non-profit. Is my blog inappropriate for resume? http://lauramcwilliams.wordpress.com/ #panic

12 minutes ago via web

Images 4.147 through 4.152 – Responses:

Image 4.147

@lauramclaura I feel like a blog is always inappropriate unless you are looking for a job as a blogger

19 minutes ago via web

Image 4.148

@lauramclaura I don't think so - shows your writing skills, a "product" you market in your job search; do you link to it on LI profile?

19 minutes ago via web in reply to lauramclaura

Image 4.149

@lauramclaura Convo starter + sets you apart, gives interviewer something to remember

14 minutes ago via web in reply to lauramclaura

Image 4.150

@lauramclaura Your blog is creative and expresses your personal worldview and law school experience. Put it below name/address /email/phone

about 13 hours ago via UberTwitter in reply to lauramclaura

Image 4.151

@lauramclaura It's a bad idea to put it on your resumé.

about 13 hours ago via Tweetie in reply to lauramclaura

Image 4.152

@lauramclaura, even though I am sure we don't hold the same opinion on politics or a few other things, I think its good...

about 12 hours ago via web

@lauramclaura also, I like ur blog, good stuff & to be honest I like your viewpoints and I admire ur honesty in them

about 12 hours ago via web in reply to lauramclaura

@lauramclaura I agree with @btannebaum, 1 thing I've learned, with any post or public opinion some will agree & sum won't,can't plese every1

about 12 hours ago via web in reply to lauramclaura

(8) Participate in #LawJobChat

A Twitter chat is an organized group discussion focused on a particular topic at a particular time. You will find organized chats for bloggers, writers, foodies, pharmaceutical professionals, small business owners, journalists, and healthcare organizations.

LawJobChat is the only Twitter chat for job-seeking lawyers. You can ask questions about your legal job search or career and receive feedback from practicing attorneys, law firm recruiters, law school career counselors, and career experts across the country. Moreover, you will begin to build relationships through your interactions with the legal community on LawJobChat.

LawJobChat occurs on the last Thursday of each month from 9:00 PM to 10:00 PM Eastern.

Visit www.twitter.com/lawjobchat to view transcripts of past chats or to find out more information about participating in future chats.

Other Twitter Chats

While LawJobChat is the only Twitter Chat focused on the legal job search, it is not the only Twitter Chat available. There are hundreds of Twitter Chats on a variety of topics. The following link contains a list and more information about all Twitter Chats:

http://bit.ly/aahSis

You'll find Twitter Chats to help you in business development, professional development, and your job search. For example, if you are a law student or a young lawyer, you may find the following three Twitter Chats interesting:

1. *#GenYChat*: focuses on engaging GenY'ers with GenX'ers and Baby Boomers - Wednesdays at 9 PM Eastern.
2. *#u30pro*: focuses on issues and trends surrounding young professionals - Thursdays at 8 PM Eastern.
3. *#jobhuntchat*: focuses on topics for job seekers in general, not specific to the legal field but still helpful – Mondays at 10 PM Eastern.

(9) Participate in Conference Tweets

Another engaging feature of Twitter is the ability to tweet from live conferences or events and respond to such tweets. Conference organizers designate a conference hashtag (# plus some logical abbreviation); attendees tweet information from conference sessions and place the designated hashtag at the beginning or end of their tweet, as shown in Image 4.153.

Image 4.153

> #LawStudents sm firm atty candidates need to be great writer, people skills, involved in community, enthusiasm for work #nalp10

Tweeting from conferences is an effective conversation starter because non-attendees following the conference tweets frequently ask questions, comment, or retweet the information.

If you aren't attending a conference, you can engage in conference discussions by following tweets and then asking questions, commenting, or retweeting.

(10) Socialize

Remember that professional connections form from common connections and interests so tweet about non-legal topics. Start a conversation about current events, sports, a movie, or a restaurant, as shown in Images 4.154 and 4.155.

Image 4.154

What do you think, Twitterverse, will the #nba #finals go 7?

15 minutes ago via TweetDeck

Image 4.155

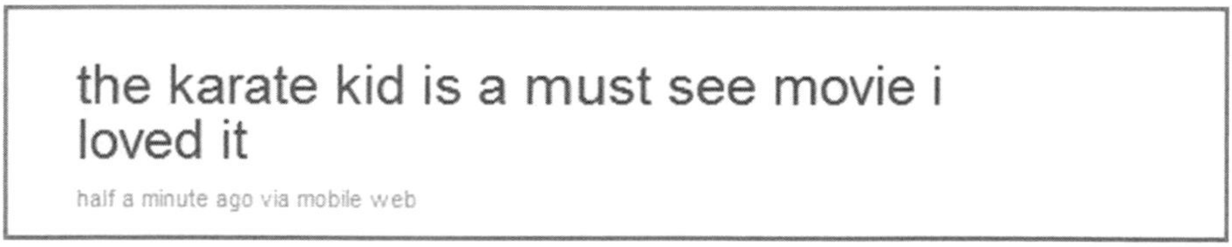

the karate kid is a must see movie i loved it

half a minute ago via mobile web

(11) Connect Offline

After you connect and engage with new contacts, certain contacts will grow into your professional network. You'll become friends with others in the legal industry, local followers from your city, or people who share a similar hobby or interest.

To solidify the relationships with your new contacts, connect offline. After you've engaged with someone 6-8 times online, pick up the phone and have a conversation. If you live in the same town, meet for coffee. When you visit another user's city, offer to meet for coffee or a meal during your visit. Images 4.156 and 4.157 provide examples of legal professionals using Twitter to arrange offline meetings.

Image 4.156

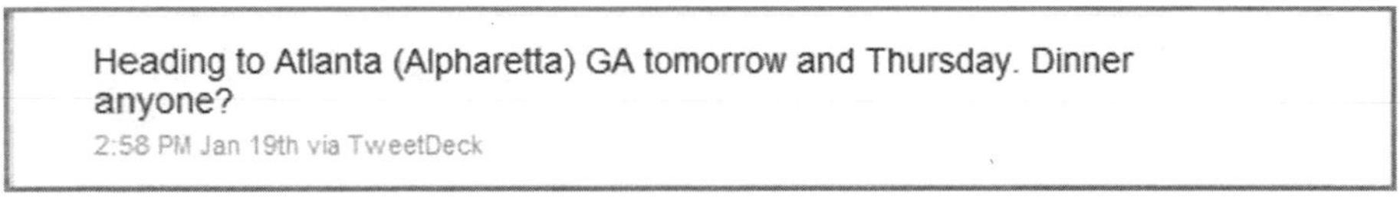

Heading to Atlanta (Alpharetta) GA tomorrow and Thursday. Dinner anyone?

2:58 PM Jan 19th via TweetDeck

Image 4.157

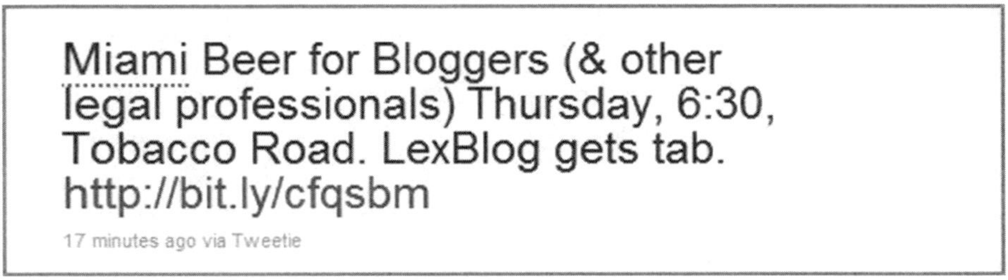

Miami Beer for Bloggers (& other legal professionals) Thursday, 6:30, Tobacco Road. LexBlog gets tab. http://bit.ly/cfqsbm

17 minutes ago via Tweetie

Find a tweetup in your town and attend. Use a third-party application like Twtvite (www.twtvite.com), as shown in Image 4.158, to find a tweetup.

Image 4.158

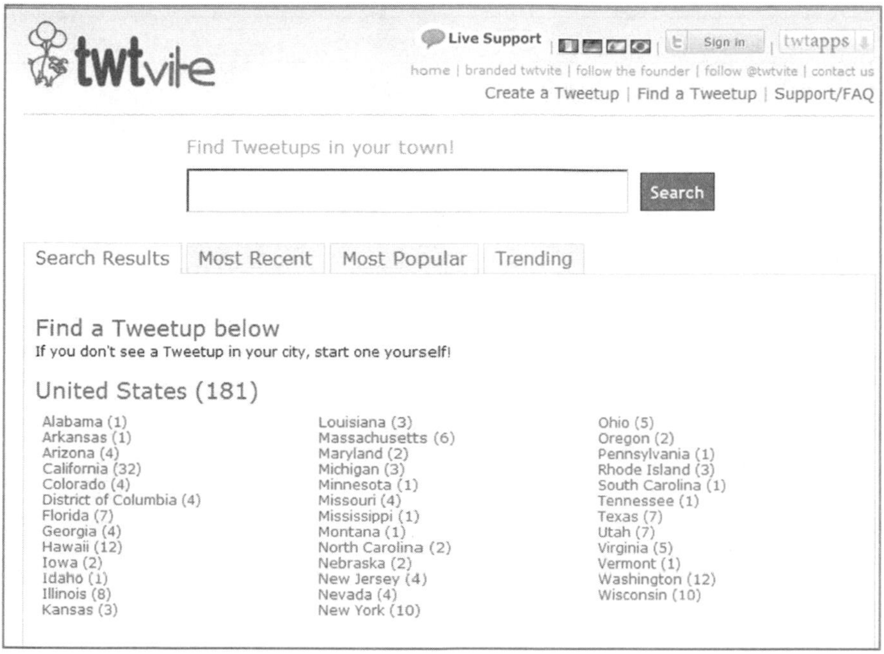

Or, attend a Tweetup held in connection with a conference. As shown in Image 4.159, the State Bar of Texas held a Tweet & Greet in connection with its 2010 annual conference which gave attorneys who tweet an opportunity to meet in person.

Image 4.159

First-ever State Bar of Texas Tweet and Greet is underway
#sbot10 http://tweetphoto.com/26562758
6:06 PM Jun 10th via TweetDeck

POINTS – PERFORMANCE (FACEBOOK)

Connect	Assimilate	Participate
Individual Profile Page		
Who: Level of Scrutiny • Strict Scrutiny - Home Invitation Rule (Majority View)	1. Status Updates 2. Wall Posts & Notes 3. Events in News Feed 4. BranchOut 5. Marketplace	Update Status 1. Personal Updates 2. Job Search Updates 3. Market Expertise in Status Updates 4. Tagged Friends in Status Updates
How: 6 Methods 1. E-mail Contacts 2. Facebook Suggestions 3. Search for People 4. News Feed 5. Friend Suggestions 6. Pages & Groups		Share/Post Professional Links 1. Practice Area Articles/Blogs 2. Legal News 3. Tag & Share
		Comment 1. Note After Networking 2. Good Luck on Professional Achievements 3. Congrats on Personal Achievements 4. Happy Birthdays! 5. Thumbs Up
Fan Page or Group		
Who: Level of Scrutiny – Rational Basis How: 6 Methods 1. Specific Search 2. Invitations 3. News Feed Notifications 4. Appendix A (law school career offices) 5. Appendix B (law firm recruiting/career departments) 6. Law Firm Facebook Pages 7. Key Word Search	1. Practice Area Insight 2. Job Postings 3. Interview Prep 4. Community Pages	1. Comment 2. Thumbs Up

POINTS – PERFORMANCE (LINKEDIN)

Connect	Assimilate	Participate

Who: Level of Scrutiny
 	
• Intermediate Scrutiny - Business Card Rule
	Searches
	
	1. Company Search → follow companies
	2. People Search
	3. Job Search
	4. Group Search
		Status Updates
		
		• Update Status
		
		   • 1x per week
		   • Variety
		
		• Comment on Others' Updates
		
		   • Comment
		   • Like
		   • Share

How: Grow 1ˢᵗ Degree Connections
 	
1. Classmates
2. Colleagues
3. Web-based e-mail
4. E-mail Applications
5. Individual E-mail
6. Existing LinkedIn Users
 	
  a. Business Card Rule
  b. Network Updates
  c. People You May Know
	News Feed
	
	1. Status Updates
	2. Profile Updates
	3. Events
	4. Application Updates
	5. Legal Updates by JD Supra
		Engage with Groups
		
		• Discussion
		• News

Write Introductions to 1ˢᵗ Degree Contacts		**Update Profile Information**
Ask for Introductions to 2ⁿᵈ and 3ʳᵈ Degree Contacts		**LinkedIn Message v. E-mail**

POINTS – PERFORMANCE (TWITTER)

Connect	Assimilate	Participate

Who: Level of Scrutiny
 	
• Minimum (Rational Basis) Scrutiny
• Cocktail Party Rule
	Job Opportunities
	
	• Specific Opportunities
	
	   • Contacts' Tweets
	   • Twitter Search
	   • TwitJobSearch. com
	
	• Potential Opportunities
		Share
		
		• Tweet About Job Search
		• Tweet About Practice
		• Share Links
		• Retweet

How: Find Legal Professionals
 	
• Published Listings
 	
   • AmLawTweeple
   • JD Supra List
   • TX Lawyers to Follow
   • MN Legal Professionals
   • LexTweet
   • Legal Birds
   • Tweet Law
   • Corporate & Securities Litigators
   • CLE Resources
   • Law School Career Services
   • 22 Tweets
	Interview Prep
	
	• Firm Search
	• Attorney Search
	• Practice Area Search
		Engage
		
		• Respond to @ replies/mentions
		• Comment on other users' links
		• Ask job search questions
		• Participate in #LawJobChat
		• Participate in conference tweets
		• Socialize

• Search Tools
 	
    • Find People
    • Tweep Search
    • Twitter Search
 	
• Other Users
 	
    • Conversations
    • Follow Fridays
    • Twitter Lists
 	
• Job Boards
 	
    • See Appendix B
 	
• Directories		

	Career Advancement
	
	• Media Opportunities
	• Writing/Speaking
	  Opportunities
	• Conference
	  Opportunities
	• News &
	  Developments
		Meet

PART 3

POLISH YOUR PERFORMANCE

The final part of the 6Ps system consists of steps to help you polish your performance and increase your chances of getting hired using the Big 3 social networking sites. The final components include:

1. Practice (Chapter 5)
2. Protocol (Chapter 6)

Chapter 5 examines how you can efficiently perform your job search using the Big 3 sites. You'll learn how to block out a set time in your daily routine for your Big 3 activities. You'll also learn how to perform certain activities in blocks to prevent distractions from the volume of information on the Big 3 sites. Finally, you'll learn about a variety of tools that can measure your performance on the Big 3 sites and receive a sample schedule to follow for efficiency.

Chapter 6 consists of pinstripes and pearls. Pinstripes are the patterns of desired behavior you should exhibit on the Big 3 sites. And, pearls are your accessories—ideas to implement to increase your chances of getting hired by standing out from your competitors.

CHAPTER 5

Practice

IF you are not using the Big 3 social networking sites in your job search, perhaps you avoid them because you assume they are a waste of time. While they can be a waste of time if you get distracted, they can also be valuable tools and lead to jobs if you use your time efficiently.

How can you use the Big 3 social networking sites efficiently? There are three required steps:

1. Block
2. Measure
3. Practice, practice, practice

BLOCK

In general, blocking requires allocating certain blocks of time for designated tasks. During that block, you perform *only* the assigned task—nothing else.

I first practiced time blocking when I started recruiting where my typical morning looked something like Table 5.1.

Table 5.1 – Time Blocking in Recruiting

Time	Activity
8:00 – 9:00 AM	Read, return e-mails
9:00 – 10:00 AM	15 recruiting calls for Position A
10:00 a.m. – 11:00 AM	Market Candidate B to 8 firms

As you can see from Table 5.1, I focused on one task during each block of time. It will help if you do this to incorporate social networking into your daily routine.

Time Block

You must block out the time you plan to spend performing your job search on the Big 3 sites. Remember from the Premise that social networking is simply one piece of the job search campaign. The total amount of time per day you allocate to your job search depends on the urgency of your job search. If you decide to spend one hour per day on job search activities, social networking is only one task to perform in your daily hour of job search activities. You may wish to spend 20 minutes per day on the Big 3 sites, 20 minutes per day searching job boards, and 20 minutes per day calling or e-mailing potential employers. Your time blocking for your job search might resemble Table 5.2.

Table 5.2 – Time Blocking in Job Search

Time	Activity
6:00-6:20 AM	Social Networking (the BIG 3)
12:00-12:20 PM	Phone calls/e-mails
7:00-7:20 PM	Job Search Boards

Consider setting a timer and refraining from other activities during each block of time. For example, don't answer your phone or review e-mails during the block devoted to your social networking activities.

> **Time Blocking Software – iFocus:** If you don't want to set a timer, there are software programs to time your activities. Several law students recently recommended iFocus to me. iFocus tracks how much time you spend on certain online activities and allows you to set limits on how much time to spend on certain sites.

Information/Activity Block

As you learned in Chapter 4, there is a lot of information to assimilate from the Big 3 sites. While most of the information will be valuable to your job search, other information may be an unnecessary distraction—especially on Facebook where more personal information is shared.

Accordingly, I recommend assimilating certain information in blocks so you can prioritize which information is more helpful for your job search. Consider using the following tools to help you assimilate information efficiently on Facebook, LinkedIn, and Twitter.

(1) The Big 3

Mobile Applications for Status Updates

Mobile applications improve your social networking efficiency and are available for all of the Big 3 sites. Many job seekers set aside a time to use social networking from their computer each day and then update their status or read others' status updates throughout the day from their mobile applications. The mobile applications allow job seekers to access the networks in down-time, such as waiting for an appointment.

(2) Facebook

The volume of information in your Facebook news feed can overwhelm you, especially if you have a large number of Facebook friends. For example, in the news feed in Image 5.1, Facebook alerts me when my friends:

1. become friends with other people
2. communicate with mutual friends
3. update their status
4. post links to articles or blogs
5. upload video or pictures
6. play the various Facebook games

Image 5.1

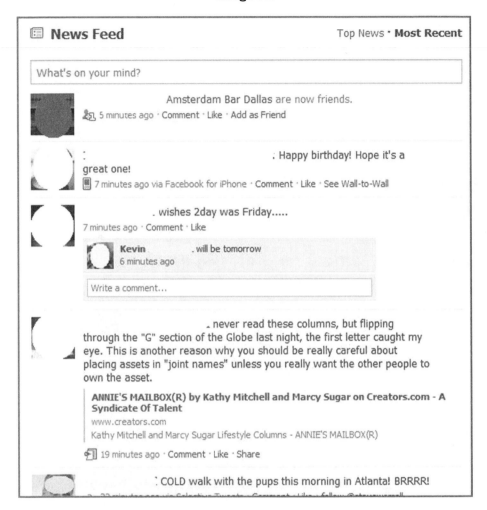

It's too easy to get distracted if you review all of this information at once. For example, while reviewing status updates you see that your friend Patti posted 167 pictures from Wendy's wedding last weekend. You then spend 20 minutes looking at these pictures when you actually just jumped on Facebook to review status updates and articles.

I recommend using the following Facebook tools so you can focus first on job search related information. Then, review all other Facebook information, if you wish, in your personal time—not during the block of time devoted to using social networking in your job search.

Lists

The Facebook List feature, discussed in Chapter 3 in connection with privacy settings, helps you place your Facebook friends into lists. You can also place the fan pages you "like" into lists. For example, you may place all law school career office pages in one list and all law firm pages in one list. Then, you can review updates by list. I recommend creating lists for at least the following: lawyer friends, law school career services pages, law firm pages, and professional organization pages. Then, review updates from these groups when performing your social networking time block dedicated to your job search.

Read all lawyer friends' status updates, updates that might contain job search information, at once rather than sifting through the news feed. Then, review career related pages updates, law firm page updates, and organization updates. The sample schedule in **Appendix E** incorporates this list concept.

Hidden Activities

Another potential nuisance in your Facebook news feed involves the game updates like Farmville, Mafia Wars, and Bejeweled. Do you really care that your friend Mark found a sad Ugly Duckling on his farm in FarmVille? And, how does that help your job search?

You can hide the game updates and prevent them from clogging your news feed:

* Go to a post in your news feed that contains a Farmville, Mafia War, or Bejeweled update.

Image 5.2

- Hover your mouse over the top right corner of a game update and the **"Hide"** button will appear.

Image 5.3

- Click Hide to either hide all updates for that particular Facebook game (Farmville) or to hide the person entirely. I chose to hide only the game because I wanted to see this person's other updates.

Image 5.4

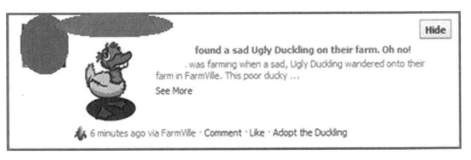

(3) LinkedIn

Initially, LinkedIn was the least overwhelming of the Big 3 because its news feed content was grouped by categories of information. For example, all status updates appeared together, then new connection updates appeared, then application updates, and so forth. For whatever reason, LinkedIn removed the categories in July 2010, so all updates now appear together in your news feed. As you can see in Image 5.5, the LinkedIn news feed now looks more like the Facebook news feed. Status updates, connection updates, and company updates are mixed together, so it takes more time for users to focus on one category of information.

Image 5.5

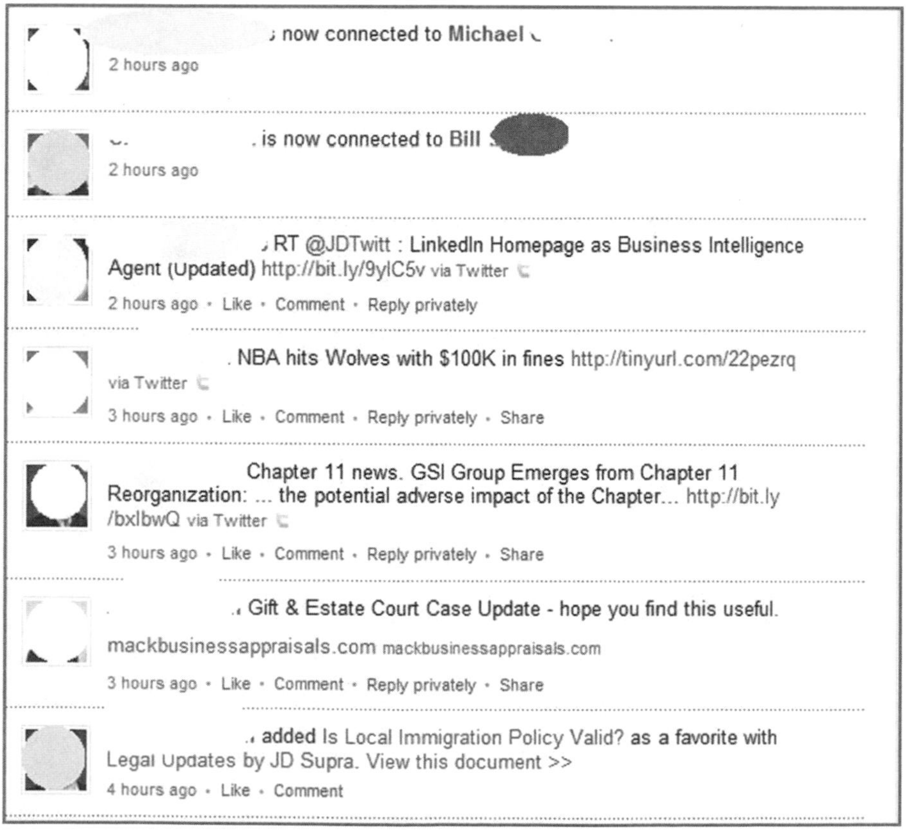

To view the LinkedIn updates by activity, or category, follow these steps:

1. Scroll through your cluttered updates under **Network Activity**.
2. At the end of your updates (but before you reach **Group Updates**), click on **See more Network Updates**.

Image 5.6

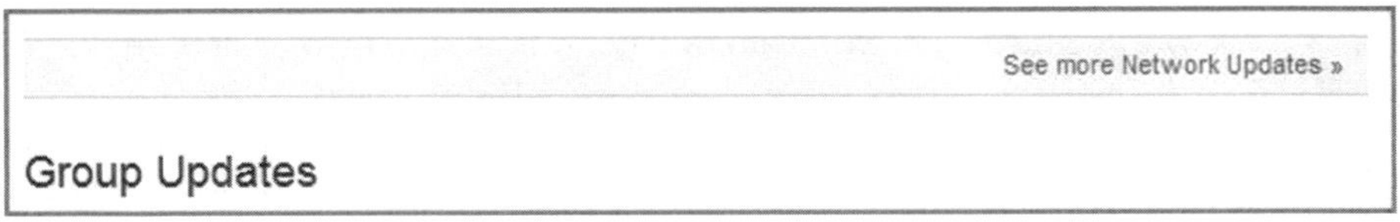

3. Notice the menu of choices—you can view updates by category of information or connection.

Image 5.7

4. Click on **Category View** to see your updates by category or activity– the way they previously appeared in your news feed. By viewing updates in categories, you can view certain updates, like status updates that may contain job leads, and skim over all other updates.

Image 5.8

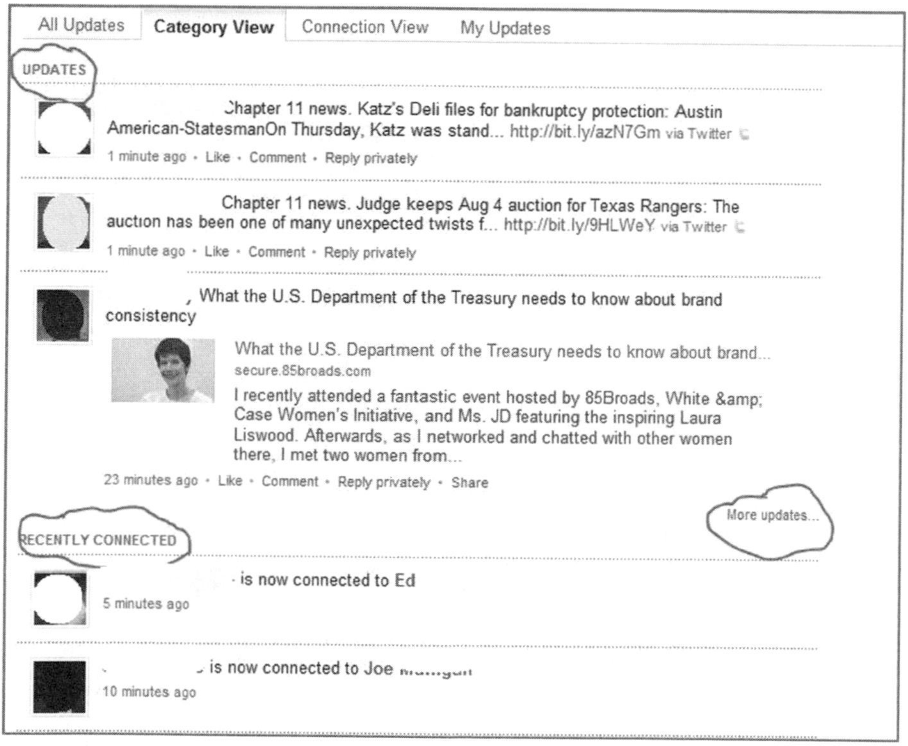

(4) Twitter

Twitter may overwhelm you initially because of the volume of information in your news feed. The people you follow will probably tweet multiple times throughout a day. Some people tweet more than 20 times a day. If you follow 500 people on Twitter and they in turn tweet at the same level, that's 10,000 tweets in one day. No one has time to review all 10,000 tweets. First, realize that whether you follow 50 people or 500, you cannot possibly review every tweet in your news feed. Second, try the following two tools to manage the information in your news feed and make sure you do review the important information for your job search.

Lists

The Twitter Lists are similar to the Facebook Friends Lists. You can place the people you follow into lists and then read tweets on a list-by-list basis. For example, you might have lists for law students, law school career services, law firms, favorite people, and non-legal people. Reading all tweets in each group allows you to focus your attention and ignore the noise and other distractions in your news feed.

Favorites

One time-consuming feature of Twitter is that many tweets contain links to articles or blog posts. While many of these links contain helpful information for job seekers, you may not have time to read all articles and blogs while reviewing Twitter updates, and, I don't recommend it. I think the articles and blogs comprise a separate activity requiring dedicated time for reviewing all articles at once.

I use the Favorite option to tag tweets with articles or blogs that sound interesting. This is essentially a bookmark. Then, I go back and read all articles and blogs at once—usually at night or over the weekend—when I have more time. The sample schedule in **Appendix E** incorporates this concept.

To "favorite" a tweet, hover your mouse over the top right corner of a tweet until a star appears. Then, click on the star.

Image 5.9

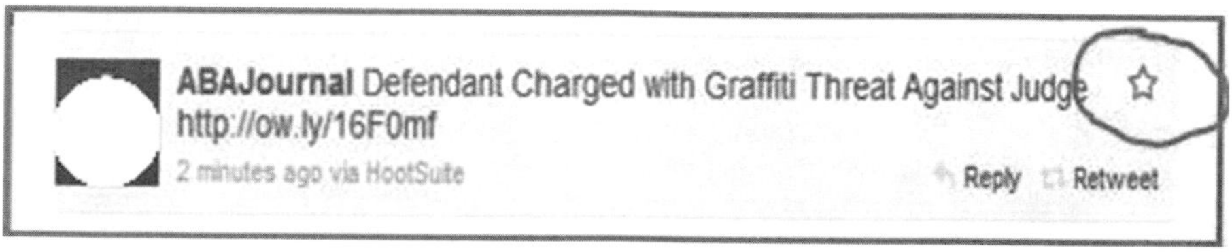

When you are ready to read the articles and blogs you have saved or added to your favorites, click on **Favorites** from the menu in the upper right corner of your Twitter home page, as shown in Image 5.10.

Image 5.10

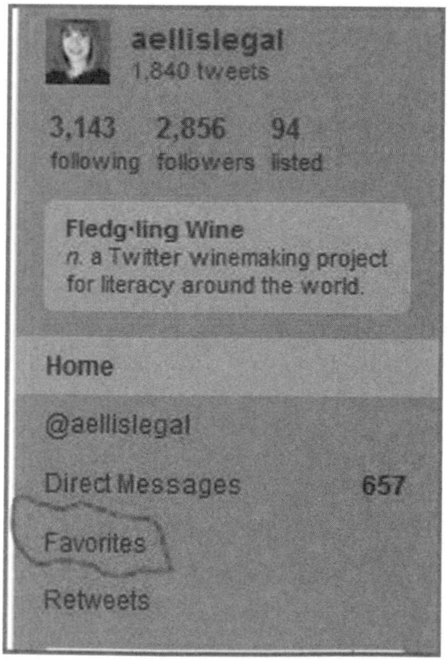

Twitter displays the tweets you added to Favorites in reverse chronological order so the most recent tweets appear first, as shown in Image 5.11.

Image 5.11

Your Favorites
jasonalba The Pregnant Job Search http://bit.ly/a3msO9 (please weigh in - I'm not the most qualified to write this post :p) 11 minutes ago via TweetMeme
lawschoolguide Blog post: Having a Child While in Law School: There's an interesting discussion over at Wish I Would Have Known r... http://bit.ly/cwUnUn 14 minutes ago via twitterfeed
Twitter_Tips Getting Past the Oprah Barrier on Twitter http://j.mp /cKV56V 26 minutes ago via API
tmj_hou_legal ConocoPhillips: Litigation Support Legal Specialist (HOUSTON, TX) http://bit.ly/9LLxJW #Jobs #TweetMyJOBS about 2 hours ago via API
richards1000 Lawyers and Innovation: An Uneasy Alliance	Freelance Law Firm http://ow.ly/1pbPJq (via @lisadimonte) about 12 hours ago via Tweetie
ChristianGAdams 8 Ways To Get More Work From Existing Clients http://bit.ly/cYqhvB about 12 hours ago via twitterfeed
j2bmarketing RT @BruceBixler49: Should You List Your LinkedIn or Twitter Address on Your Resume? http://shar.es/aLNU6 about 13 hours ago via HootSuite
allisonshields Link to today's blogtalk radio show re: social media: http://bit.ly/dA5tk2

If you want to remove a tweet from Favorites after reading the article, click the yellow star next to the tweet to remove the tweet from your Favorites.

Practice Pointer

Most mobile devices have applications to access Twitter. From those applications, you can add tweets to your Favorites. This is how I spend much of my time using Twitter. I read updates on my phone during my "downtime"—in between meetings, walking down the hall, waiting for appointments, etc. I don't open each link, though. I add them to favorites and then read some or all of them over the weekend.

Third-Party Applications

There are third-party applications you can download to help manage your activities as well—most are Twitter specific but some aggregate your activity on all Big 3 social networking sites. Three popular third-party applications include:

Tweet Deck (www.tweetdeck.com)

HootSuite (www.hootsuite.com)

Seesmic (www.seesmic.com)

MEASURE

The second step to performing efficiently on the Big 3 sites is to measure your performance. It's easy to determine whether submitting your resume to an advertised position is successful—just look at the response you receive. But, how do you measure your success on the Big 3 social networking sites? Social networking is designed to build relationships, a process which takes time. You will rarely find a job opening, submit your resume, and get hired on the Big 3 sites. Rather, you are more likely to build relationships on the social networking sites over a period of time, and the new relationships will provide job leads or other resources you need to obtain jobs. There are activities you can measure to determine whether you are building and nurturing relationships properly, including:

1. Activity Responses
2. Activity Goals

(1) Activity Responses

You can measure responses to certain activities. When your networks respond, you know that they paid some attention to the content you shared. You can review responses for the following five activities: (1) Short URLs; (2) Comments; (3) Likes; (4) Shares; and (5) Retweets.

Track Clicks on Short URLs

When you share a link to an article or blog post on the Big 3 sites, use a URL shortening service so you can track the number of people who click the link.[42]

The URL shortening service shortens the length of the link you wish to post. For example, compare:

http://www.6psbig3.com/blog/index.php/2010/06/13/law-school-career-offices-on-facebook-twitter/

and

http://bit.ly/dfGVX7

I used bit.ly (www.bit.ly), a URL shortening service to shorten the length of the original blog post. After I share the short link, I can check my bit.ly statistics to see how many people clicked on the link.

The numbers on the far left in Image 5.12 are the number of clicks for the most recent articles I shared using bit.ly and help me gauge interest in the information I shared.

Image 5.12

3 out of 143	Job Search Results - The Chronicle of Higher Education http://chronicle.com/jobSearch?viewSearch=32786681	Info Page+	June 15	Options ⚙
54 out of 54	#LawJobChat « The 6Ps of the BIG 3™ http://www.6psbig3.com/blog/index.php/2010/06/14/lawjobchat/	Info Page+	June 14	Options ⚙
59 out of 60	Law School Career Offices on Facebook & Twitter « The ... http://www.6psbig3.com/blog/index.php/2010/06/13/law-school-career-offices-on-facebook-twitter/	Info Page+	June 13	Options ⚙
4 out of 4	The 'What' List? « Above the Law: A Legal Tabloid - News, ... http://abovethelaw.com/2010/06/the-what-list/#more-21108	Info Page+	June 10	Options ⚙
15 out of 15	Senior Lawyer, Corporate Legal Services (AVP or VP - as app... http://www.linkedin.com/jobs?viewJob=&jobId=985299&fromSearch=1&sik=1275930996583	Info Page+	June 7	Options ⚙
2 out of 4	Austin social media mavens bring expertise to political con... http://austin.bizjournals.com/austin/stories/2010/06/07/story8.html	Info Page+	June 7	Options ⚙
7 out of 7	http://www.mycultivatedlife.com/2010/06/02/20-local-dallas-... http://www.mycultivatedlife.com/2010/06/02/20-local-dallas-favorites/?utm_source=twitterfeed&utm_medium=face...	Info Page+	June 6	Options ⚙
13 out of 314	Lenders foreclose on Four Seasons Resort in Las Colinas	... http://www.dallasnews.com/sharedcontent/dws/dn/latestnews/stories/060210dnbusfourseasons.5e5b123b.html	Info Page+	June 1	Options ⚙

Comments

Look at the comments on your posts or status updates. If four people comment on a link or status update you share on the Big 3 sites, like in Image 5.13 on Facebook and Image 5.14 on LinkedIn, you know you made a memorable impression.

Image 5.13

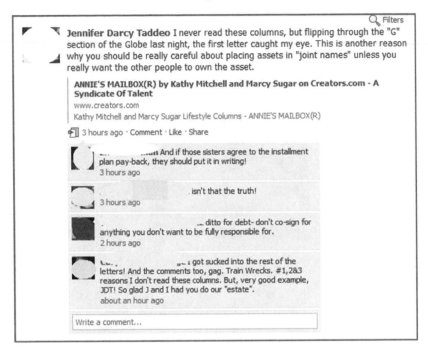

Jennifer Darcy Taddeo I never read these columns, but flipping through the "G" section of the Globe last night, the first letter caught my eye. This is another reason why you should be really careful about placing assets in "joint names" unless you really want the other people to own the asset.

ANNIE'S MAILBOX(R) by Kathy Mitchell and Marcy Sugar on Creators.com - A Syndicate Of Talent
www.creators.com
Kathy Mitchell and Marcy Sugar Lifestyle Columns - ANNIE'S MAILBOX(R)

3 hours ago · Comment · Like · Share

...And if those sisters agree to the installment plan pay-back, they should put it in writing!
3 hours ago

.isn't that the truth!
3 hours ago

ditto for debt- don't co-sign for anything you don't want to be fully responsible for.
2 hours ago

...got sucked into the rest of the letters! And the comments too, gag. Train Wrecks. #1,2&3 reasons I don't read these columns. But, very good example, JDT! So glad J and I had you do our "estate".
about an hour ago

Write a comment...

Image 5.14

Kelly Hoey Off to the ringing the opening bell on the New York Stock Exchange on Monday with Darren Spedale and StartOut!

StartOut - Building and Supporting Gay and Lesbian Entrepreneurship
startout.org

4 days ago · Like · Comment (4) · Reply privately · Share

very cool - congrats Kelly 3 days ago

Congrats Kelly! 3 days ago

Fantastic! 3 days ago

How Fun. Congratulations. 3 days ago

Add a comment...

Likes

Your contacts can "like" or give a thumbs up to a status update or link you share on Facebook (Image 5.15) and LinkedIn (Image 5.16). Receiving a thumbs up or "like" also indicates that your network appreciates your content.

Image 5.15

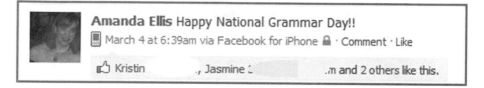

Image 5.16

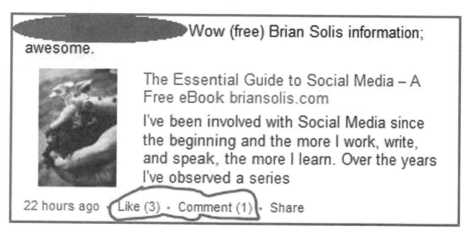

Share

Your contacts on Facebook and LinkedIn can even share links that you post. Sharing a link is stronger than a comment or "like." By sharing your link, your contact not only liked the content you shared, he or she also believed the content was worth sharing with his or her contacts.

Image 5.17 shows a link that my contact, Michael Maslanka, posted on his profile and I, in turn, shared on my profile.

Image 5.17

Amanda Ellis via **Michael P. Maslanka**: WSJ Law Blog posted about the State Bar of Texas Twitter Novel Contest ... Michael P. Maslanka's brilliant idea!

For You: Lawyer Books, Very Short - Law Blog - WSJ
blogs.wsj.com
The Texas Bar has whittled down its list of finalists in its inaugural 140-character novel contest.

May 20 at 6:19pm · Comment · Like · Share

Retweets

If a contact likes the content you share on Twitter, he or she will often retweet your content or tweet, as shown in Image 5.18.

Image 5.18

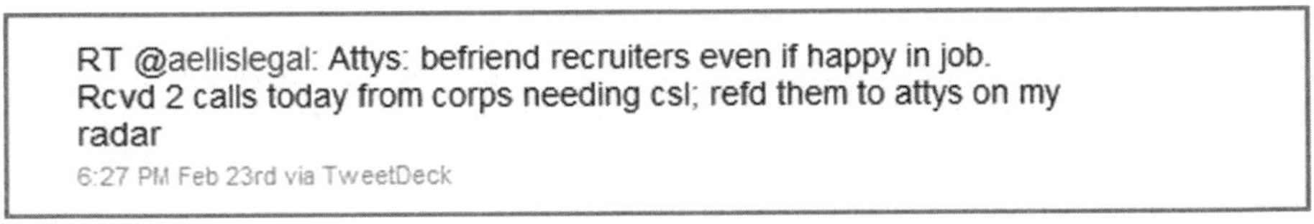

RT @aellislegal: Attys: befriend recruiters even if happy in job. Rcvd 2 calls today from corps needing csl; refd them to attys on my radar
6:27 PM Feb 23rd via TweetDeck

Check your @mentions and retweet tabs for notification of retweets. Chapter 4, page 218, and the Primer address how to check @mentions and retweets.

Image 5.19

You may even find that users who are not following you are retweeting you. One of your contacts may retweet you and then one of your contacts' contacts may retweet again.

For example, in Image 5.20, @ParaGate, my contact, retweeted my tweet about the sales cycle for law firms. Then, @documentpros_GA, one of @ParaGate's contacts, retweeted the tweet. I am not connected to @documentpros_GA, but he liked my content that another user retweeted. Thus, my original tweet reached a Twitter user who wasn't following me.

Image 5.20

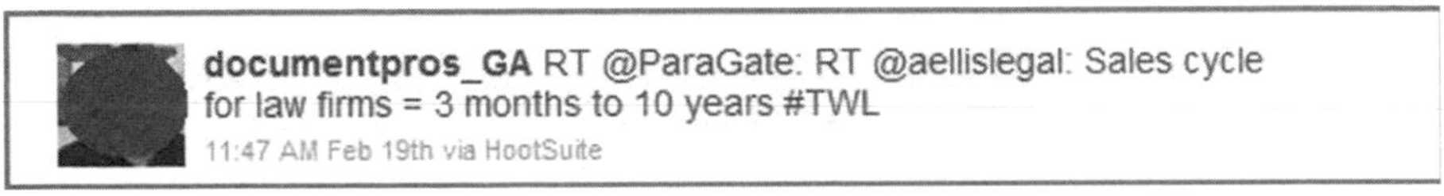

> **documentpros_GA** RT @ParaGate: RT @aellislegal: Sales cycle
> for law firms = 3 months to 10 years #TWL
> 11:47 AM Feb 19th via HootSuite

(2) Activity Goals

One characteristic of many campaigns—political, recruiting, marketing—is that the daily schedule often has no definite beginning or ending. Rather, you have a series of tasks that must be completed by certain benchmark times, *i.e.,* 20 marketing calls in one day.

You should apply this benchmarking concept to measure the social networking activities in your job search campaign because, like political, recruiting, and marketing campaigns, your job search campaign is also relationship-driven and networking intensive.

This section examines three types of activity goals, some or all of which may be appropriate for you: (1) CAP Goals; (2) Target Goals; and (3) The First-Year Plan.

CAP Goals

As you learned in Chapter 4, your performance on the Big 3 sites consists of three steps – Connect, Assimilate, Participate. Therefore, one way to measure your performance is to track your CAP activities. Table 5.3 outlines several activities and recommends a monthly goal for each. Your individual goals may vary, but Table 5.3 illustrates how you can create your own table to track such activities and measure your individual performance. Once you set your own CAP goals, use the goals to build your weekly social networking schedule, such as the sample schedule in **Appendix E** (see page 267 for how to build your schedule).

Table 5.3 – CAP Goals

The Big 3	CAP	Activity	Monthly Goal
Facebook	Connect	Connect with new friend or page	3
Facebook	Assimilate	Review status updates of the people on your "lawyer friends" list	4
Facebook	Participate	Write professional status update	3
Facebook	Participate	Share link to professional article or blog post	3
Facebook	Participate	Comment on lawyer friends' updates or wall posts	4
LinkedIn	Connect	Connect with new contact	4
LinkedIn	Assimilate	Review jobs posted by your network and on the job board	4
LinkedIn	Participate	Write professional status update	4
LinkedIn	Participate	Comment on a contact's link or status	2
LinkedIn	Participate	Send message to contact via LinkedIn instead of e-mail	2
Twitter	Connect	Connect to new professionals	4
Twitter	Assimilate	Read links tweeted by people on your "career" list	4
Twitter	Participate	Tweet a link to an article or blog	8
Twitter	Participate	Tweet in response to another user (@reply)	6
Twitter	Participate	Retweet another user's tweet	8

Target Goals

You may also want to track your interactions with specific contacts–people you may want to tap in your job search either for a referral or employment inquiry. For example, if you found an attorney on Twitter who practices in your ideal practice area and geographical market, you may want to track your interactions with this particular attorney.

Why is it necessary to track your interactions with specific targets? As explained in the Premise, it takes, on average, seven "touches" to convert a cold, or new, customer to a sale. Remember that you as a job seeker are marketing yourself to potential employers. Accordingly, traditional marketing principles apply, and it will take multiple interactions with a particular target before you receive a referral, a meeting, an interview, or an employment offer.

Table 5.4 outlines how a law student or lawyer interested in employment law may want to track his or her interactions with a key target, an employment law partner, on Twitter.

Note: All of the interactions in Table 5.4 are participation steps and would help satisfy some of your CAP goals in Table 5.3.

Table 5.4 – Target Goals

Target	Interactions						
	1	2	3	4	5	6	7
Employ-ment Law Partner (ELP)	RT* tweet by ELP	RT* tweet by ELP + add your own comment	Ask question re employment law blogs	List ELP in your #FollowFriday list	Share article of interest to ELP via Twitter	DM** ELP re meeting for coffee or phone conversation	Talk by phone or meet for coffee
*RT = retweet **DM = direct message							

First-Year Plan

If you are in your first year of law school or your first year of practice, consider yourself lucky because you have time to build your network of potential referral sources and employers before you need anything from your network. You have two or three years before you will need a new job. If you are a first-year law student, you will need a job upon graduation. If you are a first-year associate, you will likely leave your firm between your second to fifth years of practice and will need a new job at that time.[43]

Five Sources • Five Contacts = 25 New Contacts

The First-Year Plan is a 33 month plan (*i.e.*, September of your first year of law school through May of your third year of law school) focused on using the Big 3 sites to develop relationships with attorneys who may be helpful when you need a job. During the 33 months, you will use the Big 3 sites to identify and interact with attorneys from five different sources. You will also meet at least five attorneys from each source in person over the 33 month period. Therefore, your professional network will consist of at least 25 new, meaningful contacts upon law school graduation.

Five Sources

You will focus on using the Big 3 sites to identify attorneys from the following five sources:

- *Group A: Hometown/Family Contacts* – attorneys from your hometown, attorneys related to people from your hometown, attorneys who are close family friends
- *Group B: College Alumni Contacts* – attorneys who graduated from your college or university
- *Group C: Law School Alumni Contacts* – attorneys who graduated from your law school
- *Group D: Organization Contacts* – attorneys who are members of your fraternity or sorority, place of worship, or other civic or professional organization
- *Group E: Practice Area Contacts* – attorneys who practice in an area of the law which interests you

Appendix D outlines a sample first-year plan for a law student.

Note: When you use the Big 3 sites to identify, connect, and interact with attorneys in your First-Year Plan, you will satisfy more CAP goals outlined in Table 5.3.

Seven Touches

You will note that the sample law student First-Year Plan in **Appendix D** provides for multiple meetings with certain attorneys. In addition to adding contacts from multiple sources, you must also focus on nurturing the relationships you develop by interacting with your new contacts multiple times. As you learned in the Premise, it takes at least "seven touches" to convert a cold call to a sale or to build a relationship that will provide job leads. Chapter 4 outlined how you can interact with new contacts through the Big 3 sites to update them on your career and remain on their radar screens, but you also want to meet contacts in person multiple times.

Table 5.5 summarizes the multiple interactions with certain attorneys during the 33 month first-year plan outlined in **Appendix D**.

Table 5.5 – Seven Touches Effect of First-Year Plan

	Attorney 1	Attorney 2	Attorney 3	Attorney 4	Attorney 5
Source A Hometown Contacts	Months: 3, 12, 22	Months: 12, 22	Month: 18	Month: 24	Month: 29
Source B College Alumni Contacts	Months: 5, 14, 23	Months: 13, 24	Month: 19	Month: 25	Month: 30
Source C Law School Alumni Contacts	Months: 7, 17, 25	Months: 15, 25	Month: 21	Month: 26	Month: 31
Source D Organization Contacts	Months: 9, 18, 26	Months: 16, 26	Month: 22	Month: 27	Month: 32
Source E Practice Area Contacts	Months: 11, 20, 29	Months: 17, 30	Month: 23	Month: 28	Month: 33

PRACTICE

The final step to an efficient performance on the Big 3 social networking sites is practice. Simply stated, practice improves your performance.

Practice Improves Performance

A medical device company, B. Braun Medical, recently obtained astounding results from its sales managers after requiring them to practice their presentations about the company product over a six-week period. The company abandoned its old practice of simply telling the salespeople about the new product. Rather, the company required the salespeople to prepare presentations about the product and practice the presentations in front of company managers multiple times over a six-week period. The company managers critiqued each presentation, and the salespeople also watched videos of the presentations.

While the salespeople complained about the new practice requirements, 95% of the company's customers converted to the new product. Before the rigorous practice schedule, only 25% of customers converted.[44]

Thus, the medical device company achieved top performance results by requiring salespeople to practice at a high volume over a six-week period and providing feedback. You can borrow from this model to create a practice schedule for using the Big 3 social networking sites in your job search.

Six-Week Plan

I encourage you to create a schedule, or use the sample schedule outlined in **Appendix E**, to outline the activities you will perform on the Big 3 over a six-week period.

As you prepare your own schedule (or, prepare to use the sample schedule in **Appendix E**), consider the following:

- **Goals:** Incorporate your individual performance goals from the CAP Table (Table 5.3), or First-Year Plan in **Appendix D**, if applicable.
- **Prepare First!** The sample schedule or the schedule you create should be followed *after* you prepare your profiles and privacy settings.

- *My Recommendation*: Spend 3-6 hours over one weekend preparing to use the Big 3 sites—this includes all the steps discussed in Chapters 2 and 3, plus the connection step (Step 1) discussed in Chapter 4. You need polished profiles, secure privacy settings, and base contacts (and, in that order) before you start following the sample schedules below.

- *Experiment*: Chapter 4 outlined over 60 ways to perform on the Big 3 sites. You are not expected to use all 60+ methods—experiment. Try several methods and see how they work for you and your individual goals.
- *Measure*: Measure your performance using the tools discussed in the previous section (page 255).
- *Customize your Activities & Time*:
    - *CAP*: The sample schedule in **Appendix E** is designed so that you perform all three CAP levels to maximize your performance and results—if you follow the sample schedule, you will connect, assimilate, and participate on a regular basis to achieve maximum results. But, you can customize by selecting CAP activities that work for you.
    - *Time*: The sample schedule in **Appendix E** is designed as a maintenance schedule—enough activity to achieve the purpose of remaining on your contacts' radar screens. If your job search timeline is more urgent, I recommend increasing the total amount of time you spend on the Big 3 sites each week.

POINTS – PRACTICE

Block	Measure	Practice
Time • **Table 5.1** – Time Blocking in Recruiting • **Table 5.2** – Time Blocking in Job Search	Activity Responses • Facebook – Track Clicks, Comments, Likes, Share • LinkedIn – Track Clicks, Comments, Like, Share • Twitter – Track Clicks, Retweets	Practice improves Performance • B. Braun Medical Example: 25% → 95% over 6 weeks Six-Week Plan • Sample Schedule → 6 weeks (**Appendix E**) or create schedule
Information • The Big 3 - Mobile Applications • Facebook – Lists, Hidden Activities • LinkedIn – Category View • Twitter – Lists, Favorites	Activity Goals • CAP Goals (**Table 5.3**) • Target Goals (**Table 5.4**) • First Year Plan (**Appendix D**)	• Goals • Prepare First • Experiment • Measure • Customize Activities & Time

Chapter 6

Protocol

Pinstripes & Pearls[3,45]

THERE are certain desired behaviors politicians strive to exhibit in presidential campaigns. For example, the losing candidate typically calls the winning candidate on election night to concede. There is no election law addressing the call, but the call is expected.

Similarly, there are certain desired behaviors you'll want to follow when using social networking in your job search campaign. This first part of this chapter outlines certain desired behaviors.

While the desired behaviors are expected, there are other behaviors that are not expected and will set you apart if you follow them. The unexpected behaviors are like accessories. They are not required but can enhance your online image, making you more attractive to potential employers or clients. The second part of this chapter covers the distinguishing behaviors.

Think of the desired, expected patterns of behavior as pinstripes and the unexpected, accessorizing behaviors as pearls. This chapter examines both the desired behaviors (pinstripes) and the distinguishing activities (pearls).

Pinstripes

Like the pinstripe pattern in conservative business suits worn by legal professionals in courtrooms, there are certain patterns of behavior that are expected from professionals like you who use the Big 3 social networking sites. Some

---

[3] Judith Richards Hope wrote Pinstripes & Pearls: The Women of the Harvard Law Class of '64 Who Forged an Old Girl Network and Paved the Way for Future Generations (Scribner 2003) about the 15 women who graduated from Harvard Law School in 1964.

behaviors are expected on all of the Big 3 sites, while other behaviors are unique to a particular site.

The Big 3

(1) Fresh status updates on the Big 3

Keep your status updates fresh. The life of a status update will vary among the Big 3 sites because your audience varies. For example, people don't change their LinkedIn status updates as frequently as they change their Twitter updates. Here are some guidelines regarding the frequency with which you should update your status on the Big 3 sites:

- *Facebook – 4-7 times per week*. Most users check their Facebook accounts daily, so it's acceptable to update your status that frequently as well.
- *LinkedIn – at least once a week*. LinkedIn users check their accounts less frequently. If you change your update more frequently, some contacts may miss reading all of your updates. If you keep your update posted for months, it becomes stale.
- *Twitter – multiple times a day*. The volume of messages posted on Twitter is so high that you'll want to check Twitter several times throughout the day and post 5-20 updates during the day. Keep in mind that with Twitter, the update includes re-tweets, @replies and links.

(2) Don't sync status updates on the Big 3

Some people sync their Twitter and Facebook status updates; others sync their Twitter and LinkedIn updates. You should not sync your status updates for the following reasons:

- *Audience.* You communicate with a different audience on each of the Big 3 sites. For example, your Facebook audience is more personal than your Twitter audience. Do you really want to share your status updates about the struggles of potty-training your child on Twitter?

- **Frequency.** Twitter is conversational. You may post 20 times a day while sharing information and responding to other users' tweets. You are lucky if your LinkedIn audience reads status updates once a day. Most people must log on to LinkedIn to read updates and this usually happens weekly when they receive their network updates via the weekly e-mail. Your LinkedIn audience is likely going to miss one or several of your updates if you share 20 in one day.

  Moreover, your updates will clog your LinkedIn connections' news feed. The LinkedIn news feed displays only three to eight status updates in the news feed. Some employers may be annoyed to see all updates from the same person. They want to see updates from three different connections, not from the same person.

- **Confusion.** Your Twitter updates may confuse your non-tweeting LinkedIn and Facebook audiences—especially if they contain RT or @ or DM. What if your potential employer is only on LinkedIn? You don't want to annoy or confuse him with your Twitter lingo.

Practice Pointer

You can hide people from appearing in your LinkedIn news feed. If you are annoyed by your contacts who sync all of their tweets to their LinkedIn updates, hover your mouse over an update and the word "hide" will appear. Click hide to no longer receive LinkedIn updates from that contact

(3) Don't sound desperate

It's very easy for you to sound desperate on the Big 3 sites, especially as you become frustrated with your search. Don't let that frustration and desperation show in your updates. Employers don't want desperate employees; they want employees who are in demand.

Avoid updates like: Still unemployed—most frustrating experience of my life.

(4) Read links before sharing or retweeting

A common practice on the Big 3 sites is sharing links to articles or blog posts. Make sure you open the link and read the article or post before sharing. You can't always tell the slant of the article just by reading the headline.

(5) Avoid negative comments about job interviews, current job

Don't write negative comments about job interviews. One of your contacts may know someone at the firm where you interviewed. Similarly, don't post negative comments about your current job or information that may impact you negatively. For example, avoid posting updates about skipping work.

Facebook

(6) Edit your Facebook wall

There are three categories of potentially annoying or offensive information that you need to keep off your Facebook wall. You can control the annoying information by either refraining from posting or deleting when necessary. For example:

1. **Political Commentary.** Political views and intelligent discussions are acceptable in my opinion. However, be careful not to offend potential employers or referral sources with *hateful content* which can arise in a heated moment. For example, I would refrain from calling President Bush and Vice President Cheney "war-loving bast@#*$"" or posting a poll asking if President Obama should be assassinated.

2. **Mafia, Farmville, Quizzes oh my!** The Facebook games and quizzes annoy many people, so I recommend that job seekers delete this information from their walls on a regular basis. Also, refrain from inviting your entire friends list to play these games and quizzes. Many people are also annoyed by the invitations. I would only invite close friends if I knew for sure they wanted to play the games or take the quizzes.

Image 6.1

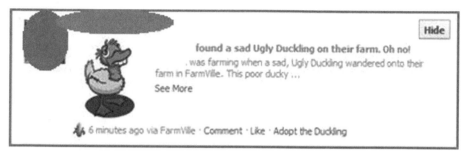

3. ***30 Links in 1 Day.*** I love sharing links to articles and blog posts on Facebook. I receive a lot of useful information by reading other friends' links, and many friends have told me they enjoy my links.

But, how many links is too many to share in one day? One of my friends recently shared 30 links in one day—articles, videos, and blog posts. People commented that she shared too many links; some even asked what she did at work all day (and, the person who posted is a lawyer). I would refrain from posting 30 links in one day. I would actually try to keep your postings under 10 per day. Here are three reasons not to post more than 10 links in a day: (1) people don't have time to read all of the information, so they will likely miss some of the information you share; (2) people grow annoyed; and (3) people question your work ethic, especially if you posted the links during business hours.

(7) Exercise caution with certain Facebook activities

1. ***Replying to Facebook messages sent to multiple parties.*** Facebook allows you to send private messages to multiple Facebook friends. However, if you reply to a message sent to multiple people, your reply is delivered to all people on the initial e-mail, like the "reply to all" feature on e-mail.

Keep this feature in mind when sending messages to multiple people. You may want to include a reminder that by hitting reply, recipients are replying to everyone on the original message. Or, you may want to re-consider whether a Facebook message is the best platform to use to convey your message.

As a recipient to an e-mail sent to multiple parties, consider whether everyone on the original message wants to see your reply before sending a reply. Perhaps it's best if you send a new message directly to the sender.

2. *Facebook Tagging.* Think before tagging friends in pictures. You may want to obtain a friend's permission before tagging him or her. As discussed in Chapter 3, users can change their privacy settings to prevent the pictures from appearing on their page. Nevertheless, if you tag someone, that picture is still present on Facebook. If you have mutual friends, those friends would be able to see the picture and recognize the mutual friend.

3. *Facebook Wall Comments v. Private Message v. Status Comment.* Think before leaving a comment on a friend's status or wall. Remember that such comments are public. If you absolutely must make a comment that is not flattering or too revealing, send a private message.

LinkedIn

(8) Fresh LinkedIn Profile (Quarterly Updates)

Review and update your LinkedIn profile regularly. As noted in Chapter 2, an increasing number of recruiters and employers search LinkedIn to find candidates. You don't want them to find an outdated LinkedIn profile. I recommend updating your profile quarterly. If you are promoted within your company, update your profile. As your experience grows, update your skills and experience section to reflect your new skill set.

(9) Exercise caution with LinkedIn Introductions

You may want to tap your 1ˢᵗ degree LinkedIn connections for introductions to 2ⁿᵈ and 3ʳᵈ degree contacts. As discussed in Chapters 3 and 4, the Introduction feature on LinkedIn allows you to write a note or introduction to the 2ⁿᵈ or 3ʳᵈ degree contact with whom you wish to connect, and LinkedIn sends the note to your mutual contact. The mutual contact will decide whether to forward it to your 2ⁿᵈ or 3ʳᵈ degree contact. Essentially, it's a virtual introduction. Instead of one of your contacts introducing you to one of his contacts at a cocktail party or business meeting, the introduction takes place via LinkedIn.

An issue may arise, however, if your mutual contact doesn't know your 2nd or 3rd degree contact that well. Remember, many people connect with other industry professionals on LinkedIn without having a solid relationship.

I recommend that you include a note to your mutual contact when requesting the introduction. Acknowledge that you are aware your mutual contact may not know the 2nd or 3rd degree contact that well. Let your mutual contact know that if that's the case, you completely understand why your mutual contact wouldn't forward the introduction to the 2nd or 3rd degree contact.

For example, pretend I am a job seeker and want to connect with Lisa, the recruiting manager at a firm on my wish list. I'm not connected to Lisa but my friend Justin is connected to Lisa on LinkedIn. Thus, Lisa is my 2nd degree contact. I may draft an Introduction to Lisa and ask Justin to forward the Introduction. Image 6.2 illustrates a blank Introduction form.

Image 6.2

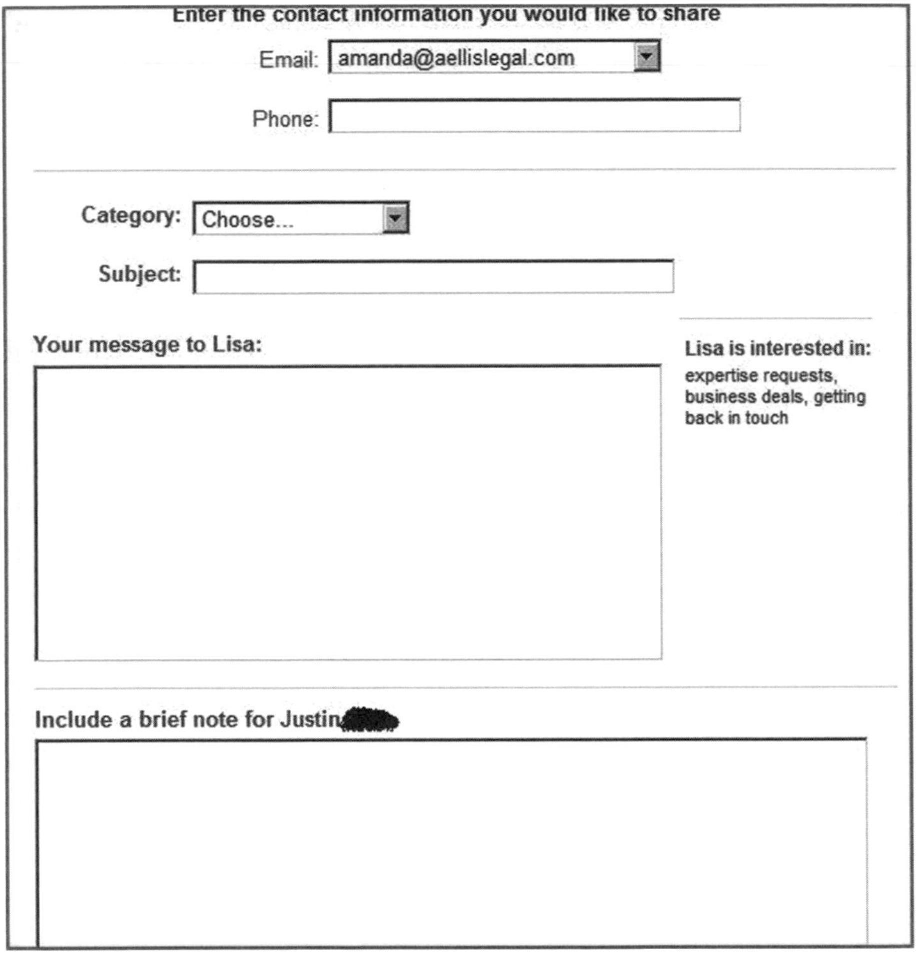

Enter the contact information you would like to share

Email: amanda@aellislegal.com

Phone:

Category: Choose...

Subject:

Your message to Lisa:

Lisa is interested in:
expertise requests, business deals, getting back in touch

Include a brief note for Justin

The first section contains my contact information. The second section contains my message to Lisa, my 2nd degree contact. And, the third section allows me to write a note to Justin, my contact, explaining why I want an introduction to Lisa. This is the section in which you can mention that your contact should only forward the Introduction if he feels comfortable doing so.

Don't take it personally if your contact doesn't forward the Introduction. In the preceding example, Justin and Lisa may not know each other that well. They may have never met in person but just happen to work in legal recruiting. In that case, Justin might not feel comfortable making an introduction. Or, some

LinkedIn users may have their own personal policy where they don't forward any introductions—if that's the case, don't take it personally.

Finally, don't abuse the introduction feature; only ask people who know you well to forward introductions on your behalf.

> ***Caveat to Law Students:*** While many career counselors may connect with you on LinkedIn, they may not want to forward introductions to their professional contacts. I would avoid sending your career counselors an introduction request—at a minimum, ask the counselor in advance whether he or she is open to receiving introduction requests from students.

(10) Don't spam LinkedIn groups

I encourage you to participate in LinkedIn groups by initiating discussions or sharing news articles, including blog posts and articles that you've written and articles mentioning you or your area of expertise. But, don't spam your LinkedIn groups.

Here are five signs you might be a LinkedIn Group spammer based on complaints I've heard from other attorneys. If you commit three to five of the offenses for three or more consecutive months, you may be considered a spammer:

- You post five different blog posts or articles for five consecutive days in the same group.
- You post the same blog post or article in multiple groups at least five times in one month.
- There are zero comments on the links you post.
- There are zero views on the links you post.
- You only post your own material (blogs or articles) and never comment on other posts or ask discussion questions to group members.

Twitter

(11) Twitter Annoyances

- ***Blog Feeds.*** Some people use Twitter only to stream their blogs to the Twitter feeds. As a result, every Twitter update will be a link to the person's blog. While there is nothing wrong with this practice, many people find it annoying because there is no interaction. The example in Image 6.3 is from a user who streams content from blogs and tweets quotes. Obviously, this approach to Twitter will not produce the most engaging or exciting Twitter user.

Image 6.3

Top 3 Work at Home Jobs For 2010 http //is gd/5SsCJ
about 2 hours ago from API

"I cannot afford to waste my time making money." Louis Agassiz
about 3 hours ago from API

Discover What to Know Before You Start a Home Business
http //bit ly/8YfDrJ
about 3 hours ago from web

"I always said that mega-mergers were for megalomaniacs." David Ogilvy
about 3 hours ago from API

Home Business Eruption - How to Start a Home Based Business
http //bit.ly/6L33a3
about 3 hours ago from API

Do You Want to Work From Home and Make Great Income?
http //short.to/12nst
about 3 hours ago from web

"A man should never neglect his family for business." Walt Disney
about 4 hours ago from API

"If you break 100, watch your golf. If you break 80, watch your business." Joey Adams
about 4 hours ago from API

Home Based Business Owners - Who is on Your Team? http //bit ly
/5KGwgp
about 4 hours ago from web

- **Automated DM.** Avoid sending automated direct messages on Twitter. Some users send automated DMs to welcome new followers such as, "Thank you for following me! I look forward to your tweets." Other users include links to their blogs or websites in the automated message, as illustrated in Images 6.4 through 6.6. Automated DMs annoy most users, so avoid them.

Image 6.4

> **:** , Need help in getting Job? Read 101 ways to find a job at http://trcb.us/jobtips Best wishes.
> 9:04 AM Feb 17th

Image 6.5

> Hi! I'm Andy. Great to connect w/you on Twitter! Look forward to sharing ideas and info. :-) Give the gift of a smile to someone today
> 9:44 PM Feb 6th

Image 6.6

> Hi! Thank you for following me. I look forward to learning more about you and to sharing GREAT information (free, of course) on marketing
> 12:21 AM Jan 25th

(12) Exercise caution with certain activities

- **@reply v. DM.** An "@ reply" or "mention" is when another user replies to your tweet or mentions your username in a tweet. Thus, two users may carry on a conversation by using the @reply feature. If you find yourself using this feature regularly, consider whether a "direct message" or "DM" is more appropriate. An "@ reply" is appropriate if the message or conversation is intended for others to see or if you are trying to engage others to join the conversation. However, if the conversation is clearly a conversation between two users, you probably want to DM instead.

- **"Pls RT".** A common practice on Twitter is to include "Pls RT" at the end of *urgent, important* messages. The "Pls RT" stands for please retweet and tells other users that you want them to retweet your message. Think of the red exclamation points that people sometimes use to flag urgent e-mails. "Pls RT" is the equivalent to the red exclamation point of tweets and should be used with the same level of caution.

Image 6.7 is an example of the proper use of "Pls RT":

Image 6.7

| I am looking for a 2L Law Intern with an entrepreneurial bent. Pls rt |
| 8:32 AM May 10th via UberTwitter |

The message in Image 6.7 is important. Moreover, this is the only tweet in over a one-week period where this person used "Pls RT." This one use of "Pls RT" does not rise to an abusive level.

You may want to use "Pls RT" if you tweet a question about an interview or your job search. But, follow the previous example and use it sparingly for it to be effective.

PEARLS

Remember, pearls are accessories. They are not a required part of a professional person's attire, but pearls enhance a professional person's appearance. Think of pearls as a conservative complement to a pinstripe environment. The pearls of social networking are activities that are not required but which will enhance your performance on the Big 3 social networking sites. You will stand out while maintaining a conservative, professional appearance.

(1) Create your brand with strategic content

You have the ability to share content on all of the Big 3 sites by posting status updates or sharing links to articles and blogs. If you consistently share content about three or four subject matters, your networks, including potential employers, will begin to see you as a brand rather than as another lawyer or law student on Twitter. You will be unique and memorable to employers.

The following examples are from Twitter, but you can create your brand across all three sites.

Law School Career Counselor: Career, Ethnic Food

Image 6.8 contains the Twitter bio of Marina Feehan, Assistant Director of the Office of Career Planning at the University of San Francisco School of Law. Note that her Twitter bio provides some information about personal and professional backgrounds. We learn, for example, that she likes ethnic food.

Image 6.8

Bio Social Media addicted attorney, now coaching law students re: Legal Careers @ USF School of Law; Fond of Ethnic Eats, All Things SF and Action Movies.

Images 6.9 through 6.11 contain a few of her tweets, and note how her tweets are about subject matters listed in her bio—career and ethnic food.

Image 6.9

JOB: Licensing Attorney - IP; RAMBUS, Los Altos, CA.
http://ow.ly/15JBA
11:10 AM Feb 10th from HootSuite

Image 6.10

READ: Large NYC Law Firms Balk at NALP Plan to Revamp Law School Recruiting Process http://ow.ly/15YYr #lawstudent #attorney #lawyer
12:09 PM Feb 10th from HootSuite

Image 6.11

FOOD: Savoring Asian Sweets to Ring in the Chinese New Year
http://ow.ly/16PMc
12:23 PM Feb 12th from HootSuite

Commercial Bankruptcy Attorney: Chapter 11 Bankruptcy, Football, Movies

Image 6.12 contains the bio of Pia Thompson, a commercial bankruptcy attorney in the Chicago area. Note that Pia's Twitter bio also provides some personal information. We learn, for example, that she's a fan of college football and movies.

Image 6.12

> **Bio** experienced bkrtcy,
> creditor's rights and workout atty,
> Wellesley grad, economist,
> college football & movie fan & a
> mom

Images 6.13 through 6.15 illustrate that Pia's tweets mirror the themes set forth in her bio—one tweet is bankruptcy related while the other two are about football and a movie, respectively.

Image 6.13

> Junior Creditors Call Tribune Co. Bankruptcy 'Fraudulent Conveyance':
> http://bit.ly/boYcwe via @addthis
> 12:29 AM Feb 3rd from mobile web

Image 6.14

> RT @espn: 13-year-old quarterback David Sills commits to USC -
> http://tinyurl.com/yk6fxbk
> 10:13 PM Feb 4th from TweetDeck

Image 6.15

> @altgeldshrugged Hot Tub Time Machine is a real movie and from
> what I've read it will be awful.
> 11:51 AM Feb 9th from web in reply to altgeldshrugged

Mix it Up! Tweets, Retweets, Questions, Answers, Links Professional, Personal

In addition to branding yourself through the content of your tweets, consider the *types* of tweets you are producing. Your followers might grow annoyed if every tweet is a link to an article. Mix it up!

Image 6.16 contains a sampling of my tweets in a three-hour period. Note that all tweets are about legal careers, but the *types* of tweets vary—I share links, retweet, and mention another user by congratulating her for landing a job interview.

Image 6.16

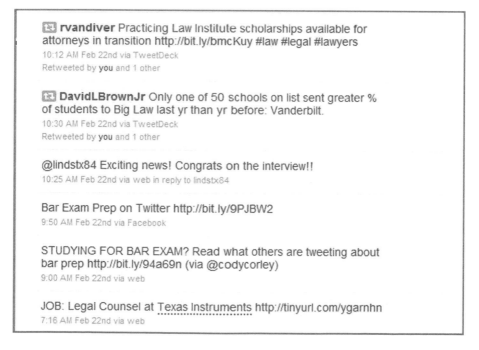

(2) Editorialize shared links

To distinguish your updates on the Big 3 sites, add your own comments when sharing a link to a blog or article. For example, most users include the title or headline of the article with the link, as shown in Image 6.17

Image 6.17

> What Women Want: Partnership Details - The American Lawyer
> http://tinyurl.com/yhjgl4v
> about 18 hours ago via my6sense

Or, on Twitter, users will retweet other tweets containing a link plus the headline, as shown in Image 6.18.

Image 6.18

> RT @kulawschool: PSLawNet Blog: Unpaid Summer Internships -
> How to make them work financially http://tinyurl.com/y87kys4 #finaid
> 11:12 AM Feb 16th via Viigo in reply to kulawschool

Both examples in Images 6.17 and 6.18 are acceptable. But, in a competitive job market, you need to be distinguishable, not simply acceptable. Consider distinguishing your links by prefacing the links with a particular point of the article rather than re-stating the title. For example, compare the tweets in Images 6.19 and 6.20 regarding the 2009 "AmLaw Summer Associates Survey." In Image 6.19, users simply retweeted the title of the article and the link.

Image 6.19

> AttorneyChan: RT @LexMonitor: RT **@AmLawDaily**: Summer
> Associates Survey 2009: Summertime Blues http://bit.ly/yesuU
> 1 day ago from Echofon

> LexMonitor: RT **@AmLawDaily**: Summer Associates Survey 2009:
> Summertime Blues http://bit.ly/yesuU
> 1 day ago from web

> BrooksLawFirm: Summer Associates Survey 2009: Summertime
> Blues http://bit.ly/yesuU (via **@AmLawDaily**)
> 2 days ago from Twitterrific

In Image 6.20, however, Kelly Hoey, a former professional development and alumni relations manager at an AmLaw firm, shared the same article but with more colorful tweets. Kelly pulled quotes from the article to provide unique content in her tweets. It is certainly more interesting to hear that a Skadden associate noted, "economic times suck," or that a Bryan Cave intern indicated, "it is a scary time to be a law student."

Image 6.20

"For the love of God," pleaded a Gibson Dunn clerk in a typical comment "please be more transparent about the offer process & outlook."

7:52 AM Sep 29th from web

A Bryan Cave intern put it this way: "It is a scary time to be a law student." http://bit.ly/lkv3H

7:51 AM Sep 29th from web

"economic times suck" one clerk at Skadden wrote bluntly in the recent summer associates survey http://bit.ly/lkv3H

7:49 AM Sep 29th from web

---

(3) Promote your brand when growing your network

People spend time browsing users' social networking profiles when they initially connect with other users. Therefore, it is important that your profile is complete when you begin adding people to your network.

Remember that your status update or your most recent tweet is part of your profile on the Big 3 sites. Review your status before adding or following new contacts or accepting invitations from others. Take advantage of the fact that your new contacts will scrutinize your profile and choose a status that adequately conveys your social networking brand.

For example, compare the tweet in Image 6.21 to the tweet in Image 6.22. Image 6.21 is acceptable but it's not distinguishable. Many conversations take place on Twitter, and Image 6.21 is an example of my conversation with another user (@jkhoey) where I'm responding to @jkhoey's question about scheduling a time to talk by phone. My new followers probably don't care about my call with @jkhoey.

Image 6.21

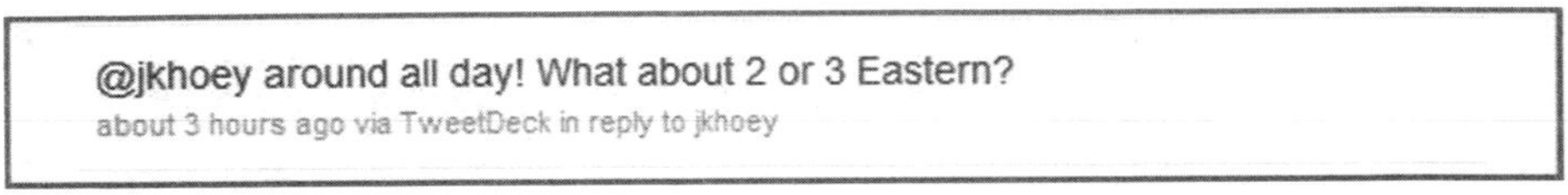

@jkhoey around all day! What about 2 or 3 Eastern?
about 3 hours ago via TweetDeck in reply to jkhoey

Image 6.22, however, contains an informative and helpful tweet. Moreover, the content relates to my brand (careers), and it's more likely to pique a new contact's interest. It's the pearl that complements my professional presence. Make sure your status is a pearl when you begin to add new contacts.

Image 6.22

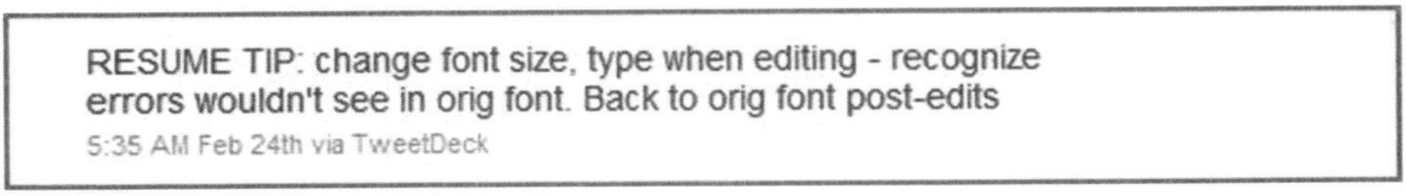

RESUME TIP: change font size, type when editing - recognize errors wouldn't see in orig font. Back to orig font post-edits
5:35 AM Feb 24th via TweetDeck

(4) Listen, learn, publish

Listen to the conversations on the Big 3 sites and determine the concerns and interests of the legal profession and the industries you represent. Turn your observations into content for articles, newsletters, or blogs.

For example, if you are speaking on a particular topic, search for the topic in LinkedIn's Answers. What questions have other people had about the topic? Can you anticipate similar questions for your presentation? How have others on LinkedIn answered the question?

Or, suppose you are writing a note on an employment law topic, but you are struggling to find a topic. Search "employment law" on Twitter to see what issues legal professionals are discussing. Search the Answers section on LinkedIn to see what employment law questions other people have asked. If five people asked questions about the same topic, perhaps that topic is one to consider for your note.

(5) Lead on Twitter

Embrace the leadership opportunities on Twitter. Because Twitter is still relatively new to the legal profession, the profession has not seen all that Twitter has to offer. You can capitalize on such missed opportunities by creating opportunities for the legal profession. Introduce your peers to tweetups, conference tweets, and twitter chats by organizing events around such activities.

For example, organize a tweetup for local attorneys in your practice area. If you service a particular industry, organize a tweetup for that particular industry. If you attend a legal or industry conference, tweet from the conference. If the conference organizers did not designate a hashtag, create your own and let others at the conference know to use it. Schedule a tweetup in conjunction with the conference.

(6) Follow different users, share different content

Share different content. If the majority of the people you follow are legal professionals, you will see content repeated on Twitter. You will find that many legal professionals on Twitter will tweet links to articles from popular legal publications, such as the *ABA Journal* or any ALM publication (Law.com, *American Lawyer, National Law Journal*).

Tweeting or retweeting links from the legal publications is acceptable but not distinguishable. You must read the articles in the legal publications, but you must also reach beyond the mainstream legal publications to find information to share that will make you distinguishable.

One way to find different, distinguishable content is to follow users outside the legal profession. You may find better information about marketing, a key component to your practice, by following marketing and PR professionals on Twitter. Or, you may discover hot industry trends for an industry you represent by following professionals in that industry. And, don't forget to follow people in your city or community.

POINTS – PROTOCOL

Pinstripes (desired patterns of behavior)			Pearls (accessories)
The Big 3 • Fresh status updates • Don't sync status updates • Don't sound desperate • Writing about job interviews • Read links before sharing			• Create your brand with strategic content • Editorialize shared links • Promote brand when growing network • Listen, learn, publish • Lead on Twitter • Follow different users, share different content
Facebook	**LinkedIn**	**Twitter**	
• Edit Facebook wall • Exercise caution with the following: (1) e-mails to multiple people; (2) tagging; (3) wall comments.	• Fresh profile • Exercise caution with Introductions • Don't spam • LinkedIn groups	• Annoyances: (1) streaming to blogs; (2) automated DM • Exercise caution with the following: (1) RT requests; (2) @reply v. DM; (3) choosing hashtag	

PART 4

PROOF LAWYERS GET HIRED USING THE 6PS SYSTEM

I noted in Chapter 4 that very few law students and lawyers currently *participate*, the third step required to successfully perform your job search on the Big 3 social networking sites. But, as more attorney job seekers complete this step, more success stories regarding social networking in the legal job search will surface. The final chapter illustrates the success lawyers and law students can achieve by mastering all of the 6Ps, including the third performance step of participation.

CHAPTER 7

Paragons

par • a • gon
- *noun*
1. a model of excellence

CHAPTERS 1-6 outlined the 6Ps, the six elements required to get hired when using the Big 3 social networking sites in your job search. This chapter illustrates the application of the 6Ps system by providing examples of two paragons of success when it comes to getting hired using social networking.

This chapter is divided into three sections:

1. *Meet the Paragons.* The first part of the chapter describes the two paragons, a lawyer and a law student who obtained jobs through one of the Big 3 sites—Twitter.
2. *Spot the 6Ps.* The second part of the chapter analyzes the presence of the 6Ps in the paragons' job searches.
3. *See the Significance.* The final section of this chapter draws on examples from the paragons' success stories to illustrate the importance of incorporating social networking in your job search.

MEET THE PARAGONS

(1) The Snarky Waitress

Bobbi-Sue Doyle-Hazard

Corporate Counsel at New England Cryogenic Center
Pennsylvania State University - Dickinson School of Law (May 2007)
Joined Twitter: Fall 2008

After graduating from Pennsylvania State University Dickinson School of Law in May 2007, Bobbi-Sue Doyle-Hazard returned to Boston to be closer to family. She exhausted all traditional job search efforts and applied to numerous positions advertised online. In April 2009, Bobbi-Sue took a job as a waitress at Abe & Louie's, a high-end steakhouse in Boston, while also handling legal matters, such as drafting wills, for friends.

Several months prior to taking the waitressing job, Bobbi-Sue joined Twitter after reading an article about the site in *Women's Health* magazine. Bobbi-Sue quickly developed a following of attorneys in the Boston area. She often tweeted about her job search but also tweeted about her life as a waitress. Some of Bobbi-Sue's funny waitress tweets amused one of her followers, a reporter from the *Boston Business Journal.*

In August 2009, the reporter wrote a story about unemployed lawyers and profiled Bobbi-Sue. The story, including a picture of Bobbi-Sue posing in her home office while wearing her waitress attire, made the front page of the *Boston Business Journal* on August 14, 2009.

On August 31, 2009, the president of the New England Cryogenics Center, Inc. ("NECC") read the story and contacted the reporter to let her know he was interested in speaking with Bobbi-Sue. The reporter conveyed the message to Bobbi-Sue, and Bobbi-Sue immediately got in touch with the president of NECC. He invited her to come in for an interview. Not only did Bobbi-Sue land a job, she landed a highly-coveted in-house job. She is NECC's first in-house lawyer.

The following interview with Bobbi-Sue provides deeper insight into her Twitter use and insight to help you in your job search.

Amanda: How frequently did you tweet?

Bobbi-Sue: I was constantly on Twitter. I had it hooked up to my phone so even when I was waitressing I could check and respond on it. I was having conversations constantly.

Amanda: What did you tweet (status updates, links to articles, conversations)?

Bobbi-Sue: A bit of everything—I posted status updates, jumped into conversations, and asked questions. I often discussed my job search on Twitter.

Amanda: How many interactions did you have with the reporter before she contacted you about the story?

Bobbi-Sue: I had more than ten interactions. The reporter started following me first. Then, I began to respond to her tweets or retweet her tweets. She did the same for me.

Amanda: What did you tweet about that led the reporter to contact you? Or, did you approach the reporter?

Bobbi-Sue: The reporter was highly amused by my tweets, whether they were professionally related or just snarky, funny things I would post about waitressing. She initially contacted me for a story in April 2009, but I wasn't a fit for that story. She contacted me again when she was working on the story about unemployed lawyers.

Amanda: Are most of your Twitter followers professional?

Bobbi-Sue: I would say 85% of the people I follow are professional contacts. The others I follow consist of friends, celebrities, and some retail establishments. I need to add some fun into my Twitter mix as well!

Amanda: Did you stop using Twitter once you obtained your job?

Bobbi-Sue: No

Amanda: How do you use Twitter now?

Bobbi-Sue: I use Twitter to keep in touch with the professional contacts I made while searching for a job, including many attorneys in the Boston area. I'll also pose questions on Twitter, such as, "Thinking about starting a Boston Running Lawyers Group – want to meet on Saturday mornings for runs?" I'll also tweet about life in general, such as, "Oh lobster rolls … how I love thee in summertime … NOM!"

Amanda: Have you met any of the professional contacts from Twitter, such as attorneys, face-to-face?

Bobbi-Sue: Yes, at least two dozen.

Amanda: What advice would you give a law student or lawyer about using Twitter in his or her job search?

Bobbi-Sue: Be yourself—but maybe a PG-13 version of yourself.

Get involved in the conversations on Twitter by contributing your own thoughts and asking questions. Don't just post status updates.

Talk about your job search. Inform your followers when you have an interview. Tweet a link to your LinkedIn profile or resume website.

(2) The Social Media Maven

Laura Bergus

Third-Year Law Student
University of Iowa School of Law – J.D. expected May 2011
Joined Twitter: June 2008

Laura Bergus obtained multiple jobs through Twitter. Laura began her 1L summer job search in January 2009, the beginning of her 1L spring semester. She purposely chose not to participate in her law school's on-campus interviews. Laura spent the majority of her time focused on using social media in her job search.

On January 8, 2009, Laura wrote a short blog post about her ideal 1L summer job. You can read the blog post in Image 7.1.

Image 7.1

Give me one reason why I shouldn't help you

Filed under: law school — Laura Bergus at 2:19 pm January 8, 2009

I'm looking for a summer law job. And I'm a first year law student, so I've been told that in "this economy" I'll be super lucky to find anything. I suppose that's true. But here's the catch: I'm offering up my insane work ethic "for free". There are just a few caveats, which will comprise my traditional unordered list:

- I have to be able to work in or around Iowa City, at least most of the time. Telecommuting is no prob.

- The offer is only good if I get to help lawyers use technology to improve efficiency, better meet their clients' expectations, etc.

- There has to be some element of real legal work (I can't be a free code monkey, which would entail knowing something to code anyway)

- I hope for a policy- or industry-level tie-in. That is, wouldn't it be great to help make something that helps everyone work more effectively??

My career services counselor at school suggested I contact the ABA's eLawyering division. Not a bad idea.

For anyone that stumbles across this, here's my dorky personal career goal:

"I hope to shape policy enabling convenient access to knowledge that people need to make important life decisions. Specifically, I think there are many opportunities for law firms and lawyers to save time and money while presenting traditional legal advice and services in ways that are easier for modern consumers to comprehend. From document automation/standardization to chat/txt/email correspondence to online portals that wholly replace a brick-and-mortar presence, a combination of today's technology and good design can ensure that the legal community excels at serving its clients' needs. I want to help lead the transformation."

If that didn't make you barf, please contact me via email or Twitter.

Laura tweeted a link to the blog post. Several of her followers then retweeted the link, and Laura's blog reached one potential employer, Montana Legal Services (MLS). The deputy director of MLS contacted another legal aid organization, Iowa Legal Aid (ILA), to let them know about Laura's blog post. Both legal aid organizations read the blog post and left comments, as shown in Image 7.2.

Image 7.2

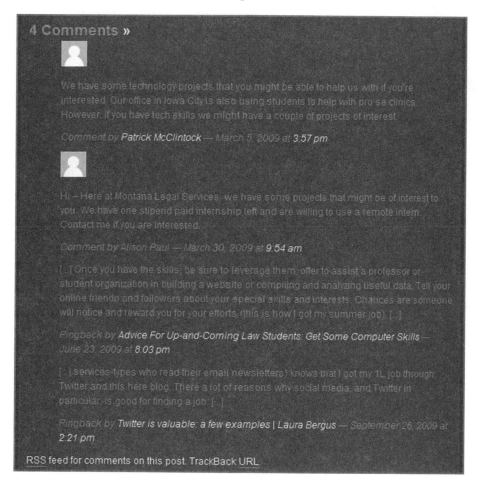

4 Comments »

We have some technology projects that you might be able to help us with if you're
interested. Our office in Iowa City is also using students to help with pro se clinics.
However, if you have tech skills we might have a couple of projects of interest.

Comment by *Patrick McClintock* — March 5, 2009 at 3:57 pm

Hi – Here at Montana Legal Services, we have some projects that might be of interest to
you. We have one stipend paid internship left and are willing to use a remote intern.
Contact me if you are interested.

Comment by *Alison Paul* — March 30, 2009 at 9:54 am

[...] Once you have the skills, be sure to leverage them: offer to assist a professor or
student organization in building a website or compiling and analyzing useful data. Tell your
online friends and followers about your special skills and interests. Chances are someone
will notice and reward you for your efforts (this is how I got my summer job). [...]

Pingback by *Advice For Up-and-Coming Law Students: Get Some Computer Skills* —
June 23, 2009 at 8:03 pm

[...] services-types who read their email newsletters) knows that I got my 1L job through
Twitter and this here blog. There a lot of reasons why social media, and Twitter in
particular, is good for finding a job. [...]

Pingback by *Twitter is valuable: a few examples | Laura Bergus* — September 26, 2009 at
2:21 pm

RSS feed for comments on this post. TrackBack URL

By April 1, 2009, Laura received offers from both ILA and MLS, and Laura
worked at the legal aid organizations during her 1L summer in 2009 and part-time
during the 2009-2010 academic year.

The MLS position was a full-time summer position, and the position with
ILA was on a volunteer basis. However, Laura's volunteering at ILA led to a grant-
funded summer job with the organization for the summer of 2010.

Laura also works as a social media and technology consultant for a small law
firm, a position that was created for Laura. The firm was interested in new technol-
ogies/social media, and an associate at the firm told the partner about Laura's social
media background. The partner viewed Laura's online social media profiles which

reflected her social media experience. The partner was impressed with Laura's online presence and decided to hire Laura as a social media consultant.

Laura's robust social media profiles also led to national media attention. *US News & World Report* featured Laura in its spring 2010 graduate school rankings issue. The reporter found Laura through the *Legal Geekery* blog and Twitter profile where Laura writes and hosts a podcast with Josh Auriemma.

Laura became involved with *Legal Geekery* after reading a tweet that *Legal Geekery* was seeking new contributors. Laura also contributes to the *Lawyerist*, a law practice blog. Laura discovered this opportunity on Twitter as well.

The following interview with Laura provides deeper insight into her Twitter use and insight to help you in your job search.

Amanda: How frequently did you tweet?

Laura: I used Twitter a little bit every day. I limited myself to 15 minutes on Twitter per day so it wouldn't interfere with my studies.

Amanda: What did you tweet (status updates, links to articles, conversations)?

Laura: Once I built up a community of legal people I was interested in following, I would hop on and join in or initiate a conversation or two every day, if I had something to add.

I also shared links to interesting blog posts. I learned that one way to get some response was to comment substantively on someone's blog and then retweet the link to the blog post.

Amanda: How many times did you share the blog post about your ideal summer job before receiving an inquiry?

Laura: Three or four times, I believe.

Amanda: Are most of your Twitter followers professional?

Laura: Yes, approximately 75% are professional.

Amanda: Did you stop using Twitter once you obtained your job?

Laura: No.

Amanda: Has your use of Twitter changed at all?

Laura: After seeing the benefits of landing multiple jobs through Twitter, I am more confident in my ability to forge real relationships, professional and personal, online.

Amanda: Have you met any of the professional contacts from Twitter, such as attorneys, face-to-face?

Laura: I've met at least a dozen Twitter contacts face-to-face. Twitter is the ultimate way to break the ice. I am amazed at my comfort level during a conversation with someone I've met on Twitter.

I try to meet my online contacts face-to-face. I'll ask a local Twitter user to meet in person for coffee. I also try to meet Twitter contacts when I travel.

Amanda: What advice would you give a law student or lawyer about using Twitter in his or her job search?

Laura: Twitter is for making and joining real conversations. Sometimes those conversations are rather banal, relating to food or television. But, so is most face-to-face small talk, especially when you are first getting to know someone. Don't be put off by a bit of this seemingly useless chatter. Pay attention and you might find someone who shares your interests in wine, music, or obscure documentaries, which can lead to deeper relationships down the road.

Don't use Twitter to broadcast; use it to engage. Look to your followers and ask yourself what they want from you.

Use Twitter to target particular areas such as practice areas, industries, and geographic regions where you are hoping to find a job.

Let people know that you are seeking a job. The reality is that most jobs are landed through a preexisting connection. If nothing else, Twitter is an easy, fast, and effective way to make lots of relevant connections.

SPOT THE 6PS

Each of the 6Ps discussed in Chapters 1-6 is present in the paragons' success stories of getting hired through Twitter. This section dissects the paragons' success stories to highlight the 6Ps.

1. *Professionalism.* You learned in Chapter 1 that Twitter is a primarily professional site. Both Bobbi-Sue and Laura maintained a primarily

professional image on Twitter and shared primarily professional content, 85% and 75%, respectively.

2. *Profile.* Bobbi-Sue's profile obviously appeared professional to attract the *Boston Business Journal* reporter as a follower. Laura's professional profile caught the attention of the small firm and *US News & World Report*.

3. *Privacy.* As recommended in Chapter 3, Bobbi-Sue and Laura did not protect their tweets. It is likely that Bobbi-Sue and Laura would not have attracted the media with protected tweets.

4. *Performance.* Bobbi-Sue and Laura completed all three CAP levels, and, therefore, yielded maximum results.

   a. *Connect.* Both Bobbi-Sue and Laura focused on connecting with other legal professionals from the moment they joined Twitter. And, they continued to grow this network of professionals.

   b. *Assimilate.* Bobbi-Sue asked questions on Twitter to learn more about job opportunities and to prepare for interviews. Laura sought out and engaged followers in legal aid technology support, an area of interest to her.

   c. *Participate.* Bobbi-Sue and Laura joined in conversations on Twitter rather than only posting status updates. And, they grew their online Twitter relationships into offline relationships by meeting Twitter followers face-to-face.

5. *Practice.* Bobbi-Sue used Twitter zealously, often checking Twitter from her phone while on breaks at her waitressing job. Laura, however, used the tool of time blocking by limiting her time on Twitter to 15 minutes per day. The differences in usage can probably be attributed to the urgency of the paragons' searches. The different practices also illustrate that you can use the social networking sites to fit your own goals and schedule.

6. *Protocol.* Note how the paragons distinguished themselves. Others on Twitter, such as the *Boston Business Journal* reporter, viewed Bobbi-Sue, the Snarky Waitress, as witty yet professional. And, Laura, the Social Media Maven, impressed others, like the small firm partner and the reporter from *US News & World Report*, with her vast knowledge in the

area of social media. Both paragons created striking yet different brands that yielded outstanding results.

SEE THE SIGNIFICANCE

In the Premise, I introduced eight reasons why social networking is an important factor in getting hired. You have read some of the reasons throughout this book. The paragons' stories illustrate several of the eight reasons as well.

1. *Search.* Employers do search candidates' online profiles and, as noted in the Premise, positive profiles can influence hiring decisions, as evidenced by Laura's job as a social media and technology consultant for the small law firm.

2. *Warm Calls.* Laura noted that Twitter is the ultimate way to break the ice. Twitter warms the cold introductions, as discussed in the Premise. Laura added that she is much more comfortable meeting someone in person if she previously engaged in conversation with him or her on Twitter.

3. *Seven Touches.* One key point about both paragons—they did not find their employers on Twitter. Rather, others in the paragons' Twitter networks spread the paragons' messages, which ultimately reached their perspective employers. Networking for a job is a high touch business, and social networks, like Twitter, are the most effective method to reach your networks with a single message.

4. *In-house Social Media Attorney.* Laura's role as a social media and technology consultant at the small firm is quite similar to the Chlorox job posting noted in the Premise. It's highly probable that both firms and corporations will seek attorneys with social media experience for various roles in the future.

5. *Perpetual Network.* Bobbi-Sue and Laura continue to nurture their initial network by engaging in conversations and meeting their followers in person. And, they continue to add new followers and meet them in person. They are nurturing and growing their perpetual network and will be prepared when they need a new job or client.

6. *Passive Candidate.* Laura was not actively seeking a job when the small firm approached her about her social media expertise. Laura

was a passive candidate whose experience permeated her profiles and intrigued a firm into hiring her.

Points - Paragons

Profes-sionalism	Profile	Privacy	Perfor-mance	Prac-tice	Protocol
BOBBI-SUE					
85%	Professional profile attracted BBJ reporter	Tweets not pro-tected	**Connect** Connected with legal professionals **Assimilate** Asked ques-tions to learn about jobs, prepare for interviews **Participate** Engaged in conversation, met two dozen Twit-ter users face-to-face	Mobile applica-tion	Brand – snarky waitress amused reporter
LAURA					
75%	Professional profile attracted partner in small firm and *U.S. News and World Report*	Tweets not pro-tected	**Connect** Connected with legal professionals **Assimilate** Learned from oth-ers about legal aid technology **Participate** Engaged in conversations Met at least a dozen Twit-ter users face-to-face	Time block (15 min-utes/ day)	Brand – social media expertise impressed reporter, partner

PARTING WORDS

YOUR job search is a campaign and requires networking, marketing, and planning. One tool that can assist with the networking, marketing, and planning in your campaign is social networking.

You may use other forms of social media in your job search as well, but the Big 3 social networking sites are three essential tools required to get hired today. Facebook and LinkedIn are necessary for nurturing existing relationships, both personal and professional, that can provide job leads. LinkedIn is also essential for researching potential employers. As illustrated by the paragons' stories, Twitter is the best tool for forging new relationships with legal professionals who may be your potential employer, colleague, or referral source.

You need all of the Big 3 sites in your job search, and you need a system such as the 6Ps to use the sites correctly and efficiently. Your mere presence on the sites won't win the campaign; rather, your performance on the sites will set you apart from your competitors and get you hired.

I wish you the best of luck, and I want to hear your success stories! Connect with me on the Big 3 sites, e-mail me, or call me.

Facebook: www.facebook.com/aellislegal
LinkedIn: www.linkedin.com/in/amandaellis
Twitter: www.twitter.com/aellislegal
E-mail: amanda@aellilsegal.com
Blog: www.6psbig3.com
Phone: 214.361.0070

Primer

FACEBOOK

Event: An event is a calendar entry for a social or business function. If you create an event, you can share the details with your Facebook friends, invite friends through Facebook, and send reminders about the event through Facebook.

Fan Page (a/k/a Business Page or Page): A fan page is a Facebook profile for a business (celebrities and "causes" often have fan pages). Fan pages are public profiles, but fan page owners can control what fans can post. For example, a page owner can choose a setting that prohibits fans from posting comments, pictures, etc.

To connect with a fan page, you click the "like" button on the page. Prior to Facebook changes in the spring 2010, you clicked on "become a fan" to connect with a fan page, so you may hear this phrase from time-to-time.

As you can see in the box below, the user who creates a Facebook fan page must certify that he is authorized to create the page for the given firm, business, or subject. A person who creates an unauthorized page violates Facebook's Terms of Use and is subject to having his Facebook account disabled. Thus, it is highly likely that a Facebook fan page affiliated with a law firm or law school is legitimate.

Image P-1

Please certify that you are an official representative of this brand, organization, or person and that you are permitted to create a Facebook Page for that subject.

☐ I am authorized to create this Page

Electronic Signature: enter full name as electronic signature

Create Page

Note: Fake Pages and unofficial "fan pages" are a violation of our Terms of Use. If you create an unauthorized Page or violate our Terms in any way, your Facebook account may be disabled. To create a Facebook Group for fans of this subject, please click here.

Friend: A person with whom you connect on your Facebook profile is your Facebook friend.

Group: An organization may have its own Facebook page called a Group. People who connect with Groups become "members" of the Group.

Anyone can create a Group; you don't have to certify that you are an authorized representative of the company, school, or institution. You frequently see Groups created for law firm alumni, law firm summer associate classes, law school classes, and professional organizations. These Groups are often created by an individual (*i.e.*, an alum) rather than by a law firm or school representative.

Groups have a variety of access options as indicated in the box below: (1) open; (2) closed; or (3) secret. If a Group is "open", you can see the information and pictures on the Group's page. If a Group is closed, you will have to request to become a Member of the Group before you can access the information on the page. An even more secure option is to make the Group secret. If a Group is secret, it wwill not appear in your search results. Membership in a secret group is by invitation, and users do not know of the Group unless invited to join.

Like: (1) You can give a "thumbs up" approval to another user's status update, wall post, or picture. (2) When you "like" the page of a business, such as a law firm or law school, you connect with that page and will receive updates from that page in your news feed.

Marketplace: The marketplace is the classified ads of Facebook where you can buy and sell items; you can also search jobs.

Member: When you connect with a Facebook Group, you become a member of that Group.

Message: You can send private messages to your Facebook *friends.*

News Feed: Your Facebook news feed is your home page that appears when you log onto the site. Your news feed contains a sampling of your friends' activities as well as birthdays and upcoming events.

Profile: Your Facebook profile is your personal Facebook page where you can share information and pictures. Chapter 2 discusses your profile in detail and Chapter 3 discusses how to protect the information you share on your profile.

Profile Picture: Your profile picture appears in the upper left-hand corner of your Facebook profile and is visible to everyone. Chapter 2 outlines the Office Desk Photo Rule for choosing an appropriate profile picture.

Status (or State Update): You can share updates to your Facebook *friends* by writing the update in the box to the right of your ***profile picture*** with the prompt, "What's on your mind?"

Image P-2

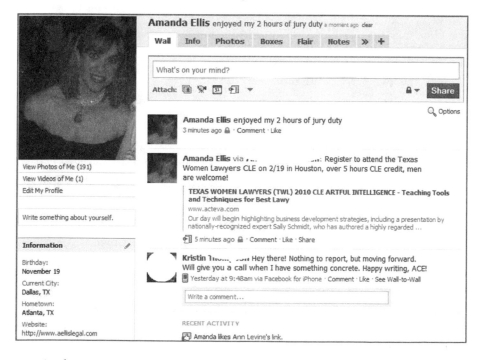

As shown in Image P-2, my current status appears to the right of my name and picture – "enjoyed my 2 hours of jury duty." If I wanted to update with a new status, I would type the new status in the box with the prompt, "What's on your mind?"

You'll also note that my status appears in the news feed of updates below the status box. If I were to change my current status, this status would remain in my news feed.

Chapter 4 discusses the Status Update feature in more detail, including how to use it in your job search.

Tag: You can tag friends in pictures, status updates, and wall posts. When you tag a friend in a picture, you label the person and the picture appears on that person's profile. Chapter 3 outlines steps to change the visibility of your tagged pictures.

When you tag a person in a status update or wall post, you mention the person's name in your update and the update also appears on the person's wall. You often will tag a person in a status update or wall post to get his or her attention or give him or her credit.

Wall: Your Facebook wall is the space on your Facebook profile where friends can write messages (visible to all your other friends) and you can share information such as pictures or articles.

Friends' Activity on Your Wall

You'll see in Image P-2 that my friend Kristin wrote a note on my wall. In addition to writing notes on your walls, your friends can also share pictures, videos or links to websites or articles.

As a job seeker, you'll want to pay extra attention to the information your friends share on your wall. If your friends post information that you do not want on your profile, delete it. If it becomes a problem, you may consider preventing your friends from posting information to your wall. This is a control in your privacy settings discussed in Chapter 3.

Share Links, Pictures, Videos

You can share information to your own wall such as links to websites or videos. For example, in Image P-2, my link to the CLE seminar for the Texas Women Lawyers is an example of my activity – I shared a link to another website about an event some of my Facebook friends might want to attend. You can also share pictures, videos, or links to articles.

Recent Activity

Finally, you'll see the very bottom notation of recent activity which indicates, "Amanda likes Ann Levine's link." When you become friends with new contacts, "like" a friend's link or comment on a friend's status or post, that activity is noted on your wall as your recent activity.

LINKEDIN

Answers: The Answers section on LinkedIn is a searchable database of questions and answers on various topics posted by LinkedIn users.

Connections or Contacts: When you connect with another LinkedIn user, that user is your 1ˢᵗ degree connection or 1ˢᵗ degree contact.

Introductions: (1) When you send an invitation to connect with a contact on LinkedIn, you can customize a note, also called an Introduction, to the contact. (2) You can also draft a note, or Introduction, to your 2ⁿᵈ and 3ʳᵈ degree contacts and ask your 1ˢᵗ degree contact who is your mutual contact to forward the note or Introduction.

Inmail: An inmail is a private message you can send to LinkedIn users with whom you are not connected.

LinkedIn Message: A LinkedIn message is a private message you can send to your LinkedIn 1ˢᵗ degree contacts.

Weekly E-mail Updates: One time each week, LinkedIn sends users updates via e-mail. Many users review LinkedIn updates when they receive their weekly e-mail digest.

TWITTER

Tweet (or update): The 140 character phrase you write in response
to the question, "what are you doing?" Typically, users respond by
announcing what they are doing at the moment, asking a question or
sharing a link to an interesting article, blog, or video. Your tweets are
<u>public</u> unless you protect them.

Example: Law student @lbergus convinces University of Iowa College
of Law to use Twitter!! See update - <u>http://bit.ly/17nsiL</u>

Username: Name created by user and preceded by the "@" symbol when
addressing a user in a tweet or retweeting a user's tweet.

Example - aellislegal

Follow: You follow another user if you want to subscribe to their updates;
you do this by clicking the "follow" button under the user's profile
picture.

Block: If you don't want someone to have access to your profile, you may
block them after they begin following you.

Retweet (RT): Forwarding another user's message to your followers.
There are two ways to retweet:

1.   *Auto retweet; and*
2.   *Manual retweet.*

Auto Retweet

To auto retweet, hover your mouse over the lower right corner of the
tweet until you see the words reply and retweet.

Image P-3

Click on Retweet and a new box will appear asking you to confirm that you wish to retweet the tweet.

Image P-4

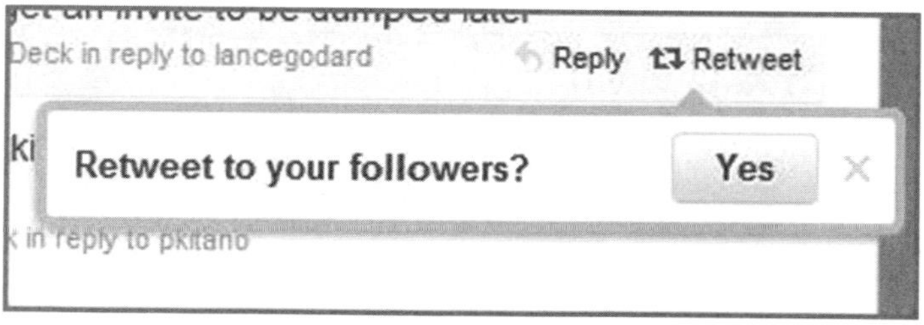

Once you retweet a tweet, the tweet appears in your stream for all of your followers to see. However, credit is given to the person who posted the original tweet. For example, in Image P-5, you can see the name of the person who posted the original tweet next to the tweet. The box with up and down arrows indicates the tweet was retweeted. And, note below the tweet tells you who retweeted the tweet.

Image P-5

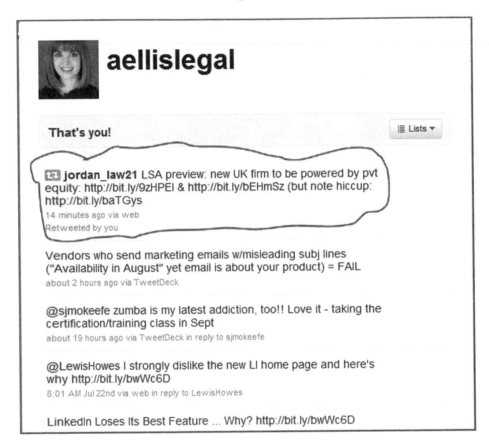

Click on the Retweet link on your Twitter home page (Image P-6) to see other users who retweeted your tweets (Image P-6) via the auto retweet feature.

Image P-6

Image P-7

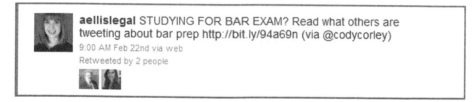

Manual Retweet

Another way to retweet is to copy and paste another user's tweet and add "RT" plus the user's username at the beginning of the tweet.

You copy and re-post another user's tweet but give credit to the user who wrote the initial tweet by writing "RT @username" (username of person who sent the original tweet).

Example: RT @bbcworld Google debuts voice service that offers free domestic calls, low cost int'l calls & speech-to-text ... http://tinyurl.com/cawfwd

Click @username (@reply/mention) on your home page to see manual retweets of your tweets, as shown in Image P-8.

Image P-8

At reply (@)/Mention: A user's <u>public</u> reply to another user's tweet. For example: @aellislegal that's sort of what I think. It shows I can be articulate and that there are issues I care about. I think I'll keep it.

Direct Message (DM): A user's <u>private</u> message to another user which you can only send as a direct message to users who are following you.

Hashtag (#): Designates a subject or topic of discussion - #subject.

Tweet-up: Twitter users in a geographical area gather to meet in person.

Law School Career Offices' Facebook & Twitter Pages

NOTE: *List was updated June 21, 2010. The list contains only law school career offices with Facebook and Twitter pages; some career offices share information on other accounts, such as the law school's main Facebook page or Twitter account. Check my blog for updates to this list – www.6psbig3.com To access a school's Facebook page, search for the title of the Facebook page listed. To access the school's Twitter page, type www.twitter.com/username. For example, to access Boston University's CDO Twitter page, type: www.twitter.com/BULawCDO*

School	Facebook	Twitter
Boston University		@BULawCDO
Case Western Reserve University	Case Western School of Law Career Services Office	
Chapman University		@ChapmanCSO
Columbia University	Columbia Law School Office of Career Services	@CLSCareers
DePaul University	DePaul University Law Career Services Office	@DePaulLawCareer
Duke University		@DukeLawCareer
Florida International University	FIU Law Career Development	
Franklin Pierce Law Center	Franklin Pierce Law Center Career Services Office	

School	Facebook	Twitter
Georgetown University		@KristenHulse (Kristen Hulse, LL.M. Advisor)
Georgia State University		@GSULawCSO
Golden Gate University		@GGULCS
John Marshall Law School	The John Marshall Law School Career Services Office	
La Verne Law School	La Verne Law Career Services	
Loyola Marymount University	Loyola Law School Office of Career Services*	
Loyola University Chicago	Loyola Law CSO (Chicago)	
Loyola University New Orleans		@nolachickadee (Amy Schwarzenbach, Career Counselor & Recruiting Coordinator)
Mercer University	Mercer Law School Career Services	
Michigan State University	MSU College of Law Career Services	
New England School of Law		@NELBostonCSO
North Carolina Central University		@pag2010 (Philip Guzman, Director of Public Service Programs) @spag1999 (Linda Spagnola, Assistant Dean for Career Services)
Northeastern University	Northeastern School of Law Career Services	
Northwestern University		@nlawcareer
Nova Southeastern University (Broad)	NSU Law Career Development	

School	Facebook	Twitter
Oklahoma City University	OCU Law Professional & Career Development Center	
Pace University		@PaceLawCCD
Pennsylvania State University (Dickinson)	Penn State Law Career Services	
Rutgers, the State University of New Jersey – Camden		@RUCamLawCPO
Rutgers, the State University of New Jersey – Newark		@RUNewarkLawCSO
South Texas College of Law	Career Resources Center - South Texas College of Law*	
Southern Methodist University Dedman School of Law		@SMUDedmanLawOCS
St. Mary's University	St. Mary's University School of Law Office of Career Services	
Stanford University		@SLSCareer
Suffolk University	Suffolk University Law School Career Development Office Rappaport Center for Law and Public Policy	@SuffolkCDO @RappaportCenter (public service and pro bono positions)
Texas Tech University		@TechLawCSC
Touro College (Fuchsberg)		@TouroLawCSO
Tulane University	Tulane Law Career Development Office	@TulaneLawCDO @KatieWOLeary (Katie O'Leary, Assistant Director CDO)
University of Alabama		@TomKsobiech (Tom Ksobiech, Assistant Dean for Career Services)

School	Facebook	Twitter
University of California Hastings College of the Law		@hastingscareers
University of Chicago		@UChicagoLawOCS
University of Detroit Mercy	University of Detroit Mercy School of Law - Career Services Office*	
University of Florida (Levin)	University of Florida College of Law - Center for Career Development	
University of Houston		@UHLCCareerDean
University of Iowa	Career Services at the UI College of Law	
University of Louisville Brandeis	University of Louisville Brandeis School of Law Career & Public Services	
University of Minnesota		@Cygnus360 (Victor Massaglia, Career Counselor) @staceytidball (Stacey Tidball, Associate Director Career & Professional Development)
University of Nebraska		@unllawcareer
University of Richmond		@URLawCSO
University of San Diego	Career Services University of San Diego School of Law	
University of San Francisco	Office of Career Planning, University of San Francisco School of Law	@usflawocp @marinafeehan (Marina Feehan, Assistant Director for Employer Relations)
University of Southern California	USC Law School Career Services	
University of Texas		@UTLawCSO @drewcarls (Drew Carls, On-Campus Interview Coordinator)

School	Facebook	Twitter
University of Tulsa College of Law		@tulawpdo
University of Virginia	Career Services at the University of Virginia School of Law	@UVALawCareer
University of Washington	UW Law Career Planning Office*	
Villanova University		@DeanPetrossian (Elaine Petrossian, Assistant Dean Career Strategy Office)
Wake Forest University	Wake Forest University School of Law Career Services	@wakelawcareers
Washburn University		@WashburnLawPDO
Washington and Lee University	Washington & Lee School of Law, Office of Career Planning	
Western New England College	Western New England College School of Law -- Career Services	
	Key: *Facebook Group – Open	

Law Firm Facebook Career Pages

NOTE: *Many law firms have Facebook pages. This list contains only firms that have a page specifically for their career or recruiting department.*

Firm	Facebook Page	Site
Carlton Fields	Carlton Fields Careers	http://www.facebook.com/#!/pages/Carlton-Fields-Careers/113629049789?v=wall&ref=ts
Curtis, Mallet-Prevost, Colt & Mosle LLP	Curtis, Mallet-Prevost, Colt & Mosle LLP Careers	http://www.facebook.com/#!/Curtis.Careers?ref=ts
Orrick	Orrick Careers	http://www.facebook.com/#!/pages/Orrick-Careers/54016070994?ref=ts

Twitter Legal Job Boards

NOTE: *To access the Twitter page for one of the job boards below, type <u>www.</u>* <u>*twitter.com/username*</u>*. For example, to access the ABA's Legally Minded job board, type <u>www.twitter.com/lm_jobs</u>*

National Legal Job Boards

@LM_Jobs - the ABA's LegallyMinded

@lawjobsinusa - national job board

@DiverseJobs - diversity jobs

@legaljobsite - job site for legal professionals

@lawjobs - job board and career site for Incisive Media's Law.com Network

@mhcareers - Martindale-Hubbell career center and job board

@Law_Crossing - legal jobs

@tmj_usa_legal - USA legal/paralegal jobs from www.tweetmyjobs.com

@GetLawyerJobs - lawyer jobs

@GetEnLeAttoJobs - entry level attorney jobs

Regional Legal Job Boards

@lbattyjobs - legal jobs in Chicago and the Midwest

@jobs_at_Legal - Atlanta legal jobs

@LegalJobsInLA - Los Angeles legal jobs from the Omni Job Board Network

@LawJobsNewYork - New York legal jobs

@jobs_NY_Legal - New York legal jobs

@nyclegaljobs - New York City legal jobs

@jobs_STL_Legal - St. Louis legal jobs

@sdlegal - San Diego legal jobs

@Jobs_SF_Legal - San Francisco area law jobs

@SocalLawCareers - Southern California legal jobs

@jobs_sat_Legal - Washington state legal jobs

@jobs_DC_Legal - Washington, DC legal jobs

International Legal Job Boards

@LawJobAustralia - Australia legal jobs

@LawJobsCanada - Canada legal jobs

@LawJobsIndia - India law jobs

@LawJob - United Kingdom law jobs

@LawJobsBIRM - United Kingdom (Birmingham) legal jobs

@LegalWeek - United Kingdom (London) legal jobs

@LegalJobsLondon - United Kingdom (London) legal jobs

Practice Area/Industry Specific Legal Job Boards

@intellectualxin - Intellectual property jobs

@getpatattorjobs - patent attorney jobs

@DotOrgJobs - philanthropy and nonprofit jobs

@lobbyingjobs -job board for lobbyists, advocacy, policy and government relations professionals

@jobsinlobbying - lobbyist jobs

@HigherEdJobs - jobs in higher education, including law schools

@AcademeJobs - jobs in higher education, including law schools

Sample Law Student
First-Year Plan

A S discussed in Chapter 5, the First-Year Plan is designed for first-year law students and first-year associates who wish to develop a professional network. You will identify and interact with attorneys from five different sources over a 33 month period and meet with at least five attorneys from each source in person over the 33 month period. The attorneys you will meet in person are labeled with a letter and number. The letter corresponds to the source. For example, A3 is the third attorney contact you will meet in person from your hometown contacts.

Month	Goal	Implementation
Year 1		
[1] September	• Complete profiles on Big 3 sites	• Chapter 2
[2] October	• Connect with former and current classmates, family friends, professional contacts • Identify hometown attorneys, schedule meeting with A1	• Chapter 4 • Announce in FB status or note that you seek to meet with attorneys from hometown or with hometown connections ("**FB Status/ Note**"). *Chapter 4* • Search BranchOut for friends and friends of friends who work at specific firms ("**BranchOut**"). *Chapter 4*
[3] November	• 1st meeting with A1	• Invite A1 to connect on LI after meeting
[4] December	• Identify college alumni contacts, schedule meeting with B1	• LI people search: enter college name as keyword, select "Law Practice" and "Legal Services" for industries, narrow for target geographical market(s) ("**LI College Search**") *Chapter 4* • Skim the FB Group/ Fan Page for your college/university to identify alumni who commented, joined ("**FB College Page**") *Chapter 4*
[5] January	• 1st meeting with B1	• Invite B1 to connect on LI after meeting

Month	Goal	Implementation
[6] February	• Identify law school alumni contacts, schedule meeting with C1	• LI people search: enter law school name as keyword, select "Law Practice" and "Legal Services" for industries, narrow for target geographical market(s) ("**LI LS Search**") *Chapter 4* • Search your law school's LI alumni group to identify alumni ("**LI LS Group**") *Chapter 4* • Skim the FB Group/Fan Page for your law school to identify alumni who commented, joined ("**FB LS Page**") *Chapter 4*
[7] March	• 1st meeting with C1	• Invite C1 to connect on LI after meeting
[8] April	• Identify organization contacts, schedule meeting with D1	• Skim FB group/fan page for organization to identify attorneys who commented, joined ("**FB Org Page**") *Chapter 4* • Search the organization's LI group page to identify attorney members ("**LI Org Group**") *Chapter 4*
[9] May	• 1st meeting with D1	• Invite D1 to connect on LI after meeting

	Month	Goal	Implementation
[10]	June	• Identify practice area contacts, schedule meeting with E1	• LI people search: enter practice area as keyword, select "Law Practice" and "Legal Services" for industries, narrow for target geographical market(s) ("**LI Practice Search**") *Chapter 4* • Search LI groups for target practice area(s) to identify attorney members ("**LI Practice Group**") *Chapter 4* • Search Twitter for practice area keywords to identify attorneys ("**Twitter Practice**") *Chapter 4*
[11]	July	• 1st meeting with E1 • Schedule 2nd meeting with A1 • Identify hometown attorneys, schedule meeting with A2	• Invite E1 to connect on LI after meeting • FB Status/Note, BranchOut
[12]	August	• 2nd meeting with A1 • 1st meeting with A2 • Identify college alumni contacts, schedule meeting with B2	• Invite A2 to connect on LI after meeting • LI College Search, FB College Search
Year 2			
[13]	September	• 1st meeting with B2	• Invite B2 to connect on LI after meeting
[14]	October	• 2nd meeting with B1 • Identify law school alumni contacts, schedule meeting with C2	• LI LS Search, LI LS Group, FB LS Page

	Month	Goal	Implementation
[15]	November	• 1st meeting with C2 • Identify organization contacts, schedule meeting with D2	• Invite C2 to connect on LI after meeting • FB Org Page, LI Org Group
[16]	December	• 1st meeting with D2 • Identify practice area contacts, schedule meeting with E2	• Invite D2 to connect on LI after meeting • LI Practice Search, LI Practice Group, Twitter Practice
[17]	January	• 1st meeting with E2 • 2nd meeting with C1 • Identify hometown attorneys, schedule meeting with A3	• Invite E2 to connect on LI after meeting • FB Status/Note, BranchOut
[18]	February	• 1st meeting with A3 • 2nd meeting with D1 • Identify college alumni contacts, schedule meeting with B3	• Invite A3 to connect on LI after meeting • LI College Search, FB College Search
[19]	March	• 1st meeting with B3	• Invite B3 to connect on LI after meeting
[20]	April	• 2nd meeting with E1 • Identify law school alumni contacts, schedule meeting with C3	• LI LS Search, LI LS Group, FB LS Page
[21]	May	• 1st meeting with C3 • Identify organization contacts, schedule meeting with D3	• Invite C3 to connect on LI after meeting • FB Org Page, LI Org Group
[22]	June	• 1st meeting with D3 • 3rd meeting with A1 • 2nd meeting with A2 • Identify practice area contacts, schedule meeting with E3	• Invite D3 to connect on LI after meeting • LI Practice Search, LI Practice Group, Twitter Practice

	Month	Goal	Implementation
[23]	July	• 1st meeting with E3 • 3rd meeting with B1 • Identify hometown attorneys, schedule meeting with A4	• Invite E3 to connect on LI after meeting • FB Status/Note, BranchOut
[24]	August	• 1st meeting with A4 • 2nd meeting with B2 • Identify college alumni contacts, schedule meeting with B4	• Invite A4 to connect on LI after meeting • LI College Search, FB College Search
Year 3			
[25]	September	• 1st meeting with B4 • 3rd meeting with C1 • 2nd meeting with C2 • Identify law school alumni contacts, schedule meeting with C4	• Invite B4 to connect on LI after meeting • LI LS Search, LI LS Group, FB LS Page
[26]	October	• 1st meeting with C4 • 3rd meeting with D1 • 2nd meeting with D2 • Identify organization contacts, schedule meeting with D4	• Invite C4 to connect on LI after meeting • FB Org Page, LI Org Group
[27]	November	• 1st meeting with D4 • Identify practice area contacts, schedule meeting with E4	• Invite D4 to connect on LI after meeting • LI Practice Search, LI Practice Group, Twitter Practice
[28]	December	• 1st meeting with E4 • Identify hometown attorneys, schedule meeting with A5	• Invite E4 to connect on LI after meeting • FB Status/Note, BranchOut
[29]	January	• 1st meeting with A5 • 3rd meeting with E1 • Identify college alumni contacts, schedule meeting with B5	• Invite A5 to connect on LI after meeting • LI College Search, FB College Search

	Month	Goal	Implementation
[30]	February	• 1st meeting with B5 • 2nd meeting with E2 • Identify law school alumni contacts, schedule meeting with C5	• Invite B5 to connect on LI after meeting • LI LS Search, LI LS Group, FB LS Page
[31]	March	• 1st meeting with C5 • Identify organization contacts, schedule meeting with D5	• Invite C5 to connect on LI after meeting • FB Org Page, LI Org Group
[32]	April	• 1st meeting with D5 • Identify practice area contacts, schedule meeting with E5	• Invite D5 to connect on LI after meeting • LI Practice Search, LI Practice Group, Twitter Practice
[33]	May	• 1st meeting with E5	• Invite E5 to connect on LI after meeting

Sample Social Networking Schedule (4 Hours/Week)

Monday	Tuesday	Wednesday	Thursday	Friday	Saturday	Sunday
FACEBOOK						
20 minutes **CONNECT** • Review new friend requests, accept		*20 minutes* **CONNECT** • Skim people you may know, request if appropriate		*20 minutes* **CONNECT** • Review new friend requests, accept	*20 minutes* **CONNECT** • Search groups & pages, join or fan if appropriate	
ASSIMILATE • Review news feed • Review law firm pages		**ASSIMILATE** • Review news feed • Review law school career pages		**ASSIMILATE** • Review news feed • Review alumni group pages	**ASSIMILATE** • Review news feed • Review professional organization pages • Review friends' pictures	
PARTICIPATE • Update status • B-day greetings • Comment on 1 law firm page		**PARTICIPATE** • Update status • Comment on friend's status or link or wall post		**PARTICIPATE** • Update status • B-day greetings • Share link posted by friend	**PARTICIPATE** • Update status • Post article or link • Comment on 1 picture	

LINKEDIN

20 minutes **CONNECT**		*20 minutes* **CONNECT**		*20 minutes* **CONNECT**	*20 minutes* **CONNECT**
• Send 1 invitation • Accept		• Review "People You May Know" section and invite 1 person • Accept invitations		• Send custom invitations to 2 lawyers met at bar event on Thurs night • Accept invitations	• Review "People You May Know" section and invite 1 person • Accept invitations
ASSIMILATE		**ASSIMILATE**		**ASSIMILATE**	**ASSIMILATE**
• Review news feed • Review profile views • Review practice area groups		• Review news feed • Review bar related groups		• Review news feed • Review events to find event for next week	• Review news feed • Conduct company and people searches to prepare for interview next Tues
PARTICIPATE		**PARTICIPATE**		**PARTICIPATE**	**PARTICIPATE**
• Update status • Comment on contact's new position/title		• Post news link on young lawyer bar group		• Update status	• Talked to mutual connections to prepare for Tuesday interview

TWITTER

20 minutes **CONNECT**		*20 minutes* **CONNECT**		*20 minutes* **CONNECT**	*20 minutes* **CONNECT**
• Reciprocate follow		• Follow 2 contacts of a user on favorite list		• Follow 2 users from #FF rec	• Review new followers
ASSIMILATE		**ASSIMILATE**		**ASSIMILATE**	**ASSIMILATE**
• Review favorite list • Review job board list		• Review law school career lists		• Review favorite list • Review legal news feed list	• Review favorite list
PARTICIPATE		**PARTICIPATE**		**PARTICIPATE**	**PARTICIPATE**
• School related tweet • 2 RTs		• Share link • 1 RT • Send 1 DM		• #FF • Respond to @ mentions	• Comment on 1 target attorney's tweets • 1 RT • Share 1 link

Chapter Notes

(ENDNOTES)

1   Plouffe, David. "Inside Obama's election win: David Plouffe,
    campaign manager, tells how he did it." The Washington Post on the
    Web 5 Nov. 2009. 25 Feb. 2010 <http://www.washingtonpost.com/
    wp-dyn/content/discussion/2009/11/02/DI2009110202428.html>.

2   Willis, Sissy. "Social Networking Key to Brown's
    Success." PajamasMedia Weblog. 29 Jan. 2010.
    25 Feb. 2010 <http://pajamasmedia.com/blog/
    social-networking-key-to-browns-success/?singlepage=true>.

3   "McCain v. Obama on the Web: Engagement and Participation." Pew
    Research Center's Project for Excellence in Journalism Weblog. 15
    Sept. 2008 25 Feb. 2010 <http://www.journalism.org/node/12773>.

4   "social network." Dictionary.com's 21st Century Lexicon. Dictionary.
    com, LLC. 25 Jul. 2010. <Dictionary.com http://dictionary.reference.
    com/browse/social network>.

5   Slevin, Peter, and Jose Vargas. "Obama Tries New Tactics to Get
    Vote Out in Iowa." The Washington Post on the Web 31 Dec. 2007
    25 Feb. 2010 <http://www.washingtonpost.com/wp-dyn/content/
    article/2007/12/30/AR2007123002795.html>.

6   Yan, Sophia. "How Scott Brown's Social-Media Juggernaut Won
    Massachusetts." Time on the Web 4 Feb. 2010 25 Feb. 2010 <http://
    www.time.com/time/nation/article/0,8599,1960378,00.html>.

7   Zuckerberg, Mark. "500 Million Stories." Facebook Weblog.

21 July 2010 24 July 2010 <http://blog.facebook.com/blog. php?post=409753352130>.

8   Schroeder, Stan. "Facebook Users Are Getting Older. Much Older." Mashable Weblog. 25 July 2009 24 July 2010 < http://mashable. com/2009/07/07/facebook-users-older/>.

9   Rao, Leena. "LinkedIn Tops 70 Million Users; Includes Over One Million Company Profiles." TechCrunch Weblog. 20 June 2010 20 July 2010 <http://techcrunch.com/2010/06/20/linkedin-tops-70-mil- lion-users-includes-over-one-million-company-profiles/>.

10   Schonfeld, Erick. "Nearly 75 Million People Visited Twitter's Site in January." TechCrunch Weblog. 16 Feb. 2010 24 July 2010 <http:// techcrunch.com/2010/02/16/twitter-75-million-people-january/>.

11   Neal, David. "There are 75 Million Twitter Users." The Inquirer Weblog. 27 Jan. 2010 24 July 2010 <http://www.theinquirer.net/ inquirer/news/1589058/there-75-million-twitter-users>.

12   Cross-Tab. "Online Reputation in a Connected World." Microsoft on the Web. Abstract. 16 March 2010 <http://www.microsoft.com/ privacy/dpd/research.aspx>.

13   *Ibid.*

14   *Ibid.*

15   Wallen, Jan. "Are you on the radar screen of companies and people who can hire you?" Examiner.com Weblog. 16 Oct. 2009 25 Feb. 2010 <http://www.examiner.com/x-25594-LinkedIn- Examiner~y2009m10d16-Are-you-on-the-radar-screen-of-companies- and-people-who-can-hire-you>.

16   Carton, Bruce. "Company Requires 'Tweet' As Part of Law Firms' RFP Response." Legal Blog Watch Weblog. 21 Jan. 2010 25 Jan. 2010 <http://legalblogwatch.typepad.com/legal_blog_watch/2010/01/ twitter-required-company-requires-tweet-as-part-of-law-firms-rfp- response.html>.

17   Weiss, Debra Cassens. "Sign of the Times: Clorox Seeks Lawyer for Social Media Issues." ABA Journal on the Web 25 Jan. 2010 25 Jan. 2010 <http://www.abajournal.com/news/article/ sign_of_the_times_clorox_seeks_lawyer_for_social_media_issues/>.

18   Matthews, Steve. "LinkedIn Lawyers Hit 840K." Law Firm Web

Strategy Weblog. 4 Jun 2009 20 May 2010 <http://www.stemlegal.
com/strategyblog/2009/linkedin-lawyers-hit-840k/>.

19 Bodine, Larry. "More than a Million Lawyers on LinkedIn."
Law Marketing Weblog. 8 Dec. 2009 20 May 2010
<http://blog.larrybodine.com/2009/12/articles/tech/
more-than-a-million-lawyers-on-linkedin/>.

20 Nations, Daniel. "How Barack Obama is Using Web 2.0 to Run for
President." About.com Weblog. 20 May 2010 <http://webtrends.
about.com/od/web20/a/obama-web.htm>.

21 Woodard, Niki. "Fred Thompson's Campaign Web Site Was Already
In Full Swing." Pew Research Center's Project for Excellence in
Journalism Weblog. 7 Sept. 2007 25 Feb. 2010 <http://www.jour-
nalism.org/node/7367>.

22 Cross-Tab. "Online Reputation in a Connected World." Microsoft
on the Web. Abstract. 16 March 2010 <http://www.microsoft.com/
privacy/dpd/research.aspx>.

23 Williams, Doug. "The Non-Secret Secret of Legal Profession
Marketing." Texas Women Lawyers 2010 Conference. Houston, Texas.
19 Feb. 2010.

24 Cornelius, Doug. "Compliance and Recommendations on Social
Networking Sites." Compliance Building Weblog. 24 Mar. 2009
1 July 2009 <http://www.compliancebuilding.com/2009/03/24/
recommendations-on-social-networking-sites-and-compliance/>.

25 Meinhardt, Jane. "Law Marketers Win Key Ruling with Florida
Bar Settlement." Tampa Bay Business Journal on the Web 27 Nov.
2009 27 Nov. 2009 <http://tampabay.bizjournals.com/tampabay/
stories/2009/11/30/story4.html>.

26 Baldas, Tresa. "Lawyers Warn Employers Against Giving Glowing
Reviews on LinkedIn." The National Law Journal on the Web 6 July
2009 3 Apr. 2010 <http://www.law.com/jsp/nlj/PubArticleNLJ.jsp?id=
1202432039774&slreturn=1&hbxlogin=1>.

27 Cross-Tab. "Online Reputation in a Connected World." Microsoft
on the Web. Abstract. 16 March 2010 <http://www.microsoft.com/
privacy/dpd/research.aspx>.

28 Cuyler, Aviva. "Lawyers and Law Firms on Facebook." Legal
Marketing Scoop Weblog. 28 July 2009 2 Aug. 2009 <http://

scoop.jdsupra.com/2009/07/articles/law-firm-marketing/
lawyers-and-law-firms-on-facebook/>.

29   Matthews, Steve. "LinkedIn Lawyers Hit 840K." Law Firm Web
     Strategy Weblog. 4 Jun 2009 20 May 2010 <http://www.stemlegal.
     com/strategyblog/2009/linkedin-lawyers-hit-840k/>.

30   Bodine, Larry. "More than a Million Lawyers on LinkedIn."
     Law Marketing Weblog. 8 Dec. 2009 20 May 2010
     <http://blog.larrybodine.com/2009/12/articles/tech/
     more-than-a-million-lawyers-on-linkedin/>.

31   RecruiterEsq. 2009. 25 Feb. 2010 <http://www.recruiteresq.com>.

32   Lurssen, Adrian. "145 Lawyers (and Legal Professionals) to Follow on
     Twitter." Legal Marketing Scoop Weblog. 9 Sept. 2008 16 Sept. 2008
     <http://scoop.jdsupra.com/2008/09/articles/law-firm-marketing/145-
     lawyers-and-legal-professionals-to-follow-on-twitter/>.

33   Smith, D. Todd. "Texas Lawyers to Follow on Twitter." Texas
     Appellate Law Weblog. 23 Dec. 2008 24 Dec. 2008 <http://
     www.texasappellatelawblog.com/2008/12/articles/technology/
     texas-lawyers-to-follow-on-twitter/>.

34   PracticeLaw. 2009. Minnesota Bar Association. 25 Feb. 2010. <http://
     www.practicelaw.org/161>.

35   LexTweet. 2008. LexBlog. 20 Dec. 2009 <http://lextweet.com>.

36   LegalBirds. 2008. Justia. 20 Dec. 2009 <http://legalbirds.justia.com>.

37   Tweetlaw. 2009. 25 Feb. 2010 <http://tweetlaw.com>.

38   Carton, Bruce. "Updating My 15 'Must Follows' on Twitter."
     Compliance Week Weblog. 17 Feb. 2010 21 Feb. 2010
     <http://www.complianceweek.com/blog/carton/2010/02/17/
     updating-my-15-must-follows-on-twitter/>.

39   Mandatory CLE Unplugged. 2010. uMCLE.com. 3 May 2010
     <http://www.umcle.com/socialmedia/twitter/>.

40   22 Tweets. 2009. The Godard Group. 20 Feb. 2010 <http://22tweets.
     com>.

41   "Paul Rosenberg." Wikipedia.com. 20 May 2010 <http://en.wikipedia.
     org/wiki/Paul_Rosenberg_%28music_manager%29>.

42   Leaman, Rebecca. "How to Shorten URLs and Track Clicks."
     Wild Apricot Weblog. 3 Feb. 2009 20 May 2010 <http://

www.wildapricot.com/blogs/newsblog/archive/2009/02/03/how-to-shorten-urls-and-track-clicks.aspx>.

43 Johnson, Joshua. "Associate Attrition and the Tragedy of the Commons." The Crit Vol. 1, Issue 1. Spring 2008. Abstract. 20 May 2010 <http://www.thecritui.com/articles/Johnson%5B1%5D. Formatted.1.pdf>.

44 Colvin, Geoff. "The unconventional performance idea that works." The Washington Post on the Web. 19 May 2010 20 May 2010 <http://views.washingtonpost.com/leadership/panelists/2010/05/the-unconvential-performance-idea-that-works.html>.

45 Hope, Judith Richards. Pinstripes & Pearls: The Women of the Harvard Law Class of '64 Who Forged an Old-Girl Network and Paved the Way for Future Generations. New York: Scribner, 2003.